Conscience and Catholicism

Conscience and Catholicism

Rights, Responsibilities, and Institutional Responses

Edited by

David E. DeCosse and Kristin E. Heyer

ORBIS BOOKS

Maryknoll, New York 10545

ORBIS BOOKS
Maryknoll, New York 10545

Fathers and Brothers MARYKNOLL™

Founded in 1970, Orbis Books endeavors to publish works that enlighten the mind, nourish the spirit, and challenge the conscience. The publishing arm of the Maryknoll Fathers and Brothers, Orbis seeks to explore the global dimensions of the Christian faith and mission, to invite dialogue with diverse cultures and religious traditions, and to serve the cause of reconciliation and peace. The books published reflect the views of their authors and do not represent the official position of the Maryknoll Society. To learn more about Maryknoll and Orbis Books, please visit our website at www.maryknollsociety.org.

Published by Orbis Books, Maryknoll, New York 10545-0302.

Manufactured in the United States of America.
Manuscript editing and typesetting by Joan Weber Laflamme.

Library of Congress Cataloging-in-Publication Data

Conscience and Catholicism : rights, responsibilities, and institutional responses / edited by David E. DeCosse and Kristin E. Heyer

pages cm

Includes bibliographical references and index.

ISBN 978-1-62698-144-7 (pbk.)

1. Conscience—Religious saspects—Catholic Church—Congresses. 2. Christian ethics—Catholic authors—Congresses. 3 Catholic Church—Doctrines—Congresses. I. DeCosse, David E., editor.

BJ1278.C66C655 2015

241'1088282—dc23

2015009612

We dedicate this volume to the joint doctoral faculty in theological ethics at Boston College

Contents

Acknowledgments

Many people have been instrumental in helping bring this volume to fruition. We would especially like to thank Michael and Phyllis Shea for their very generous gift to the Markkula Center for Applied Ethics to support the Project on Conscience and Roman Catholic Thought. Their gift enabled us to envision and complete this project. We are grateful to Jim Keane at Orbis Books for his enthusiasm for the project and his editorial savvy in shepherding the book to completion, and to Rosario Garriga Hughes for her generous help with translation. We would also like to express gratitude to our wonderful colleagues at Santa Clara University: Kirk Hanson, executive director of the Ethics Center; Monica DeLong, director of operations at the Ethics Center; Shruti Saxena and Venkata Sai Kishore Modalavalasa, graduate assistants at the Ethics Center; Elizabeth Purner of the Graduate Program in Pastoral Ministries at Santa Clara University; Gary Macy, chair of the Religious Studies Department; Thomas Massaro, S.J., dean of the Jesuit School of Theology of Santa Clara University; and the joint ethics faculty from the Jesuit School of Theology in Berkeley and at Santa Clara. We would also like to thank the many staff at Santa Clara who helped make possible the expert seminar we held in September 2014, out of which the essays in this book have developed. We are deeply grateful to the participants in that seminar—who are the contributors to this book—for their collegial spirit from its earliest planning stages and the excellent quality of their contributions.

Finally, we dedicate this book to the joint doctoral faculty in theological ethics at Boston College. In doing so we wish express our deep gratitude for our formation during our respective years in the doctoral program there and for their mentorship, which continues to shape our scholarly and vocational endeavors in profound ways.

Introduction

David E. DeCosse and Kristin E. Heyer

Few notions in Catholic theology today have as much rhetorical power as "conscience." Yet behind such rhetorical power lies a host of theological challenges. Beyond various concerns about its function and formative sources, conscience is variously understood as capacity, act, habit, sanctuary, place of encounter, and transcendent encounter itself. Given its sacred nature and the dignity of others' claims, conscience can strike notes of inviolability and provisionality alike, and its exercise requires both deep courage and deep humility. This book attempts to address its complexity by appealing to the significance of a nuanced theology of conscience in light of history, context, and praxis.

One particular challenge to the theology of conscience gave proximate rise to this book. In recent years Catholic bishops in the United States have been locked in a conscience-related dispute with the Obama Administration over contraceptive coverage in national healthcare policy. For many bishops the federal policy posed a profound threat to the Catholic conscience. As this line of thinking went, the policy would require Catholic institutions like hospitals and universities to provide employees with insurance coverage for contraception, even though Catholic moral doctrine regards the use of artificial contraception to be an intrinsic evil. In this dispute "conscience" for the bishops largely functioned as a mark of group identity: "conscience" is equated with the Catholic conscience and is understood as legitimately operative only when it is in conformity with Catholic moral doctrine. Yet this way of understanding conscience marked a departure from a more appropriately broad theological idea. On the one hand, the consciences of non-Catholic employees at Catholic institutions played almost no role in the arguments of many bishops. Moreover, the Catholic theological tradition offers a robustly different, personalist view of conscience—one drawing on such figures as Thomas Aquinas and emerging in key documents of the Second Vatican Council—from the one being advanced by many bishops. Still more, it has become increasingly clear that the papacies of both John Paul II and Benedict XVI engaged in a decades-long effort to constrain conscience and force compliance with the directives of the hierarchical magisterium of the church. In January 2012, David DeCosse published an extended essay in *National Catholic Reporter* making these points (the essay is included as an appendix to this book). Not long afterward Michael and Phyllis Shea made a generous gift to the Markkula Center for Applied Ethics at Santa Clara University to support work on issues raised in the essay and related to conscience and Catholicism. Soon thereafter we conceived the idea of hosting an expert seminar of theologians from around the United States and the world to examine the contemporary challenges to the theology of conscience.

That seminar was held at Santa Clara University, the Jesuit university in Silicon Valley, September 10–12, 2014, and it featured the authors of the essays in this book. From the project's conception its goal was to consider conscience in a comprehensive way, including the dimensions of conscience that raise claims to rights, impose burdens of responsibility, and factor in the complex interplay of institutional policies. For two days the group (from the United States and six other countries) engaged in close conversation about drafts of the essays now included in this volume. We were of varied gender, racial, and ethnic backgrounds. Some of the scholars teach; others work in administration; one just received her doctorate; one is a retired archbishop. Some were members of vowed religious communities; others were lay scholars. Given the dominant view of conscience advanced in the last decades by John Paul II and Benedict XVI, the participants and topics were chosen to open up space for advancing an alternative view of conscience with deep roots in the Catholic tradition.

While the problematic issue of the American bishops' construal of conscience in their clash with the federal government may have occasioned the conference, other related questions drove the conversations at the seminar and drive the conversation of this book. Chiefly, is it possible to consider a Catholic theology of conscience apart from close attention to context and to the varied expressions of context across history, praxis, and culture? In the opening chapter of the book Jesuit moral theologian James Keenan shows the different ways in which the theology of conscience developed after the Second World War in Western Europe and in the United States, respectively. In Europe, Keenan notes, a rich, personalist theology of conscience arose in response to the catastrophic obedience of millions of Europeans to fascist, totalitarian regimes. By contrast, the American Catholic theology of conscience remained sharply confined within ecclesiastical boundaries; one's conscience at most was free to obey the directives of the hierarchical teaching authority of the church. In the United States this constrained view was cracked open by the response to *Humanae Vitae*, the 1968 encyclical that reaffirmed the Vatican's opposition to artificial birth control. But even that opening was problematic, as it cast the theology of conscience into two reflexive modes: authority or dissent. Keenan argues that it is time that the church (especially in the United States) revisits the profound postwar work of the Europeans.

To be sure, invocations of conscience can devolve quickly into a sharply polarized discourse of authority or dissent. Such polarities can be cloaked in theological or philosophical fineries like infallibility and autonomy. Yet it is important to probe behind such fineries. In his essay retired San Francisco Archbishop John Quinn turns to the great nineteenth-century theologian John Henry Cardinal Newman's account of conscience in relation to the definition of papal infallibility at the First Vatican Council in 1870. Quinn evokes Newman's subtle exposition of the doctrine of conscience—notably, in Newman's eyes, that conscience is of higher authority even than the pope. Quinn also considers how Newman's very favorable view of the primacy of conscience did not prevent Newman from also accepting the conciliar definition of papal infallibility. Of course, what made such an acceptance possible was Newman's vivid sense of the limited, contextual nature even of such an apparently absolute papal claim. For instance, the claim of infallibility did not extend to the governance of the church but to doctrinal definitions. Moreover, the claim derived much of its intelligibility from the broader infallibility of the church itself.

In the first two essays, then, the theology of conscience is related to time: how we understand conscience theologically is inseparable from history. Yet conscience is also very much a function of place. Here Japanese Jesuit moral theologian Osamu Takeuchi's essay offers a compelling account of how a Catholic theology of conscience can be developed in conversation with Asian culture. In particular, such a conversation invites the integrated consideration of the personalist, relational, and transcendent dimensions of conscience—dimensions too long neglected in, for instance, the neo-Scholasticism that dominated Catholicism in the twentieth century and that still holds powerful sway over much of Catholic education and formation. Of course, such cultural conversations are in a sense always ensuing, whether we recognize them or not, affecting how theology understands conscience and how well theology can speak to the differentiated cultures of a truly global church. The document *Gaudium et Spes* from the Second Vatican Council, with its beautiful evocation of conscience as "the most secret core and sanctuary" of a person, is often considered a high-water mark of the theology of conscience in the last fifty years. But the document's moving discussion of the inner, transcendent dimension of conscience is matched by an emphasis on the ways in which conscience connects Catholics to those outside the church: "In fidelity to conscience, Christians are joined with the rest of men in the search for truth, and for the genuine solution to the numerous problems which arise in the life of individuals from social relationships."[1] Takeuchi's essay—as well as essays by others in this volume—recovers the social dimension of conscience envisioned at the council.

Takeuchi takes aim at a particular construct of conscience that has long held sway in Catholic theology: the solitary individual exercising conscience as an intellectual judgment on a moral act. To be sure, there are aspects of such a construct that are important. Yet there are other aspects that have been rightfully called into question by contemporary scholarship on, for instance, the emotions. Stephen Pope, who has written extensively on evolution and moral theology, turns in this book to Jonathan Haidt's moral psychology in order to argue that Catholic theology should pay far more attention than it has to the formative role of emotions in the judgments of our conscience. Drawing on Haidt's powerful image, Pope argues that reason is at best riding the "elephant" of our emotions as it seeks to make judgments of conscience. Among other things the deep structure of conscience to which Pope points—a structure involving emotion, imagination, sense, as well as reason—complicates the question of the formation of conscience. In turn, the question of formation is further problematized when we consider that the conscience of a Catholic is always shaped amid a cultural context, one that bears within it powerful ways in which the forces of such deep structures emerge as intuitions about morality and instincts about judgment. And what if such intuitions and instincts are profoundly destructive?

In his essay Bryan Massingale tackles the problem of conscience formation in the context of a culture of racism. Massingale, whose recent work has focused on racial justice, wrote the essay during the months in which the ongoing problem of African American men dying in encounters with law enforcement erupted in the deaths of two more such men, Michael Brown in a suburb of St. Louis and Eric Garner on Staten Island in New York City. No simple formation in the rational categories of church teaching has seemed up to the task of converting the conscience of many American Catholics from an indifference or hostility to the plight of these men. For Massingale, the power of unconscious racial bias to distort the formation of conscience requires the cultivation of qualities of authentic interracial solidarity. Theologian Lisa Fullam of the Jesuit School of Theology of Santa Clara University addresses a related issue in her essay: the cultural malformations of conscience that are all too readily applied to women. Fullam describes these malformations in terms of the social sin of sexism, which both oppresses women and thwarts their flourishing. How to resist the insidious pull of such forces in the shaping of conscience? Fullam turns

---

[1] Second Vatican Council, *Gaudium et Spes*, no. 16.

to a rereading of the stories of Joan of Arc and Teresa of Avila as exemplary models of resistance to the sexism of their times and thus apt models today for countering this malformation.

When we speak of the contexts of conscience, we cannot neglect the political arena. Of course, different political contexts can generate many different ways of thinking theologically about conscience. Today, in many places throughout the world, however, the political context posing a special challenge to a theology of conscience is constitutional democracy—especially as such democracies grapple with legal issues related to claims of gender and sexuality at odds with official Catholic teaching. Thus Irish theologian Linda Hogan in her essay takes on the issue of the legalization of marriage for gay and lesbian couples in Ireland. Here, Hogan cautions, the claims of conscience too often invoke false absolutes and become conversation stoppers. Moreover, such claims often proceed on the ready identification of the politically pluralist contexts of constitutional democracies with ethical relativism. By contrast, Hogan argues for the need for epistemic humility in the face of our claims of conscience, which are capable of truth but which are also the result of the inescapably historical and situated way by which we arrive at moral judgments at all. The conscience of a Catholic in a constitutional democracy inhabits a context of moral pluralism that mandates conversation.

Argentine theologian Emilce Cuda also considers the question of conscience and the legalization of marriage equality. Argentina shares with Ireland a constitutional democratic political structure and a largely Catholic population. But the political context of Argentina is also marked by much greater poverty than the political context in Ireland. For Cuda, the question of the formation of conscience of Catholics on the issue of marriage equality cannot properly be understood apart from consideration of this whole context—which she calls the "democratic popular" context. Conservative Catholics in Argentina opposed gay marriage on the basis of Catholic sexual teaching. Yet the support for gay marriage on the part of many Argentinians (including many Catholics) involved conscience grappling in a discursive space with a wider field of values—not only sexual ethics but also concerns about equality, justice in the exercise of political power (as it pertained to gays and lesbians and as it pertained to the poor), and social peace. The conscience of a Catholic is shaped amid discourse and cannot be shaped at the expense of such a wider field of values. Cardinal Jorge Mario Bergoglio of Buenos Aires (now Pope Francis) provides for Cuda a salutary model of such conscience formation.

We noted above the claim of *Gaudium et Spes* that closely links conscience to the search with others for the common good in any given context. How theology considers this dimension of conscience will no doubt be affected by the power of the church in the context in question. Thus Philippine Jesuit moral theologian Eric Genilo addresses in his essay the issue of conscientious objection by Catholic public officeholders to the 2012 national law making contraception (but not abortion) more broadly available throughout the country; the law was strongly opposed by the Philippine bishops. May an officeholder who objects to the law undertake conscientious objection in the performance of official duties and thus actively undermine the implementation of a duly adopted law? Genilo concludes that such a public servant cannot, and he makes his case largely on the grounds of the normative importance of connecting the individual exercise of conscience with the demands of the common good. Yet the challenge for thinking about the relationship of conscience to the common good in the Philippines is one of dominance and restraint. How does a dominant religion like Catholicism in the Philippines think theologically about the claims of the entire common good, even if such claims may challenge Catholic doctrinal positions?

In India, the challenge for the theology of conscience is often influenced by an opposite set of contextual factors, for instance, by the relatively tiny size of the Indian Catholic community amid the religious pluralism and dominant Hinduism of the country. With the attainment of national power in 2014 by the Hindu nationalist party this contextual configuration has presented the church in India with a particularly challenging problem: the existence and threat of laws banning religious conversions (laws largely understood as efforts to limit conversions from Hinduism to other religions). Indian moral theologian Eugine Rodrigues turns to the work on conscience and religious freedom of such theologians as John Courtney Murray and Louis Janssens to show how a Catholic understanding of conscience is violated by such anti-conversion laws—a finding made not only on behalf of all Catholics but also on behalf of all Indians of whatever background. Her analysis also shows how, from the perspective of Catholic theology, the issue is not only one of the dignity of individual conscience. Rather, it is also one in which the protection of conscience is at the same time considered an indispensable help to the creation of a participatory, dialogical common good in India.

One of the key tenets of the theology of conscience of Cardinal Newman was his presumption that the moral law was general, not universal. Or, as Newman put it, "exceptions there must be in all concrete matters."[2] In such a theology, conscience occupies the gaps where the standard rules do not

[2] John Henry Newman, "A Letter Addressed to His Grace the Duke of Norfolk," in *Conscience, Consensus, and the Development of Doctrine*, ed. James Gaffney (New York: Image Books, 1992), 457.

apply. Of course, for the last decades the Vatican has insisted on the objective, universal nature of the moral law; on the prerogative for the hierarchical magisterium to define those laws and the policy implications of those laws; and on the responsibility of Catholics to form their consciences in conformity with such exacting, universal standards. According to this view Newman was wrong: there are no gaps where the rules do not apply. In few fields have these divergent theologies of conscience come more into conflict than in healthcare. In her essay ethicist Carol Bayley of Dignity Health provides an insider's perspective on what is perhaps the most noteworthy American instance of a case that appears to fall outside the standard rules: the situation at a Phoenix Catholic hospital involving a mother of three with a life-threatening pregnancy. Bayley also describes how what was formerly called Catholic Health Care West became Dignity Health, a change in name driven by a conscience-related struggle over sterilization at a non-Catholic hospital in the Catholic Health Care West network. For Bayley, the conscience of a Catholic is primarily formed by the imperative to love. Moreover, she argues, it was precisely such an imperative that drove the actions of the healthcare personnel involved in each story. Yet the situations with Catholic Health Care West occurred in the developed world where, even given tragic circumstances, extensive medical and social resources exist. In Africa the challenges of conscience in Catholic healthcare often arise in vastly poorer circumstances, as Nigerian Jesuit Agbonkhianmeghe Orobator shows in his essay. Here the ecclesiastical precepts that exist—for instance, the ban on condoms even for those infected with AIDS—are challenged even more. The consciences of healthcare workers must be alive to the concrete situations of those whom they serve—situations that are marked by great desperation and injustice. Precepts too often seem to float above such desperate contexts. By contrast, Orobator argues for the formation of conscience on the basis of an ongoing attention to the concrete situation of the one being served, to relationship, dialogue, and love. Across these disparate healthcare delivery contexts the challenges posed raise strikingly parallel questions for Bayley and Orobator regarding connections between ecclesiology and models of conscience.

Throughout this volume, then, there is a persistent exploration of the social and contextual dimensions of conscience. Does this, then, imply that an organization in itself can have a conscience? And how might Catholic institutions themselves think about adjudicating their own claims to identity with the claims of conscience of others in civil society and even others—many of whom, for instance, may be non-Catholic—who are a part of Catholic institutions themselves? The final essays in the volume take on these problems of the so-called institutional conscience. Economist and theologian Daniel Finn draws on critical realist sociology to argue that institutions cannot be understood to have a conscience. To be sure, he says, institutions have collective agency and moral responsibility. Such agency and responsibility arise out of a complex interplay of individuals and relationships, however, and thus such interplay does not amount to the more specified subjectivity appropriate to conscience. Jesuit theologian William O'Neill of the Jesuit School of Theology of Santa Clara University concludes the book by providing a casuistry of sorts by which Catholic institutions today can think through the complex questions related to balancing their own claims of identity amid other consonant and competing values in both pluralist, political society and within the Catholic institutions themselves. O'Neill fittingly brings the volume to an end by emphasizing the importance of context in such a casuistry. Personal claims of conscience obviously have great significance. Yet such claims, when considered in institutional contexts, must be assessed in light of a broad range of values and virtues that are present in the Catholic tradition, even if submerged in the last several decades.

Taken together, the essays in this volume offer a counterbalance to recent emphases in Catholic thought in their attention to how context, culture, and institutions shape conscience. We close this introduction with suggestions drawn from this volume for ongoing areas of work on the theology of conscience. One such area pertains to institutional realities. The Catholic tradition's non-voluntary and structural dimensions of social sin illuminate the interplay that emerges in human life between ideological biases and institutional participation—an interplay that conspires to obstruct conscience formation.[3] Another area points to how renewed attention to the affections can alert us to various "elephants" that exert significant influence on our reasoning, both in ways that foster scotosis, an intellectual blindness, and in ways that may trigger remorse or better permit us to pursue the good in complex contexts. Furthermore, relationality emerges as crucial for conscience formation, a social emphasis consistent with the etymology of the word *con-science* ("knowing together with") and the social nature of moral knowledge and of persons themselves. Nevertheless, several essays' emphases warn of the need to guard against confirmation bias and "group think." The joint reflections of the book also suggest a connection between truncated conscience discourse (whether primarily adversarial, stopgap, or conformist) and truncated conscience formation, suggesting both the need

---

[3] Building upon sociological understandings of internalized structures, several theologians articulate stages of social sin that shed light on the relationship between its voluntary and non-voluntary dimensions. See, e.g., Gregory Baum, *Religion and Alienation: A Theological Reading of Sociology* (New York: Paulist Press, 1975), 200–203, and Kristin E. Heyer, "Social Sin and Immigration: Good Fences Make Bad Neighbors," *Theological Studies* 71/2 (June 2010): 410–36.

and desire for more robust and far-reaching formation. How can persons be better empowered by engagement with the Christian story to recognize distortions and to "do the truth in love" in complex situations? With an accent on conscience that connotes an ongoing search rather than premature closure, we hope this collection will foster ongoing discernment and further open up a conversation in a global church.

1.

To Follow and to Form over Time

A Phenomenology of Conscience

JAMES F. KEENAN, S.J.

In this essay I examine the evolution of the conscience over the course of the twentieth century, noting that developments in Europe have far outdistanced those in the United States and arguing that we need to rely on the Europeans' more developed understanding of conscience as the origin of all moral decision making. I close with an illustrative coda: making an application of conscience to a case of conflicting virtues for a university professor.

The Weak, Sick, Conforming Conscience of the Laity of the First Fifty Years

As Stephen Schloesser has shown us, we cannot understand Vatican II without understanding World War II.[1] The civilian death toll alone is staggering: around forty-seven million persons, including about twenty million due to war-related famine and disease. The military toll was about twenty-five million, including about five million prisoners of war.

European moral theology emerged from the rubble of World War II having to face the now-haunted conscience of the postwar modern world. Though John Gallagher writes, "World War II was to have an impact on European Catholic theology that was not totally unlike that which World War I had on Protestant Christianity," few Catholic ethicists other than

[1] Stephen Schloesser, "Against Forgetting: Memory, History, Vatican II," *Theological Studies* 67 (2006): 275–314.

Gallagher and Charles Curran seem to note the war's impact on their field of investigations.[2] The evident failure of the moral manuals in shaping Catholic consciences to resist rather than to participate in the barbarism of Fascism and Nazism led Catholic moral theologians throughout Europe to a complete repudiation of the manuals immediately after the war.

When I think of the moral manuals and their impact on English-speaking Catholics during the time of the war and its aftermath, I frequently refer to three specific editions by, respectively, Jesuit Thomas Slater (1855–1928),[3] Jesuit Henry Davis (1866–1952),[4] and Capuchin Father Heribert Jone (1885–1967).[5] These specific editions allow us to consider the very first English moral manual, the most important English edition during World War II, and the most international manual to appear from Germany, just four years after its surrender. No other moral manuals had more influence on English-speaking clergy and the church throughout the world than these three.

Though many are familiar with Thomas Slater's famous apologetic definition of the moral manuals, it bears repeating for its insight:

> The manuals of moral theology are technical works intended to help the confessor and the parish priest in the discharge of their duties. They are as technical as the text-books of the lawyer and the doctor. They are not intended for edification, nor do they hold up a high ideal of Christian perfection for the imitation of the faithful. They deal with what is of obligation under the pain of sin, they are books of moral pathology.[6]

Slater acknowledged that if readers were looking to learn how to become better disciples, they should look elsewhere: to the manuals of ascetical, devotional, or mystical theology, where they would find the "high ideal of Christian perfection."

Slater concluded the stunning preface by bisecting the natural law's fundamental principle, to do good and avoid evil: "The first step on the right road to conduct is to avoid evil." Undoubtedly the Catholic moral life came with low expectations.[7]

---

[2] John Gallagher, *Time Past, Time Future: An Historical Study of Catholic Moral Theology* (Mahwah, NJ: Paulist Press, 1990), 141.

[3] Thomas Slater, *A Manual of Moral Theology for English-speaking Countries* (London: Benziger Brothers, 1906).

[4] Henry Davis, *Moral and Pastoral Theology in Four Volumes*, 4th edition (New York: Sheed and Ward, 1943).

[5] Heribert Jone, *Moral Theology*, 8th ed., trans. Urban Adelman (Westminster: Newman Press, 1951).

[6] Slater, *A Manual of Moral Theology for English-speaking Countries*, 5–6.

[7] Ibid., 6.

Slater's claim that moral theology was only about avoiding evil was shared by the other manualists. For instance, Davis writes: "It is precisely about the law that Moral Theology is concerned. It is not a mirror of perfection."[8] The manuals of moral theology were not designed to help one become a disciple, but rather to help keep a penitent from becoming lost forever.

Regarding conscience, Slater described it as meaning "a dictate of the practical reason deciding that a particular action is right or wrong."[9] He invoked "certainty," a key concept for the manualists. "In order to act lawfully and rightly, I must have at least moral certainty of the imperfect kind that the proposed action is honest and right."[10]

Since perfect certainty about a moral judgment is often elusive, the required degree of moral confidence for right action is imperfect certainty: Is one at least adequately convinced that one's action is right or not? If one lacked imperfect certitude, then one experienced practical doubt; acting out of such a conscience was not lawful. The conscientious but doubtful Catholic had to search for imperfect certainty and, therefore, needed to consult an expert: the parish priest. The doubtful Catholic usually did this in the confessional.

Like Slater, Henry Davis defined conscience as "an act of practical reason."[11] He noted that "if conscience were never interfered with by passion or ignorance there would be only one kind of conscience, namely the true conscience."[12] The simplicity of his assumptions allowed him to describe a variety of ways by which one lacks a true conscience. He gave a startlingly long list of categorically problematic consciences (the false, doubting, perplexed, scrupulous, and laxed conscience), allowing us to see just how easily and frequently the average Catholic departs from the true conscience.[13]

On the obstacles to acting out of conscience, Jone provided a host of nervous conditions that diminished the agent's moral responsibility: neurasthenia, hysteria, compulsive disorders, melancholia, hypochondria, inferiority, and more.[14] While we see in Davis a tendency to find the conscience of the agent more ignorant, confused, and incompetent than in Slater, in Jone we find the penitent more prone to psychological disorders. In both cases, while compassion for the sinner was probably what motivated them, the newer

---

8 Davis, *Moral and Pastoral Theology in Four Volumes,* 1:4.

9 Slater, *A Manual of Moral Theology for English-speaking Countries*, 53.

10 Ibid., 60.

11 Davis, *Moral and Pastoral Theology in Four Volumes,* 1:65.

12 Ibid.

13 Ibid., 1:67–78.

14 Jone, *Moral Theology*, 29–37.

writers still found more occasions to view the ordinary penitent as less capable, less responsible, and less mature. For them, the average lay person was really not capable of discerning and executing morally right conduct.

Moreover, during these first fifty years of the twentieth century, other church developments further conspired to infantilize the laity. For instance, along with its promulgation of the Code of Canon Law in 1917, Vatican congregations and offices spoke on moral matters more and more frequently and more and more specifically throughout the century. To the extent that they did, to that extent were moralists no longer theologians reflecting on the questions facing the contemporary world, questions that were routinely addressed from the sixteenth to the nineteenth century in the casuistic and moral manuals.[15] These earlier moral theologians wrote mostly on the fifth, seventh, and eighth commandments, developing teachings on war and international law; on money lending, pension funds, and annuities; and on lying, oath taking, and witnessing. That is, they helped construct ways for Catholics to participate in the emerging political, financial, and legal world order of modernity.

Nothing like this happened in the first fifty years of the twentieth century. On the contrary, these later manualists attended to the continuous output of normative teachings from the Roman Curia throughout the twentieth century that were set on controlling Catholic identity and life within the church. The more "urgent" questions in the manuals reflect the Vatican's internal-ecclesial agenda: fulfilling the laws of the church, fasting and abstinence, avoiding servile work, attending to Catholic education, and avoiding condemned books or movies.

As the century unfolded, manualists were more and more concerned not with facing the challenges of the world but with conforming to the rigors of the church. In fact, in the United States, where the manualist tradition continued to the end of the 1960s and still is alive and well in many seminaries, these same obsessive, conforming identity issues drive moral theology.

Moral manualists became also more and more opposed to innovation. They chided those who looked for moral theology to be more integrated into both dogmatic or fundamental theology and ascetical or devotional theology. In fact, the more other theologians tried to persuade the manualists in this more holistic direction, the more the manualists receded from moral theology into canon law. In a particularly salient way the manualists from the United States resisted and derided the developments coming from Europe.

---

[15] Albert Jonsen and Stephen Toulmin, *The Abuse of Casuistry* (Berkeley and Los Angeles: University of California Press, 1988); John Mahoney, *The Making of Moral Theology* (New York: Oxford University Press, 1987).

As a result of these developments, the manualists were unable to address the real critical issues of the day.[16] For instance, though writing during the war, Davis spends a mere two paragraphs in talking about killing the innocent during war, but two full pages on a Vatican norm on girls' dresses at mass on Sunday.[17] Jone dedicates one sentence to the moral possibility of hydrogen warfare but provides a timetable to reckon how many minutes "our clocks are ahead of or behind true local time." The table assists in matters regarding private celebration of the mass, recitation of the divine office, receiving holy communion, and observing the laws of fasting and abstinence. More than 100 US cities are provided. As he notes, midnight in Albany is 12:05 am.[18]

The European Repudiation of the Manuals and Their Turn to Conscience

On the eve of the war a few European moral theologians recognized that the moral manuals were an embarrassment and needed to be repudiated. They were notably Fritz Tillmann, Émile Mersch, Gustav Ermecke, Johannes Stelzenberger, Bernard Häring, Gerard Gilleman, and Rene Carpentier.[19] Their initiatives provided enough theological foundations and directionality before the war that after the war the replacement of the manuals could begin to take place.

Belgian Benedictine Dom Odon Lottin (1880–1965) led the charge in the aftermath of World War II. In 1946, he published his first moral theological synthesis, *Principes de Morale*. Not a manual for hearing confessions, it is instead a theological foundation for anyone interested in the formation of conscience.[20] In 1954, he published his revolutionary *Morale Fondamentale*, in which he critiques the wretched past of moral theology, blaming the priest-confessor's singular focus on sin as principal cause for moral theology's failure.[21] He also attacks moral theologians and probabilists in particular, calling their command of the field of moral theology "profoundly regrettable" and noting that the probabilists never instructed the laity to be

[16] See examples in James F. Keenan, *A History of Catholic Moral Theology in the Twentieth Century: From Confessing Sins to Liberating Consciences* (New York: Continuum, 2010), 9–34.

[17] Ibid., 30.

[18] Jone, *Moral Theology*, 209, 357.

[19] Karl-Heinz Kleber, *Historia Docet: Zur Geschichte der Moraltheologie* (Münster: LIT Verlag, 2005), 89.

[20] Odon Lottin, *Principes de Morale* (Louvain: Abbaye du Mont César, 1946).

[21] Odon Lottin, *Morale Fondamentale* (Tournai, Belgium: Desclee and Cie, 1954).

virtuous; all they did was offer a variety of actions as not sinful, that is, as permitted.[22] What clergy and moral theologians should do, Lottin argues, is assist the laity to lead positive conscientious lives.[23] His striking break with the manualists is seen by the hermeneutical context in which he establishes the conscience as foundational to the moral life. No longer do we find the manualists' pathology of conscience: doubtful, laxed, scrupulous, uncertain, or erroneous. Here we find instead extensive writings on the "formation" of conscience, some forty-five pages. Here too we find the resolution of doubt, not by consulting a priest who looks up what a probabilist permits, but rather by forming a mature conscience. Thus, after establishing that the end of morals is to form the conscience, he dedicates the remaining 130 pages to the virtuous life and to the formation of the prudential judgment.[24] The Christian conscience is formed by the virtues—and these are acquired, developed, and maintained by learning what prudence means.[25]

By turning to the virtues and prudence, Lottin liberates the Christian conscience from its singular docility to the confessor priest. He instructs church members to become mature, self-governing Christians and insists that Christians have a lifelong task, a progressive one, as he called it, toward the ideals of both the natural and supernatural virtues.[26] This emphasis on the personal is not a move away from community; rather, Lottin argues that our personal good is derived from the common good.[27] By turning to prudence, then, Lottin urges his readers to find within themselves, their community, their faith, the church's tradition and its scriptures, the mode and the practical wisdom for determining themselves into growing as better Christians.

Then there is Bernard Häring.[28] In 1936 he was asked to prepare to teach in the field of moral theology. "I told my superior that this was my very last choice," Häring remembered, "because I found the teaching of moral theology an absolutely crushing bore."[29] He wrote:

> In 1936 when I came to study moral theology under the guidance of a professor who was a canon lawyer, he used the manual of Aertnys-

22 Ibid., 331.

23 Ibid., 297–339ff.

24 Ibid., 341–470.

25 Ibid., 363–69, 379–81, 448–52.

26 Ibid., 54ff.

27 Ibid., 189–201.

28 On Häring, see Joseph Römelt, "Bernhard Häring," ed. Konrad Hilpert, *Christliche Ethik im Porträt* (Freiburg: Herder, 2012), 705–27; James F. Keenan, "Bernard Häring's Influence on American Catholic Moral Theology," *Journal of Moral Theology* 1/1 (2012): 23–42.

29 Bernard Häring, *My Witness for the Church* (Mahwah, NJ: Paulist Press, 1992), 19.

> Damen; we students found ourselves in crisis and even disgusted. For my personal in-depth development I found other ethical writers of great value. Thus I created a deviation between the official morality for the preparation of the office of confessor and the personal work for a morality to live and to announce.[30]

His own experience of the war intervened and shaped the breadth and depth of his project.[31] Häring witnessed to how many Christians recognized the truth, were convicted by it, and stood firm with it. The war experiences irretrievably disposed him to the agenda of developing a moral theology that aims for the bravery, solidarity, and truthfulness of those committed Christians he met in the war.[32]

At the same time he also witnessed to

> the most absurd obedience by Christians toward a criminal regime. And that too radically affected my thinking and acting as a moral theologian. After the war, I returned to moral theology with the firm decision to teach it so that the core concept would not be obedience but responsibility, the courage to be responsible.[33]

Repudiating the manualists' obediential moral theology, he summoned conscientious Christians to a responsive and responsible life of discipleship.

In 1954, the same year that Lottin published *Morale Fondamentale,* Häring published in German the sixteen-hundred-page magisterial three-volume manual *Das Gesetz Christi (The Law of Christ: Moral Theology for Priests and Laity)*.[34] The opening words of the foreword were decisive: "The principle, the norm, the center, and the goal of Christian moral Theology is Christ."[35]

Among its innumerable contributions are five central themes: an entirely positive orientation; an emphasis on history and tradition; human freedom as the basis of Christian morality; the formation of the conscience; and the relevance of worship for the moral life. Here he writes with a deep

---

[30] Bernhard Häring, *Teología Morale Verso il Terzo Millennio*, class notes (Rome: Alfonsianum University, 1987). This was the last course Häring offered.

[31] Häring, *My Witness for the Church,* 132.

[32] Bernard Häring, *Embattled Witness: Memories of a Time of War* (New York: Seabury Press, 1976).

[33] Ibid., 23–24.

[34] Bernhard Häring, *Das Gesetz Christi* (Freiburg: Verlag Wewel, 1954). Translated by Edwin G. Kaiser as *The Law of Christ: Moral Theology for Priests and Laity* (Paramus, NJ: Newman Press, 1961).

[35] Häring, *The Law of Christ*, vii.

confidence in the theological competency and interest of the educated, conscientious Catholic.

At Vatican II Häring served on pre-conciliar and conciliar commissions, but most important, he was the secretary of the editorial committee that drafted the *Pastoral Constitution on the Church in the Modern World (Gaudium et Spes),*[36] and he was referred to as "the quasi-father of *Gaudium et Spes*."[37] We see his style throughout it. The anthropological vision is based on the human as a social being. Moral issues are not treated as primarily individual, but rather as communal and even global. Even though sin is pervasive in the document, the vision is fundamentally positive, as the church stands with the world in joy and hope. A new moral theological foundation emerges: here the church conveys a deep sympathy for the human condition, especially in all its anxieties, and stands in confident solidarity with the world. The entire experience of ambivalence that so affected the world in its tumultuous changes of the 1960s is positively, but realistically, engaged.[38] Finally, in looking at contemporary moral challenges, the church encourages an interdisciplinary approach in understanding and promoting a globalized vision of modernity.

Out of this framework, the council shaped the now famous conciliar definition of conscience in paragraph 16, evidently indebted to Häring's extensive description of conscience in *The Law of Christ*.[39]

The teaching on conscience is, I think, the emblematic expression of the hopeful expectations raised by Häring and affirmed by Vatican II. Universally, conscience becomes from that time the point of departure for revisionists, as witnessed by the plethora of books and essays that appear later on the topic.

The American Rejection of the European Turn to Conscience

Unlike Europe, America did not come out of the war in doubt about its actions, except for the bombings of Hiroshima and Nagasaki, and perhaps of Dresden and Tokyo. Americans, and Catholics in particular, came out of the war more confident than ever. They had no need to repudiate the manuals.

---

[36] Häring also assisted in other documents, among them *Optatam Totius* and the chapters on the laity and the call to holiness in *Lumen Gentium.*

[37] Charles Curran, "Bernard Häring: A Moral Theologian Whose Soul Matched His Scholarship." *National Catholic Reporter* 34 (July 17, 1998).

[38] Philippe Bordeyne, *L'Homme et son angoisse: La Theologie Morale de 'Gaudium et Spes'* (Paris: Cerf, 2004).

[39] Häring, *The Law of Christ*, 1:135–89.

The developing role of the moral theologian as primarily the interpreter and parser of church internal laws, therefore, had an extended lifespan in the United States, giving it a chilling maturity that is with us today. Charles Curran, in his compelling *Catholic Moral Theology in the United States: A History*, makes a similar point: "Catholic moral theology in the United States continued to use the manuals as the textbook for the discipline and followed existing approaches in sexual and medical ethics. As a result, theologians in this country were not prepared for the new perspectives ushered in by the Second Vatican Council."[40]

From 1940 on, American moral theologians writing the "Moral Notes" section in *Theological Studies* treated developments in European moral theology. John Lynch, and then John Ford and Gerald Kelly, were parsimonious in granting entrance in their roles as gatekeepers of acceptable innovation. While editing "Moral Notes" myself, I surveyed the journal's first twenty-five years (1940–65) and found substantive innovations in the field of social ethics, whether from John Ryan, Paul Furfey, John LaFarge, or John Courtney Murray,[41] but I found hardly any innovation at all in fundamental moral theology by Lynch, Ford, and Kelly; instead, I found steady resistance to Janssens, Häring, Alfons Auer, and others. Other than Ford's compassionate care for alcoholics and some comments on conscientious objection in war, everything they write on fundamental moral theology is manualistic. The exceptional essay by Ford on "Obliteration Bombing" is exactly that, an exception.[42]

In fact, these theologians are more rigid, authoritative, and intolerant than even their predecessors, Slater, Davis, and Jone. They invert the order of authority that the high casuists and early manualists use, acknowledging the authority of the papacy and of Roman dicasteries before that of the argument itself—in fact, sometimes without even considering the argument's authority. For Ford and Kelly, a magisterial claim is itself the guarantor of its truthfulness. As they insist on that guarantee, they reject the appeal to conscience: "It is only through conformity with the teaching of the Church that the individual conscience can have security from error. The 'autonomy of the individual conscience' cannot be reconciled with the plan of Christ and can produce only 'poisonous fruit.'"[43]

---

40 Charles Curran, *Catholic Moral Theology in the United States: A History* (Washington, DC: Georgetown University Press, 2008), 59.

41 See also ibid., 63–82.

42 John Ford, "The Morality of Obliteration Bombing," *Theological Studies* 5/3 (1944): 261–309; see Eric Genilo's perceptive analysis, *John Cuthbert Ford: Moral Theologian at the End of the Manualist Era* (Washington, DC: Georgetown University Press, 2007).

43 John Ford and Gerald Kelly, *Contemporary Moral Theology I: Questions in Fundamental Moral Theology* and *Contemporary Moral Theology II: Marriage Questions*

Their dependence on the agenda that Rome sets is far more in evidence than even Davis and Jone and is summarized in this stunning statement:

> An earnest student of papal pronouncements, Vincent A. Yzermans, estimated that during the first fifteen years of his pontificate Pius XII gave almost one thousand public addresses and radio messages. If we add to these the apostolic constitutions, the encyclicals and so forth, during the same period of fifteen years, and add furthermore all the papal statements during the subsequent years, we have well over a thousand papal documents. . . . Merely from the point of view of volume, therefore, one can readily appreciate that it was not mere facetiousness that led a theologian to remark, that even if the Holy See were to remain silent for ten years, the theologians would have plenty to do in classifying and evaluating the theological significance of Pius XII's public statements.[44]

Ford's and Kelly's approach eventually faced critique by their peers. Daniel Callahan describes the authors as "loyal civil servants" and "faithful party workers" and dismisses their work "as years behind the (theological) revolution now in progress."[45] Later, David Kelly identifies the period from 1940 to 1968 as one of "ecclesiastical positivism." During that time "divine will is seen to be expressed in a specific source of revelation, the authoritative pronouncements and interpretations of the Roman Catholic magisterium."[46]

As we can now see, in countries where moral theologians write from 1946 to 1968 on conscience, their bishops (who were once these theologians' students) are able to invoke conscience in light of church teaching; not so in the United States. We cannot primarily blame our bishops for this; the blame falls on American moral theologians.

A turn to the birth-control debate is a good illustration of the divide between the Americans and the Europeans. When the encyclical *Humanae Vitae* appears in 1968, the episcopal conferences receive the encyclical differently: the French, German, Canadian, Scandinavian, and Dutch bishops author a variety of responses that encourage the laity to follow their consciences as they receive the encyclical; the United States Conference of

(Westminster, MD: Newman Press, 1964), 1:111.

44 Ibid., 1:20–21.

45 Daniel Callahan, "Authority and the Theologian," *Commonweal* 30/11 (June 5, 1964): 319–23.

46 David Kelly, *The Emergence of Roman Catholic Medical Ethics in North America* (New York: Edwin Mellen Press, 1979), 231.

Catholic Bishops stands univocally in strong solidarity with the encyclical itself, with hardly a word on conscience.[47]

Though discussion on birth control starts in 1957, still, among moralists there is little new until 1963, when John Rock writes his bestselling book, *The Time Has Come*.[48] Then, Janssens breaks ranks with his fellow moralists and argues that the use of anovulant drugs is no different in intentionality from using a "natural" method that depends on a woman's infertile period.[49] A variety of Europeans follow this train of thought, but again the response from Kelly, Lynch, and Connell is a critical one.[50]

At the council itself European moralists are largely trying to look at birth control through a different lens from that of a legal hermeneutics. They are looking to find out what a person in conscience should do, searching for the moral truth without confining themselves to the ecclesial positivism of the Americans and of bygone days. The council's spirit and style are emboldening them to do so. And in doing so, European moral theologians develop a way of describing what in conscience as a disciple of Christ one should consider in the case of contraception, or as it was eventually called, responsible parenthood.

No small event in the formation of this consensus is the intellectual conversion of Josef Fuchs, who is added to the papal commission studying birth control, ostensibly because he seems less inclined to change than other commission members, notably Häring. After hearing the testimony of married couples, Fuchs abandons his conviction that moral truth is found necessarily and primarily in long-held norms articulated by the magisterium.[51] The competency of a moral decision depends on the adequacy of the human judgment in conscience and, to Fuchs, the married couples' understanding of the specific claims on them is more comprehensive and more adequate than the general teachings of Rome. Fuchs acknowledges here that one finds moral truth through the discernment of an informed conscience confronting reality: "Many confuse objective morality with the prescriptions of the Church. . . . We have to realize that reality is what is.

---

[47] John Horgan, *Humanae Vitae and the Bishops* (Dublin: Irish University Press, 1972).

[48] John Rock, *The Time Has Come: A Catholic Doctor's Proposals to End the Battle over Birth Control* (New York: Alfred A. Knopf, 1963).

[49] Louis Janssens, "Morale conjugale et progestogènes," *Ephemerides Theologicae Lovanieneses* (1963): 787–826.

[50] Francis Swift, "An Analysis of the American Theological Reaction to Janssens' Stand on The Pill," *Louvain Studies* 1 (1966): 19–54.

[51] Mark Graham, *Josef Fuchs on Natural Law* (Washington, DC: Georgetown University Press, 2002); James F. Keenan, "Josef Fuchs and the Question of Moral Objectivity in Roman Catholic Ethical Reasoning," *Religious Studies Review* 24/3 (1998): 253–58.

And we grow to understand it with our reason, aided by law. We have to educate people to assume responsibility and not just to follow the law."[52]

Conscience Today

In the United States the turn to conscience did not come out of the profound remorse that the Europeans had at the end of the war; rather, the turn to conscience was born as a way of opting out of *Humanae Vitae*. As I have argued above, the United States never developed the robust notion of conscience that one finds among the Europeans.[53] For that reason, I suggest that we turn to what the Europeans have and are developing so as to develop a notion of conscience that is largely about self-governing and not primarily a mode for dissenting (note, for instance, how, like the laity on *Humanae Vitae*, the United States bishops have invoked conscience as a way of opting out of the Affordable Care Act).

Seventy years after the war the Europeans maintain a remarkable and enduring defense of conscience as the locus for moral responsibility to the call of discipleship. For them, only an active, vigilant conscience is a Christian conscience. Conscience is not simply an act or a habit, as the medieval Scholastics claimed; it is deeper, more profound, more fundamental to the person. It is, as Klaus Demmer notes, at the origin of every decision.[54]

In the twenty-first century we need this more robust notion of conscience that requires more from the ordinary Christian and that sees the conscience as the source of moral agency.[55] For this reason we can say that we need always to heed and form and follow our conscience. Moreover, the revisionists' notion of conscience is in the pursuit of the good, animated by its call to love God, self, and neighbor. Conscience has a highly relationally oriented understanding; it is not simply the agent making a judgment, but

---

[52] Robert Kaiser, *The Politics of Sex and Religion: A Case History in the Development of Doctrine 1962–1984* (Kansas City, MO: Leaven Press, 1985), 154.

[53] Keenan, *A History of Catholic Moral Theology in the Twentieth Century,* 141–83. For further development, see idem, "Redeeming Conscience," *Theological Studies* 76/1 (2015).

[54] Klaus Demmer, *Living the Truth: A Theory of Action* (Washington, DC: Georgetown University Press, 2010), 118–50.

[55] For further development, see James F. Keenan, "Catholic Conscience Awakening: The Evolution of Our Contemporary Dependence on Conscience," ed. Stephan Goertz, Rudolf B. Hein, Katharina Klöcker, *Fluchtpunkt Fundamentalismus: Gegenwartsdiagnosen katholischer Moral* (Freiburg: Herder, 2013), 305–25.

rather the way that the disciple hears and responds to the triple command to love through virtue.

That triple command is only made possible in its realization by grace. Bringing grace into the language of conscience becomes then a way of understanding the accompaniment of God with us from the very first stages of God's call to the very final stages of our lives, most particularly in those moments where we are convinced in conscience of taking a stand. It also serves as a way of reminding us that it is precisely in conscience that we are most alone with the God who accompanies us, as *Gaudium et Spes* teaches us.

Finally, it is good for us to consider a favorite insight from Demmer. When asked if bishops should instruct the faithful what their own positions were on specific moral/civic issues, he argued that bishops should attend to their primary charge: to remind all Christians that they each have a conscience to be followed.[56] If bishops spent their moral energy on this, then maybe the people of God would get somewhere. But he felt that bishops neglected this. Still, one would ask, what if bishops did preach, teach, and admonish all their communities to follow their consciences, could they still take moral stances and urge Christians to follow this or that course of action? Demmer would remind the bishops that their second task is to instruct Christians that, knowing they have to follow their consciences, now they need to form their consciences. Because conscience formation is not first about knowledge of the right, but about the more complex task of living the right, they have to form their consciences by becoming better people, more competent at living and doing the truth. Demmer would remind them, however, that this second task was a lifelong one and that getting started on the right road is a long process. "It takes time to gain a foothold in truthfulness," he once wrote.[57] But then, Demmer would be asked, if bishops did teach us to follow and form our consciences, could they then take moral stances? Exasperated, he would say, well, if they do both, I think they could have their say.

An Application

I have finished a book on an institution that rarely considers ethics, the university. This might seem surprising, but I think the case can easily be

[56] Klaus Demmer, "La competenza normativa del magistero ecclesiastico in morale," in Klaus Demmer and Bruno Schüller, *Fede cristiana e agire morale* (Assisi: Cittadella, 1980), 144–72.

[57] Demmer, *Living the Truth*, 143.

made.[58] Here, then, I propose a case wherein we may see a case of a contemporary Christian conscience at a university.

Consider: At a Catholic university a relatively new faculty member learns that the university administration has recently cracked down on a group of students that is calling for responsible sexual conduct on campus by offering fellow students condoms. The students had been offering condoms for two years without any comment from the university. After the crackdown the students are ordered not to make any condoms available or else. What is not clear is the sanction, whether suspension or expulsion. The student newspaper calls the action of the university administration irresponsible because the university has done nothing to promote responsible sexual conduct except to say that sexual activity outside of marriage is illicit. Faculty response is not public, though many raise their eyebrows as if saying, "Are we in the twenty-first century?"

You are a senior tenured faculty member. A recently hired junior tenure-track faculty member comes to you and says, "I've been following this story, and a group of students has asked me to be on a panel addressing this issue. I am sympathetic to the students, but if I do this it will be my first public presentation on campus. By the way, the students told me that no other faculty member has agreed to speak. What do you think?"

In listening to the younger colleague, I would say something like this. The conscience of a faculty member should always be engaged at a Catholic university. In fact, the basic reason for a Catholic university to exist is twofold: to educate those in need and to engage publicly the moral challenges of our time. Though other Catholic institutions might not get as involved in controversial issues, it is precisely the Catholic university that must provide the safe space for such discourse.

That being said, I would say, you are right to wonder about what to do. I can only tell you how I try to work out my conscience on such matters. I believe that we define ourselves on our campuses by what we teach in our classes, by our availability to our students and colleagues, and by what we convey to others in the public forum. I tend to bring these issues up in my class on HIV/AIDS and ethics to develop a sense of consciousness raising with my students, not only about the world but also about their own campus lives. I try to help my students to understand that they too need to be involved in these matters. So, in my class, I try to teach my students that they need to form and follow their consciences.

Outside my class I only agree to be on panels on matters to which I think I bring a specific competency or a specific presence. For instance, recently

---

[58] James F. Keenan, *University Ethics: Why Colleges Need a Culture of Ethics* (New York: Rowman and Littlefield, 2015).

my university had a panel entitled "Are Women Treated Fairly Here?" I learned I was the only male faculty member who agreed to be on the panel. I made a point of that in my presentation. So often on issues more related to women, men stay out of the issue, and regardless of their position, their absence says volumes about their solidarity with women on campus.

I think on our campus there are issues that affect us, such as matters on responsible sexual conduct, fairness to women, equal respect for all, unexamined racial segregation, the embarrassing reality of classism that cuts across the campus, the unexamined treatment of staff and contingent faculty, the need to more transparently include gay, lesbian, and transgender students, staff and faculty, and more. These are matters that we need to be mindful of because they are essential issues for our community. As educators we have a special obligation to bring them to the fore in our classes and in our department meetings when it seems necessary and appropriate.

We enter into the university community by stages. In order to know when is the appropriate time and what is the appropriate issue that you should get involved on this panel, I would suggest you ask yourself three questions. Is this a justice issue that I should be a spokesperson for? Are there students on this campus whom I ought to be there to support? Am I concerned sufficiently with care for myself; that is, how ready am I to be confronted on campus in public debate? These three matters on justice as the fair treatment of persons, on fidelity to those to whom I owe it, and on an adequate regard for my own well-being seem to be the questions that a prudent faculty member out of conscience ought to consider and be vigilant about.[59] I would suggest that rather than making a quick decision about whether to be on the panel or not, you ask yourself these questions. I would also suggest that you think to the future about which campus issues you would want to speak publicly on.

Finally, would you mind if I brought up to the faculty the fact that no other faculty member accepted the student invitation to be on this panel? I think it might be worth our consideration as to why this is the case.

---

[59] For a development of these virtues, see James F. Keenan, "Proposing Cardinal Virtues," *Theological Studies* 56/4 (1995): 709–29; idem, "Virtue Ethics and Sexual Ethics," *Louvain Studies* 30/3 (2005): 183–203.

2.

Newman and the Problem of Conscience in Relation to Papal Infallibility

John R. Quinn

John Henry Newman's treatment of conscience is largely related to problems connected with the dogma of papal infallibility. His most extensive public treatment of conscience occurs in his *Letter Addressed to His Grace the Duke of Norfolk*,[1] and my observations in this essay deal chiefly with the *Letter*, even though there is a vast amount of material on conscience scattered throughout his personal correspondence[2] and in the final chapter of the *Apologia*.[3] Newman's lucid and profound elaboration is timely in today's church, in which conscience can be reduced to personal opinion and infallibility can be inflated to include every teaching and decision of the pope.

The *Letter* was occasioned by a fiery pamphlet by William Gladstone, who served sixty years in the House of Commons and led four governments as prime minister and served as leader of the opposition for three terms, and for four terms as chancellor of the exchequer.[4] Gladstone's pamphlet—*The*

[1] John Henry Newman, *A Letter Addressed to His Grace the Duke of Norfolk*, in *Certain Difficulties Felt by Anglicans in Catholic Teaching*, vol. 2 (Westminster, MD: Christian Classics, 1969), 176–347.

[2] See *The Letters and Diaries of John Henry Newman*, vol. 27, *The Controversy with Gladstone*, ed. Charles Stephen Dessain and Thomas Gornall (Oxford: Oxford University Press, 1975).

[3] John Henry Newman, *Apologia Pro Vita Sua*, ed. Martin J. Svaglic (Oxford: Clarendon Press, 1967), chap. 5.

[4] Gladstone's first term as prime minister ran from December 3, 1868, to February 17, 1874. He was leader of the opposition from February 17, 1874, to January 17, 1875. The reason Gladstone's first government fell was the defeat of his Irish University Bill. "The Irish members (of Parliament) voted against the Bill after the Irish bishops

Vatican Decrees in Their Bearing on Civil Allegiance—was published in November 1874, while he was leader of the opposition to the government of Benjamin Disraeli. The pamphlet sold 150,000 copies before the year's end. By the time Newman published his *Letter to the Duke of Norfolk* in 1875, Gladstone was no longer in the leadership of the Commons but remained a singularly important public figure.

Referring to the infallibility decree of Vatican I, Gladstone denounced Rome in his 1874 tract for creating "a policy of violence and change in faith . . . when no one can become her convert, without renouncing his moral and mental freedom, and placing his civil loyalty and duty at the mercy of another."[5] A basic theme running through what Gladstone wrote was that Vatican I had made Catholics the mental slaves of the pope, and in political matters demanded obedience to the pope rather than to the crown. Papal primacy and infallibility, therefore, were primarily understood by Gladstone in terms of their effect on the relationship of Catholic citizens to the state.

Given Gladstone's prestige and the vitriol of his language, there was an overwhelming sentiment among British Catholics that a public response had to be made. Newman was universally believed to be the most distinguished Catholic capable of making the response, which took the literary form of a letter addressed to the Duke of Norfolk. Several interesting things lay behind the choice of the duke as the addressee of the *Letter*. For one thing, he had been a pupil at Newman's Oratory School in Birmingham. But there was also a certain irony at work in the choice of the duke. He was a member of a pre-Reformation Catholic family and earl marshal of England. The earl marshal is the eighth of the Great Offices of State and above the office of the lord high admiral. He has the role of organizing the coronation of the monarch and all state funerals, and some earls marshal have even served as regent of England. Using the duke as the addressee was thus a way of saying how absurd Gladstone's attack on Catholics was, since he was really saying that even the earl marshal of England could not be a loyal citizen.

In the *Letter*, contradicting the broad claims of Gladstone, Newman established the fundamental truth that the infallibility of the church and of the pope is limited in its object and constrained by its circumstance. A definition can be infallible only when it is directed to the universal church and at the same time has as its object a divinely revealed truth. Consequently, papal infallibility does not extend to purely secular matters or to political matters. In some detail and with convincing power Newman eliminated

had condemned it, and Gladstone was convinced, mistakenly, that these had acted on instructions from the Pope" (see "Introductory Note," in *The Letters and Diaries of John Henry Newman*, 27:xiii).

[5] W. E. Gladstone, "Ritualism and Ritual," *Contemporary Review* 24 (1874): 674, quoted in Ian Ker, *John Henry Newman* (New York: Oxford University Press, 1990), 679.

Gladstone's objection to the council decree by showing its moderate and limited scope. To prove that infallibility is not a personal or arbitrary quality of the pope, he quoted a book by Fessler, an Austrian bishop, that had been praised by Pius IX himself. This is the passage Newman cited, "The Pope is not infallible as a man, or a theologian, or a priest, or a bishop, or a temporal prince, or a judge or a legislator, or in his political views, or even in his government of the Church."[6]

Having laid out the object and limits of papal infallibility, he went on to tackle Gladstone's affirmation that infallibility made Catholics mental slaves, did violence to their consciences, and made it impossible for them to be loyal citizens. In the first place Newman distinguishes between papal teaching authority, which articulates general religious truths such as Christ died for the salvation of all, and conscience, which makes the judgment here and now that something should or should not be done. "Conscience is not a judgment upon any speculative truth, any abstract doctrine, but bears immediately on conduct, on something to be done or not done. . . . Hence conscience cannot come into direct collision with the Church's or the Pope's infallibility."[7] Conscience is not a teacher of truth but a judge of action, and as Newman notes, conscience can be mistaken.

Gladstone was focused more on disciplinary orders or directives of the pope than on strictly doctrinal pronouncements. He erroneously thought that Vatican I taught that the pope is infallible in all his acts and directives. Thus he believed that a Catholic would be obliged to obey a papal order to kidnap the queen or to throw a bomb into the Houses of Parliament. Gladstone's preoccupation about the possibility of the pope fomenting a rebellion of some kind was influenced not only by extreme ultramontane ideas then in the air, but also by the awareness of such historical events as the excommunications of Henry VIII and Elizabeth I, both of which were followed by social upheavals and bloodshed. These same preoccupations of papal interference continued to concern the British government in the nineteenth century, when Catholic emancipation in Ireland was under discussion. Under existing laws Irish Catholics were required to take an oath rejecting the authority of the pope and another rejecting the church's teaching on transubstantiation—the doctrine of the true, not merely symbolic, presence of Christ in the Eucharist. They did not have voting rights and could not serve in the military or the judiciary or other professions. The Irish were a subjugated people, and Britain feared that if religious emancipation, that

---

[6] *Letter,* 325n.3. Newman quoted from a French translation of Fessler. Fessler's work was later published in English as *The True and False Infallibility of the Pope* (New York: Catholic Publication Society, 1875).

[7] Ibid., 256n.2.

is, the lifting of these various restrictions, were enacted, the Irish would be increasingly inclined to rebellion and that the pope might urge them on.

Gladstone, wrong in his understanding of the meaning and scope of papal infallibility, was also wrong in his belief that the pope was behind the failure of his Irish University Bill in 1873. Among other things this bill was aimed at giving nondenominational university education to Irish Catholics. The bill failed and brought down Gladstone's government. He was very bitter over this and believed that the Irish bishops, under Roman influence, had been behind the failure in some way.[8] Newman describes Gladstone's state of mind in a passage he cites in the *Letter:* "This step on the part of the bishops showed . . . the new and mischievous force which had been acquired at Rome by the late acts there."[9] The "late acts" were the *Syllabus of Errors,* Pius IX's condemnation of the errors of modernity, and the primacy and infallibility decrees of the council.

Newman strongly rejected this exaggerated view of papal authority: "I am far from saying that Popes are never in the wrong. . . . I am not bound to defend the policy or acts of particular Popes."[10] And in a subsequent "Postscript" to the *Letter,* he writes: "Were I actually a soldier in her Majesty's service in a just war, and should the Pope suddenly bid all Catholic soldiers to retire from her service . . . I should not obey him." Thus Newman refuted Gladstone by showing that infallibility does not apply to policy or disciplinary decrees.

During the council Newman had been concerned that an excessive notion of papal infallibility might prevail, but he relaxed when he saw the infallibility definition itself and realized that it was moderate and surrounded by conditions. He wrote, "I saw the new definition yesterday, and am pleased by its moderation. . . . Personally I have no difficulty in admitting it."[11] He judged the decree moderate because such voices as Archbishop Henry Edward Manning of Westminster and William Ward, editor of the widely read Catholic publication *The Dublin Review,* had been promoting a decree that would make a wide range of papal pronouncements infallible, including the *Syllabus.* But the decree did not do this. Newman found further reassurance about the infallibility decree in the realization that papal infal-

[8] Irish historian F. S. L. Lyons says of this bill: "With the massive insensitivity which that most subtle of men could sometimes muster, he thus succeeded in a single stroke in alienating every section of Irish opinion." While Gladstone blamed Rome and the Irish bishops for the failure of the bill, in fact he was blinded to the reality that no one wanted the bill, including Gladstone's cabinet. The House of Lords broke out in laughter when they heard the bill's provisions. See Edward Short, *Newman and His Contemporaries* (New York: T&T Clark, 2011), 229.

[9] *Letter,* "Introductory Remarks," 181.

[10] *Letter,* 217.

[11] *Letter,* 301.

libility is not "to be of everyday use, but . . . as a protection or remedy in great emergencies or on supreme occasions, when nothing else will serve, as extraordinary and solemn acts of [the church's] religious sovereignty."[12] Thus Newman asserted the principle of authority while at the same time asserting its limited scope. Infallibility was an emergency power.

For Newman, the primordial infallibility is not that of the pope but that of the church. The revelation given by Christ to the apostles is given to the church; it is the church that is infallible. This prompted modern theologian Yves Congar to point out that the divine revelation is not given to any single individual but to the whole church, and that for this reason it is necessary to persevere in the communion of the church in order to possess the whole of the gospel. It was the infallibility of the church that was one of the major truths behind Newman's painful decision to forsake his Anglican roots and become a Catholic. He said that Anglicans tended to base themselves on the axiom that the norm of truth is "what has always been, what is universal, and what is held by all *(quod semper, quod ubique, quod ab omnibus)*." But Newman, through his study of the fathers and of history, saw that the doctrine of the faith had developed over time. He therefore embraced as normative the truth enunciated by Augustine, "*Securus iudicat orbis terrarum*" (the verdict of the whole world is conclusive). By this phrase Newman understood that the norm of truth is not simply what was held in the past. The norm of truth must also include what the faith of the universal church is now. He was thus reassured when the text of the decree on infallibility explicitly stated that the pope, under the conditions stipulated, has that infallibility which the church possesses. The pope is not only the guardian of ancient tradition but also the authentic witness of the faith of the church now.

For a time after the council was adjourned, he was not sure that papal infallibility had been defined as a dogma of faith, because some eighty bishops were absent at the final vote, thus calling the moral unanimity of the vote into question. Some of these bishops just did not think that papal infallibility should be defined at all because it had not been debated long enough among theologians and because they feared it would cause serious misunderstandings for governments and problems of conscience for individuals. Some left because they could not accept the clause in the final decree that infallible declarations of the pope are "infallible in their own right and not because of agreement by the Church," a clause often cited in its Latin original, *ex sese et non ex consensu ecclesiae.* However, correctly understood, this statement was intended to exclude the Gallican idea that the pope's decrees had to be subsequently approved by the bishops. The clause

---

[12] *Letter,* 209.

was meant to counteract any Gallican idea that the pope is in a canonical sense subject to or merely the executor of the will of the episcopate. Such clarifications are found in the *Acts of the Council* but were not placed in the actual text of the decrees, so as not to give any hint of support for the Gallican positions.

When, during the months following the council, it became evident that most of the bishops publicly accepted the dogma, Newman's concern about unanimity was put to rest. Fessler's book also served to remove these concerns. Yet, even when he accepted papal infallibility as a dogma of faith, Newman continued to believe that much greater balance and clarity would be achieved when the theologians wrote about it; further, he explicitly held that a future council would bring needed balance and perspective to the doctrine. In other words he expected that writings of theologians and a future council would make more explicit that papal infallibility is limited by divine revelation and by divine tradition and is exercised in the communion of the episcopate. He anticipated that because the council focused so strongly on the pope, the role of the episcopate had not been sufficiently expressed and thus a future council would make more explicit that the bishops as well as the pope are of divine institution in the church.

Gladstone's concerns were how the government would deal with Catholic citizens whom he erroneously thought to be under the supreme authority of a pope infallible in both secular and religious matters and whom he feared might be directed by such a pope to act against the laws of the country. Newman had dealt with these broad issues raised by Gladstone by showing that infallibility did not extend to purely secular or political matters.

But he did experience continuing concern over the problems of conscience of many people who consulted him and sought his guidance in their personal perplexities. To help these people during the first months after the council, he repeatedly said that for a long period the church had acted as if the pope could make infallible declarations concerning revealed truth. It was a fairly common position of theologians, for example, that the condemnation of Jansenism by Pius VI in 1796 was an infallible papal teaching. Thus on July 30, 1870, he wrote, "But the definition is what the Church has acted upon for some centuries, and a very large body of Catholics have long held."[13] It was a theological opinion held by many but not a dogma of faith.

As a way of helping perplexed people, Newman adds but does not elaborate upon another very important consideration: "Perhaps it is *necessary,* in time to come, for the seat of government to be strengthened." And he explains, "If terrible times were imminent, an increase in papal authority

---

[13] Letter to Madame Jacques Blumenthal, July 30, 1870, in *The Letters and Diaries of John Henry Newman,* 25:170.

might be absolutely necessary to keep things together."[14] The intention of strengthening the seat of government, that is, the pope, was rooted not only in doctrinal principles but was influenced in the minds of many bishops at Vatican I by the five year imprisonment of Pius VII by Napoleon, during which the pope was incommunicado. The demand that all the clergy of France should take the oath of the Civil Constitution of the Clergy denied the authority of the pope and in effect created a French church. This severely divided the priests and bishops into those who took the oath and those who didn't, and these severe divisions rendered the French episcopate incapable of dealing with the grave problems of the church resulting from the revolution. Napoleon, who saw that he had to address the serious problems of the church if he was to unite France, wanted to remove and reconstitute the French episcopate and reorganize and reduce the number of dioceses. But he came to see that the people and a large part of the clergy would never accept this if it was done without or against the pope.

Ultimately, by a stunning primatial act, the pope agreed to remove the entire French episcopate and reconstitute it. The bishops at Vatican I, never forgetting how Pius VII in fact saved the church in France in the face of the impotence of the bishops, perceived that possible future crises or world conditions might necessitate definitive action by the pope in crisis situations that could not wait for extended consultation or the convening of a synod or council, or even situations in which the pope was arrested or imprisoned. Walter Kasper writes:

> The Fathers of the First Vatican Council experienced specific historical conditions that led them to formulate things the way they did. The Council majority saw the church besieged from all sides and in an almost apocalyptic situation. . . . This is why they reverted to the modern idea of sovereignty, in such a way that he could act even if he were to be prevented from communicating with the Church.[15]

Sovereignty is in general understood as supreme authority that is absolute and incommunicable, that is, an authority beyond which there is no appeal. The council used strong language not only to provide for extreme situations but also to put to rest any idea of Gallicanism, that is, of the pope being limited by the authority of the bishops. They did not want to stipulate conditions in the text of the decree because they were aware that they could

[14] Ibid.

[15] Walter Kasper, "Introduction to the Theme and Catholic Hermeneutics of the Dogmas of the First Vatican Council," in *The Petrine Ministry,* ed. Cardinal Walter Kasper (Mahwah, NJ: Newman Press, 2006), 19.

not foresee exactly what kind of future crises might arise, and they wanted to make it clear that the pope could act in any crisis situation. The text of the decree purposely set the papal primacy in the context of the tradition of the church and of previous councils, and the *Acts of the Council* shows that the text was to be understood and interpreted in this sense.

While Newman made reference to considerations of this kind when dealing with those who were personally troubled, he also encouraged them not to act precipitously, to take their time. He encouraged them to pray and to have strong faith in God's providence over the church. But he was outraged at priests and bishops who demanded immediate acceptance of the council teaching. His long personal experience of dealing with people led him to the conviction that people need time and that harsh measures are reprehensible. People were unsettled and perplexed due to the propaganda urging that the *Syllabus* be defined as infallible, and this state of anxiety was augmented by the absence of general public knowledge of the actual proceedings of the council. Newman was trying to help people get through this while respecting their troubled consciences.

The most far-reaching point made by Newman, in my opinion, is what he calls "the supreme authority of conscience."[16] Joseph Ratzinger writes: "For Newman, conscience represents the inner complement and limit of the Church principle. Over the pope as the expression of the binding claim of ecclesiastical authority there still stands one's own conscience, which must be obeyed before all else. If necessary even against the requirement of ecclesiastical authority."[17] Ratzinger was aware of the frequently cited words of Newman, "Certainly, if I am obliged to bring religion into after-dinner toasts, (which indeed does not seem quite the thing) I shall drink—to the pope, if you please,—still, to Conscience first, and to the Pope afterwards."[18]

But are there no limits to conscience? Newman points out that conscience "is the highest of all teachers, yet the least luminous."[19] He is careful to distinguish the popular idea of conscience from the authentic Catholic understanding. About the widespread popular understanding of conscience he writes: "When men advocate the rights of conscience, they in no sense mean the rights of the Creator, nor the duty due to Him, in thought and deed, of the creature; but the right of thinking, speaking, writing and acting, according to their judgment or their humour, without any thought of God

---

[16] *Letter,* 246.

[17] Joseph Ratzinger, "The Dignity of the Human Person," in *Commentary on the Documents of Vatican II,* vol. 5, ed. Herbert Vorgrimler (New York: Herder and Herder, 1969), 134.

[18] *Letter,* 261.

[19] Ibid., 254.

at all. . . . It is the right of self-will."[20] The true Catholic idea of conscience means "the rights of the Creator . . . the duty to Him, in thought and deed. . . . Conscience has rights because it has duties."[21] And he says again, "I am using the word 'conscience' . . . not as a fancy or an opinion, but as a dutiful obedience to what claims to be a divine voice, speaking within us."[22]

Newman goes on to speak of the required conditions if conscience is to refuse obedience to papal authority. "If in a particular case it is to be taken as a sacred and sovereign monitor, its dictate, in order to prevail against the voice of the pope, must follow upon serious thought, prayer, and all available means of arriving at a right judgment on the matter in question."[23] Various factors affect the ability of conscience to hear accurately this voice of God speaking in the depths of the human person, things such as original sin, about which Newman spoke so powerfully in the *Apologia*, prejudice, social conditioning, and other such factors. Hence, the need for thought, consultation, study, and prayer, which Newman mentions. The Catholic of mature faith dealing with conflict with papal authority would always have the humility to say, "Maybe I am wrong," and pausing to consider this possibility would also be an element of such discernment.

Newman's chief framework for his public treatment of conscience is focused on the relation of the Catholic citizen to the civil power and what response such a citizen's conscience would require him or her to make in the event that the pope would intervene in the political affairs of the nation. Until the twentieth century the popes did not say very much about problems of personal morality. This happened at the time of the contraception controversy in the late 1960s and issues of homosexuality so widely aired today. Matters of personal morality do not enter into Newman's thinking on conscience.

But Newman's emphasis on the individual ultimately confronted by the supreme tribunal of his or her conscience establishes a principle in opposition to increasing secular and civil totalitarianism. Newman's doctrine of the primacy of conscience, though framed in terms of the citizen in conflict with papal interference in purely political matters, means also that above the power of the state there stands within the human person, the citizen, a sovereign zone of freedom to which the state does not have access and that it cannot control. There was something of a prophetic intuition here of the yet unimagined totalitarianism of the Nazi and the Communist eras. And so there is no question that Newman lays the groundwork for the great affirmation of *Gaudium et Spes* that "The Church is the sign and

[20] Ibid., 250.
[21] Ibid.
[22] Ibid., 255.
[23] Ibid., 257–58.

the safeguard of the transcendence of the human person" (no. 76).[24] As Joseph Ratzinger said of Vatican II, "Merely by the weight it attributes to the subject of conscience within the framework of its doctrine of man, it takes its place in the line of thought deriving from Newman."[25] Newman, along with Kierkegaard, gives a new focus to conscience as the center of Christian anthropology. This anthropology is based on the truth that the human person is created by God and for God—his or her origin and destiny is beyond the state and not confined to this world. This is what is meant by affirming "the transcendence of the human person." Newman, focusing on showing that a Catholic citizen does not take orders from the pope in purely political matters and that the pope's infallibility does not extend to such matters, clearly upholds the primacy of conscience without developing a detailed exposition of the issue.

In summary, then, Newman represents "in an unprecedented way the discovery of the individual who is called directly by God and who, in a world which scarcely makes God known any more, is able to become directly certain of God through the voice of conscience."[26]

---

[24] The Latin original is *tutamentum*, which means "defense," suggesting an active, watchful, protective stance; "safeguard" seems to convey a more passive idea.

[25] Ratzinger, "The Dignity of the Human Person," 5:134.

[26] Ibid.

3.

Three Modes of the Embodiment of Conscience

Osamu Takeuchi, S.J.

Conscience is often understood in Catholic thought solely as an intellectual judgment on a moral act. Understood in this way conscience is very act centered, individualistic, and rational. But it is very difficult for such an understanding of conscience to be brought into dialogue with Japanese and broader Asian culture, which, among other things, has a profoundly communal and religious sensibility. Are there resources in the tradition of Catholic theology on conscience that could be brought into more fruitful dialogue with Japanese culture? Are there resources in Japanese and Asian culture that can deepen the Catholic understanding of conscience?

In this essay I explore both questions in the hope of arriving at a Catholic notion of conscience that can be more conversant with Japanese and Asian culture. At the heart of my argument is the claim that we have three essential responsibilities: to ourselves, to the community, and to God. These responsibilities are the modes of the embodiment of conscience. The first responsibility considers our fundamental option. Its purpose is to be an authentic human person. Here the key word is *virtue,* by which we can be what we should be. The second responsibility explores the common good. Here the key word is *harmony/peace*, by which we can be good members of the community. The third responsibility concerns the relationship between God and human beings. Here the key idea is the encounter between ethics and spirituality. On one hand, becoming good is the purpose of ethics/morality. On the other hand, becoming holy is the purpose of spirituality. Conscience, or *ryōshin* in Japanese, is, as it were, the intersection of ethics/morality and spirituality. Strictly speaking, conscience is not the voice of

God but the place where we can listen to that voice. This essay discusses these three points by embracing both Christian and Confucian thought.

Being a Good Person: *Ryōshin* or Conscience

Even though the notion of conscience is polyvalent and ambiguous, it is universally accepted that conscience plays a core role in the formation of human beings. Conscience is found in everyone and does not necessarily have a theological connotation. In other words, the faculty of conscience is not restricted to a particular religion. Therefore, one can find a concept of conscience in Eastern thought even if such a concept does not exactly correspond to that in Western thought.

In East Asia the concept that corresponds most closely to conscience in the West is *liang hsin/ryōshin* (良心).[1] Mencius (孟子: 372–289 BCE) is the first person who explicitly used this term. His basic idea of morality is based on *liang hsin*. *Liang hsin* is thought of within the context of both morality and philosophy, especially in Confucianism.

Mencius strongly believes that *liang hsin* springs from one's heart/mind, which is "good by nature." Therefore, *liang hsin* originally means good heart/mind of human beings and does not depend on acquiring education and/or experience. He regards the heart/mind as more important than the five organs. However, this does not mean that Mencius had the same idea of human beings as do Western thinkers who claim the distinction of body and mind. According to him, there is a natural hierarchy within the structure of human beings, and in that hierarchy heart/mind holds a preeminent position. One has to nourish and cultivate it as much as one can in order to be a true human person.[2]

While conscience has been understood as a faculty of intellectual judgment on the distinction between good and evil, *ryōshin* has been understood

---

[1] 良心 comprises two ideograms, 良and 心. By itself良connotes good, and 心 refers to the heart/ (understood both metaphorically and physically). "Heart" is an English translation of *kokoro* (心) and "mind" of *seishin* (精神). *Kokoro*, which is a Japanese term, is the center by which a human person can be a human person. The physical heart also is the center of circulation of blood and *ch'i* (気: material/vital force). All human acts, such as emotion, affection, feeling, and thought, are based on it. *Seishin*, on the other hand, is a concept opposed to body or flesh. Sometimes *seishin* contains an intellectual nuance. However, *kokoro* is highly implicit and polyvalent. Therefore, it is almost impossible to translate *kokoro* into one word. *Ryōshin* is the Japanese pronunciation of 良心 of the Chinese *liang hsin*.

[2] The Book of *Mencius*, 6A:15 [Book Six, Part I, Chapter 15]. I quote the text from Wing-tsit Chan, *A Source Book in Chinese Philosophy* (Princeton, NJ: Princeton University Press, 1963).

as the basis of conscience in the Confucian tradition. *Ryōshin* is more deeply rooted in human nature than conscience understood too narrowly in intellectualist terms. In other words, *ryōshin* is regarded as a human disposition that transcends mere rational judgment. The main role of *ryōshin* is to determine how to cultivate oneself to become an authentic self.

Kokoro or Heart/Mind

It is not easy to define *kokoro* (心: heart/mind), but one may be able to confirm its meaning from one's experience. That is, *kokoro* lies in the center of us. This means that *kokoro* is not a part of us but concerns the whole self. In other words, *kokoro* involves the sum of our faculties, such as intellect, passion, affection, and volition. In this sense one may be able to say that *kokoro* is the original point of the human being as *personal* existence. *Kokoro* is the dwelling place of conscience, where a fundamental option is executed and a human being encounters God.

"No good tree bears bad fruit, nor again does a bad tree bear good fruit. . . . The good person out of the good treasure of the heart produces good, and the evil person out of evil treasure produces evil; for it is out of the abundance of the heart that the mouth speaks" (Lk 6:43–45). This is a simple expression, but at the same time it teaches us an important lesson: Good deeds arise from a good heart and evil ones from a bad heart. Thomas Aquinas said that action follows being. This means that one's moral duties and possibilities are grounded in one's being. In other words, "the moral 'ought' is founded on the 'is,' the given reality of the individual."[3]

To bear good fruit one must be a good human person. It is virtue that makes this possible. Virtue is neither a mere abstract concept nor a system of studies, but rather is that which one should acquire and nourish from one's daily experiences. Both in the West and in the East many have pointed out the importance of virtue.

Confucianism: Virtue Ethics

Traditional Western thought holds that there are four cardinal virtues (prudence, justice, fortitude, and temperance). Christianity adds three theological virtues (faith, hope, and love). Frankly speaking, Confucianism is an ethic of virtues. In other words, human beings can and should become true human persons by acquiring and nourishing virtues.

---

[3] James T. Bretzke, S.J., *Consecrated Phrases: A Latin Theological Dictionary*, 2nd ed. (Collegeville, MN: Liturgical Press, 2003), s.v. "*Agere sequitur* (esse)."

Mencius is often recognized as the one who developed concretely the thought of Confucius (551–479 BCE). While Mencius retained Confucius's cardinal ideas of morality, he developed them in his own way. For example, while Confucius's ethics is based on "a Heavenly-ordained social structure," that of Mencius is grounded in "*hsing* (性: human nature)." In other words, Mencius grounded Confucius's essential understanding of morality in human nature rather than in heaven (*T'ien*).[4]

Mencius regards humanity as "good by nature." This may sound naive, but it is the origin of all his thought and is generally called the "theory of the original goodness of human nature" (性善説: *seizen-setsu*).[5] This theory derives from Confucius's theory of *chung-shu* (忠恕: conscientiousness and altruism).[6] *Chung* is to be sincere to oneself and *shu* is to be sincere to others. One needs *chung* in oneself and *shu* in one's relationship to others. Goodness is almost equivalent to sincerity in this conception.

In order to demonstrate his theory, Mencius presents four innate feelings universally present in human beings.[7] These are called the Four Beginnings (*ssu-tuan*: 四端): the feeling of commiseration (惻隠之心: *sokuin no kokoro*), the feeling of shame and dislike (羞悪之心: *shūo no kokoro*), the feeling of respect and reverence (恭敬之心: *kyōkei no kokoro*/辞譲之心: *jijō no kokoro*), and the feeling of right and wrong (是非之心: *zehi no kokoro*). The Four Beginnings are never abstract concepts but rather concrete metaphors of moral "sprouts."

These moral sprouts are weak and fragile; therefore, one has to nourish and cultivate them. In other words, as innate moral "sprouts" they should be "extended and developed." Mencius sees a symbiosis between moral and physical development. He regards human nature as a moral quality, while Kao Tzu (告子: 420–350 BCE) limits human nature to physiological instinct or biological characteristics such as appetite and sexual desire.[8]

The feeling of commiseration has priority over the other three feelings, and the feeling of right and wrong holds the last position. In other words, for Mencius, having compassion for others is more important than the judgment of right and wrong. This is one of the notable differences from Western moral thought. We should remember that *ryōshin* is regarded as a

---

[4] *Mencius*, 6A:1–6, 2A:6, 4B:26. Confucius did not mention human nature except in the *Analects*, 5:12 and 17:2. For Confucius and Mencius, *T'ien* had some sense of agency and ultimacy as the Source of all or the Ancestor. For Neo-Confucians, it has metaphysical ultimacy along with the Great Ultimate (*T'ai-chi*).

[5] This is a translation of the Chinese *hsing-pen-shan* (性本善), *seizen-setsu* (性善説) in Japanese. See *Mencius*, 2A:6.

[6] *Analects*, 4:15.

[7] *Mencius*, 6A:6.

[8] Ibid., 6A:4.

human disposition that transcends mere rational judgment. The main role of *ryōshin* is to determine how to cultivate oneself to become an authentic self. According to Mencius, being good as a human person is more important than exercising the intellectual faculty of judgment. This sense of morality is never individualistic but rather is communal; that is, it should be executed in harmonious relationship to others.

The Four Beginnings are each the beginnings of *four virtues*, that is, *jen* (仁: humanity), *i* (義: righteousness), *li* (禮: propriety), and *chih* (智: wisdom). These four virtues spring from the human heart/mind, and humans do not conform to them as external ideals. Mencius presents the four *actualities* of each virtue. "The actuality of humanity consists in serving one's parents. The actuality of righteousness consists in obeying one's elder brother. The actuality of wisdom consists in knowing these two things and not departing from them. The actuality of propriety consists in regulating and adorning these two things."[9]

Making a Good Community: *Wa*

So far we have surveyed the understanding of virtues in Confucianism in China. There is another exquisite virtue peculiar to Japan: *wa* (和: harmony/peace).[10]

The ethical/moral ethos of the Japanese is, to be sure, influenced by Shintoism, Buddhism, and Confucianism. Hence, it is not easy to specify a particular virtue that is dominant to the Japanese. However, we may be able to point to *wa* as a distinct virtue for many people in Japan.

The term *wa* is used separately, but it is also compounded in such words as *nyūwa* (柔和: gentleness), *wakai* (和解: reconciliation), *chōwa* (調和: harmony), and *waon* (和音: chord). Still more, *wa* represents Japanese style and Japan itself. In this way, *wa* contains a unique connotation and is one of the most important virtues in Japan.

One of the characteristics of *wa* is harmony. *Wa* is not merely social (justice, fairness), but also concerns a more internal and substantial matter. In fact, *wa* has been thought of as one of the most important virtues in both Taoism and Confucianism. It is closely related to the way in *Lao Tzu*:

> Tao (Way) is empty (like a bowl),
> It may be used but its capacity is never exhausted.
> It is bottomless, perhaps the ancestor of all things.

---

[9] Ibid., 4A:27.

[10] There are some other translations of *wa*, such as "solidarity" or "cooperation."

> It blunts its sharpness,
> It unites its tangles.
> It softens its light.
> It becomes one with the dusty world.
> Deep and still, it appears to exist forever.
> I do not know whose son it is.
> It seems to have existed before the Lord (4).[11]

Wing-tsit Chan comments on the above as follows:

> This chapter shows clearly that, in Taoism, function is no less important than substance. Substance is further described in *Lao Tzu*, chs. 14 and 21, but here, as in *Lao Tzu*, chs. 11 and 45, function (*yung*, also meaning use) is regarded with equal respect. There is no renunciation of phenomena as is the case with certain Buddhist schools.[12]

In addition, we also have the famous passage, "Confucius said, 'The superior man is conciliatory but does not identify himself with others; the inferior man identifies with others but is not conciliatory.'"[13]

Seventeen Articles of the Constitution

Prince Shōtoku (574–622 CE) drafted the *Seventeen Articles of the Constitution* in 604 CE. This is the first set of legal statutes in Japan. He conceived the future form of the state of Japan by using the Confucian virtues, while he personally professed Buddhism. In this constitution he describes the thought of *wa* (harmony) as follows:

> Harmony (*wa*) should be valued and quarrels should be avoided. Everyone is apt to form a clique, and there are few people who are reasonable. Therefore some disobey their lords and fathers, and feud with their neighbors. But when superiors are in harmony and inferiors are friendly, then they discuss affairs in cooperation, everything will be reasonable spontaneously. Then there is nothing which cannot be accomplished.[14]

---

11 Lao-Tzu, *Tao-Te Ching,* at http://www.kingsacademy.com.

12 Wing-tsit Chan, *A Source Book in Chinese Philosophy*, 141.

13 *Analects*, 13:23.

14 Asia for Educators, Columbia University, *The Constitution of Prince Shotoku*, http://afe.easia.columbia.edu.

Though Confucianism does not traditionally conceive of *wa* this way, it has a similar way of using it. That is, *wa* contains not only the importance of mutual cooperation and harmony, but that of obedience and confidence. In this way the *Seventeen Articles of the Constitution* does not aim at the relationship among ranks based on paternal structure, but at the realization of *wa* by way of mutual self-restraint. At the same time, it does not deny personality and diversity, but rather aims at making one belong to the communal.

It is remarkable that, though based on the thought of Buddhism, this constitution uses *wa* in a Confucian sense. *Wa* should be disciplined by propriety; one has to know the importance of *wa* and to realize it.[15] In other words, the heart of harmony is required when one pursues propriety.

Harmony and the Common Good

In Confucian thought every community should have a harmony based on heaven (*T'ien*). This harmony is revealed by the realization of the common good. The term *common good* is actually not a term particularly emphasized or developed in Confucian thought, but it has implications similar to the concept in a Christian context.[16] The life of human beings is oriented to the realization of the common good. In other words, there is a reciprocal relationship between person and community, or society, in the embodiment of harmony.

The common good is not a mere congeries of goods or the total sum but rather a good for the whole society that should be participated in/shared by each human person. When one considers the common good in the Confucian context, the concept of heaven plays a key role. The common good is also closely related to both *t'ien-ming* (天命: Mandate of Heaven) and the four cardinal virtues (*jen* [humanity], *i* [righteousness], *li* [propriety], and *chih* [wisdom]). The quality of these moral principles is essentially communal. Therefore, it is in the community that the notion of the common good is properly understood and realized. Moral community is the matrix in which the good is realized and in which one can find moral identity.

---

15 "Yu Tzu said, 'Among the functions of propriety (*li*) the most valuable is that it establishes harmony. The excellence of the ways of ancient kings consists of this. It is the guiding principle of all things great and small. If things go amiss, and you, understanding harmony, try to achieve it without regulating it by the rules of propriety, they will still go amiss'" (*Analects*, 1:12).

16 James T. Bretzke, S.J., "The Common Good in a Cross-Cultural Perspective: Insights from the Confucian Moral Community," in *Religion, Ethics, and the Common Good*, ed. James Donahue and M. Theresa Moser, R.S.C.J. (Mystic, CT: Twenty-Third Publications, 1996), 84.

It is true that Confucian society has a strong hierarchical system, but an autocratic government was not originally intended.[17]As Bretzke points out, "Confucianism would envision an ethico-political system of mutual trust and aid designed to foster a true community dedicated to a common moral purpose of justice and righteousness for all—in other words, a fair approximation of the moral meaning of the common good."[18] In Confucian society the starting point for understanding a human person is not individualistic but a "betweenness" or the relationship of one person with another.

In this way, the common good is the aim of the whole human community and of each person within the community. In treating the common good in a Catholic context, Vatican II explains in *Gaudium et Spes*:

> Because of the increasingly close interdependence which is gradually extending to the entire world, we are today witnessing an extension of the role of the common good, which is the sum total of social conditions which allow people, either as groups or as individuals, to reach their fulfillment more fully and more easily. The resulting rights and obligations are consequently the concern of the entire human race. Every group must take into account the needs and legitimate aspirations of every other group, and even those of the human family as a whole. (GS, no. 26)

Conscience and the Common Good

Conscience and community are closely related. In other words, as a place where one can hear the voice of God, conscience has communality.

In considering conscience one cannot help presupposing an ability to decide or discern good and evil. What one can find here is not the infallible voice of God but one's concrete adaptation to the absolute requirement of the fundamental conscience.[19] Nevertheless, this adaptation is so creative that it is not restricted to the narrow perspective of the subjectivist *sola cum*

---

[17] Ibid., 94.

[18] Ibid.

[19] Josef Fuchs, *Moral Demands and Personal Obligations* (Washington, DC: Georgetown University Press, 1994), 161. In this regard Fuchs asks one to pay attention to the following: "Such a conviction would not contain the direct voice of God, a voice that one need only 'hear' perceptively and then obey; rather, it would be the last word of the situational conscience reflecting on its own reality, containing not the infallible voice of God but the human person's attempt to give a concrete 'body' to the absolute requirement of the fundamental conscience."

se ipsa (alone with itself) but is, in the true meaning, a creative and living *solus cum solo* (alone with the alone), that is, living in deep communion with God.[20] Therefore, one may say that the conscience is not directly the voice of God but the human way of responding to God.

Conscience should not consist of what people appropriate from outside, but what is found in themselves, and conscience should not be restricted only to religious matters. In other words, moral obligation, doing good and avoiding evil, is obligatory for everyone, and conscience is the source of all moral obligations.[21] This moral obligation is affected not only by time and space but also by social and historical differences.

Among the many understandings of conscience, many emphasize the objectivity or universality of conscience. Conscience can be "described as an experience and insight into the objective and absolute ethical requirement that always exists *a priori* in the human person, an insight that cannot be rejected." Alternately, conscience can be "described as an organ, not an oracle."[22] The first understanding is illuminating: Even those who do not accept the notion that conscience is the voice of God may be able to accept that the objective and absolute ethical requirement of "doing good and avoiding evil" exists a priori.

Human beings made in the image of God are also communal and social beings. Vatican II says: "The fact that human beings are social by nature indicates that the betterment of the person and the improvement of society depend on each other. Insofar as humanity by its very nature stands completely in need of life in society, it is and it ought to be the beginning, the subject and the object of every social organization" (GS, no. 25). In other words, the individual and the community should be in harmony while having diversity. For this harmony, society should precede the individual, but this does not mean that an individual may or should be sacrificed for the sake of society. It is the common good that both an individual and community should aim at together. About this, Vatican II says:

> Individuals, families, and the various groups which make up the civil community, are aware of their inability to achieve a truly human life by their own unaided efforts; they see the need for a wider community where each one will make a specific contribution to an even broader implementation of the common good. For this reason they set up

[20] Ibid.

[21] James F. Keenan, "Josef Fuchs at Eighty: Defending Conscience from Rome," *Theology Digest* 42/3 (Summer 1995): 138.

[22] Fuchs, *Moral Demands and Personal Obligations*, 155.

> various forms of political communities. The political community, then, exists for the common good: this is its full justification and meaning and the source of its specific and basic right to exist. The common good embraces the sum total of all those conditions of social life which enable individuals, families, and organizations to achieve complete and effective fulfillment. (GS, no. 74)[23]

Called to Be a Good and Holy Person: Conscience as Sanctuary

Conscience is not merely the criterion by which one performs right or wrong actions. Rather, conscience is deeply engraved in each person, enabling each to become a true human person. Fidelity to conscience is the ground on which one is good or evil. Moral goodness is trying one's utmost to do good and avoid evil. This is the "sincerity" of one's conscience, and here is another bridge between the Western notion of conscience and Japanese *ryōshin*.

Conscience is the place where the personal relationship between God and the human person exists. Therefore, one can say: "Conscience is the source of all moral obligations: there we are each called by God to love and to develop ourselves so as to know what constitutes right living."[24]

The understanding of conscience as the "voice of God" belongs to the religious sphere and is even somewhat mystical.[25] According to Josef Fuchs, "Especially since the Second Vatican Council (*Gaudium et Spes*, 16), it has become common to describe the conscience as a *sacrarium* in which we find ourselves responsibly before God—*solus cum solo* (alone with the Alone)."[26] In fact, the council describes conscience very concisely and clearly: "Conscience is the most secret core and the sanctuary of the human person. There they are alone with God whose voice echoes in their depths" (GS, no. 16).

---

[23] The common good consists of three essential elements: respect for the person as such (*Catechism of the Catholic Church* [CCC] 1907), the social well-being and development of the group itself (CCC 1908), and peace, that is, the stability and security of a just order (CCC 1909). See also *Pacem in Terris*, no. 46.

[24] Keenan, "Josef Fuchs at Eighty," 138.

[25] Josef Fuchs, *Christian Morality: The Word Becomes Flesh,* trans. Brian McNeil (Washington, DC: Georgetown University Press, 1987), 121; idem, *Personal Responsibility and Christian Morality,* trans. William Cleves et al. (Washington, DC: Georgetown University Press, 1983), 218.

[26] Fuchs, *Moral Demands and Personal Obligations,* 154.

Ryōshin and Conscience: Relationship, Transcendence, and Embodiment

Ryōshin is essentially a relationship. Relationship itself constitutes a moment of self-transcendence; that is, it implies a personal insufficiency or a capacity for others. I would like to use these terms in the following sense: *Transcendence* is an internal reality of *ryōshin,* and *embodiment* an external reality of *ryōshin.* In the former there is the dignity of *ryōshin,* and in the latter the communality of *ryōshin.*

Behind this consideration there is the understanding that Jesus is an embodiment of the unseen God and of the conscience or *ryōshin* of God. This is the reason why embodiment is an essential concept in this particular argument about conscience and shows how the concept of embodiment also facilitates the conversation about conscience specifically between Catholic and Japanese notions of culture.

As transcendence, *ryōshin* is regarded ontologically as a precept of *synderesis*: doing good and avoiding evil (Thomas Aquinas). However, this way of thinking risks ignoring embodiment. As embodiment, *ryōshin* is interpreted anthropologically and is understood as a faculty cultivated in relationship to others (from the Confucian heritage). This way of thinking, however, risks slighting the Transcendent as the fundamental source of human life. It is not enough to appreciate either of them singly; one needs a comprehensive appreciation of both.

Thus, relationship represented by transcendence and embodiment is essential for *ryōshin*. One can understand that *ryōshin* does not remain on an individual level, but rather develops into a "communality." The fuller the formation of *ryōshin* is, the closer a relationship to others will be. There is an essential relationship between the individual and community. Therefore, the formation of *ryōshin* is oriented toward the "common good." In this way, *ryōshin* is not merely a notion but rather is truly realistic. One experiences *ryōshin* in the real world as one experiences the community through transcendence and embodiment.

Conscience plays a very important role when one considers the relationship between God and human beings. Conscience grounds human existence ontologically and promotes the growth of personality ethically. Conscience is not, however, merely a discernment and judgment of right/wrong and good/evil. Rather, it reveals the fundamental disposition for human beings to live as human beings. Becoming a good person (ethics) and becoming a holy person (spirituality) essentially neither contradict nor oppose each other; rather, they should be integrated. And the place where ethics and spirituality encounter each other is no less than conscience itself. Conscience cannot be reduced to a mere ethical category; rather, it should also be thought of in relationship to spirituality.

Ryōshin is essential to human life and human realization or cultivation. One can confirm this proposition from two points of view. First, one can examine this ontologically. All living things find their origin in life itself or the Transcendent. In other words, every living thing can exist by participating in life itself. What does it mean to be authentically human? It is to live according to *ryōshin*. This concept is present in all cultures, though it is outstanding in cultures with a Confucian heritage. *Ryōshin* is, precisely speaking, not the voice of God but rather a "place" where one can listen to it. Therefore, *ryōshin* may and should be understood as a place where ethics and spirituality encounter. One can find this in two characteristics of *ryōshin*—embodiment and transcendence. That is, ethics reveals the embodiment of *ryōshin* as a norm of human conduct, and spirituality reveals transcendence as a relationship between God and human beings.

Conclusion

I began this essay by noting the problematic Catholic view that understands conscience too narrowly as an intellectual judgment on a singular moral act by a solitary individual. Such a view of conscience has not only proved problematic within Catholicism but also provides little point of contact for a conversation about conscience with Japanese and Asian culture. By contrast, by turning to the resources of Japanese and Asian culture, we can see conscience-like concepts like *ryōshin* and others that emphasize sincere inwardness, social harmony, and a religious sensibility. These characteristics of Japanese and Asian thought invite us to consider similar characteristics in the Catholic tradition of thought about conscience—even if such Catholic characteristics had been long out of view until the Second Vatican Council. For Catholicism to speak effectively and well to Asian culture about conscience, it must consider such things. In turn, Asian culture can learn from the riches of the Catholic tradition on this matter. It is time for *ryōshin* and conscience to converse.

4.

Conscience, Catholicism, and the New Science of Morality

Stephen J. Pope

This essay attempts to use insights from what is called the new science of morality to shed light on the Catholic debate over conscience. It proceeds in three stages: first, it offers a brief summary of the moral foundations theory of psychologist Jonathan Haidt and his collaborators; second, it employs this theory to offer a diagnosis of the conditions that shape the Catholic debate over conscience; and third, it examines what contributions moral foundations theory can make to making progress in mutual understanding.

The New Science of Morality

Adam Smith and Charles Darwin provided, respectively, the moral and biological foundations of the so-called new science of morality developed in contemporary moral psychology, particularly by psychologist Jonathan Haidt.[1] Haidt's moral foundations theory treats morality as a set of social norms that bind people into groups. Moral psychology draws from a variety of social scientific disciplines to suggest that human behavior is much less the product of rational processes and more the effect of largely preconscious emotional forces.

Moral judgments are "evaluations (good vs. bad) of the actions or character of a person that are made with respect to a set of virtues held to be

[1] Jonathan Haidt, *The Righteous Mind: Why Good People Are Divided by Politics and Religion* (New York: Vintage, 2012).

obligatory by a culture or subculture."[2] Most of our moral judgments are made rapidly on the basis of moral intuitions. Intuitions are "the sudden appearance in consciousness of a moral judgment, including an affective valence (good-bad, like-dislike), without any conscious awareness of having gone through steps of searching, weighing evidence, or inferring a conclusion."[3]

Haidt maintains that our moral intuitions come from our capacity to generate positive and negative moral emotions in response to particular situations. Evolutionary processes crafted this capacity because it enabled our predecessors to respond effectively to challenges from their social and/or natural environments. Early humans, for example, would have been more likely to leave descendants if they immediately ran from lions rather than trying to reason about what to do when they saw one staring at them from the tall grass. Reasoning comes into play when routine responses to typical scenarios don't work.

We do not normally reason to seek the truth, Haidt argues, but to support our emotional reactions.[4] We engage in moral reasoning when someone challenges us to explain the choices lying behind our actions. When we can't give good reasons, we are in a state of being "dumbfounded," that is, rendered unable to offer a verbal account of our intuitive convictions.[5] The frequency of being dumbfounded indicates that most of us make moral assessments before rather than after we start thinking carefully about what we ought to do.

Haidt describes the dual-process model of cognition as something like the relationship between a rider (controlled processes, reasoning, planning, deliberating) and an elephant (automatic processes, emotions, intuitions). In his scenario the rider thinks he is in charge, but in fact the elephant is the one who controls where the rider is going. The elephant does almost all the work. The rider's main job is to explain to other riders what the elephant is doing and why it is a good idea. The rider also tries to make the elephant look good and to recruit other elephants to its herd.

It is important to note that the rider is not the person but only the consciously aware and reasoning person. The person is the rider/elephant in its environment, and most important, the other elephants with which it associates. Conscience is the rider/elephant as it generates morally significant intuitions, particularly approval or disapproval, and reflects on those intuitions.

---

[2] Jonathan Haidt, "The Emotional Dog and Its Rational Tail: A Social Intuitionist Approach to Moral Judgment," *Psychological Review* 108 (2001): 817.

[3] See Jonathan Haidt, *The Happiness Hypothesis: Finding Modern Truth in Ancient Wisdom* (New York: Perseus, 2006), 818.

[4] Haidt, *The Righteous Mind*, 29.

[5] Ibid.

Our cognitive "rider" engages in a second-order, strategic activity that is strongly shaped, and usually driven, by our more determinative underlying moral emotions (the "elephant"). The basic structure of the emotion has been shaped by natural selection to deal with the challenges of survival and social cooperation. Emotions are primary because they come first, they operate very quickly (in an "affective flash"), and they provide powerful motivation for behavior. Subjects have been found to make snap judgments about others from perceptual cues picked up in a tenth of a second of when they first encounter someone.[6] When our bodies are uncomfortable, we make harsher judgments of the same individuals, and we view the same person differently when we are with one group of people rather than when we are with another.

Haidt thinks we are mostly elephant. This might account for why moral philosophers are no more ethical than the average person. Philosophical moral reflection does not, on average, improve the conduct of ethicists.[7] It might also account for two other findings: (1) people who say they are religious believers do not act more altruistically than their nonreligious peers; and (2) people who attend religious services are more likely than others to engage in altruistic service and to donate to charity.[8]

Just as the elephant's movement is strongly influenced by the movement of the other elephants in the herd, so our emotions are powerfully shaped by the moral emotions of the people in our groups. Like the other elephants in our herd, we usually screen out evidence that disconfirms our intuitive judgments.

We are capable of reasoning in more ways than just rationalizing our choices. Insight into our own biases can help us be more humble about the reliability of our intuitions and judgments. Reasoning can play an important social function when we talk to other people in ways that enable us to understand, try to reconcile, and perhaps revise our moral judgments in light of information or insights we had not previously taken into account. Reasoning with others can help us become aware of holding bigoted assumptions, challenge them, and refuse to act on them.

Moral decision making is both universally human in its general form and culturally relative in its content. Moral foundations theory has an evolutionary psychological take on the contextual nature of conscience that is emphasized by Linda Hogan, Bryan Massingale, and Lisa Fullam

---

[6] Ibid., 69.

[7] Ibid., 104ff. See also Joshua Rust and Eric Schwitzgebel, "The Moral Behavior of Ethicists and the Power of Reason," in *Advances in Experimental Moral Psychology*, ed. Hagop Sarkissian and Jennifer Wright, 91–109 (New York: Bloomsbury Academic, 2014).

[8] Haidt, *The Righteous Mind*, 308, 310.

in this volume. The natural history of our species has bequeathed us a set of "learning modules" that generates action-guiding moral intuitions. Every culture constructs its particular moral code on top of six evolved psychological systems ("learning modules" or "moral systems") that concern, respectively, (1) care vs. harm, (2) fairness vs. cheating, (3) loyalty vs. betrayal, (4) authority vs. subversion, (5) purity/sanctity vs. disgust/degradation, and (6) liberty vs. oppression. Moral foundations theory does not try to present some scientific version of natural-law ethics but rather a descriptive account of the basic patterns of evolved sensitivities that we see displayed in everyday morality.

Each of these variables (1) evolved because it met an adaptive challenge, for example, care evolved because it led individuals to promote the well-being of their children; (2) is engaged by widespread, characteristic emotional "triggers" common to many, for example, care is triggered by distress or suffering in one's child; (3) has a set of current, more occasional emotional triggers, for example, we can feel sympathy for a whining puppy; (4) gives rise to a characteristic emotion, for example, compassion (or empathy) in the case of care, and (5) is the object of certain socially sanctioned virtues, for example, care is habituated in kindness.

Cultures can be distinguished according to how they relate to the six variables. People who live in modern cultures (as displayed, for example, in American college students) emphasize care, fairness, and liberty more than authority, tradition, and purity. Inhabitants of more-traditional rural cultures resonate more with loyalty, authority, and sanctity. Only societies steeped in the first two systems, for example, could think it is permissible to do what is disgusting (that is, that violates the purity/sanctity code). Cultures grounded in loyalty, authority, and sanctity have ways of interpreting what counts as harm, care, and liberty (regarding, for example, arranged marriages or adult circumcision) that appall inhabitants of modern and postmodern societies.

Haidt draws two implications from this framework, one negative and the other positive. First, since traits that were adaptive in communities of the past might no longer be so for us, we need to avoid the trap of presuming the normativity of our own first-order moral intuitions. Sometimes these intuitions are absorbed from religious traditions or implicitly communicated by religious institutions. This highlights the importance of conscience formation but also moral education, experience, and conversation.

Second, increased knowledge of the underlying bases of our moral sensibilities can help us become more self-directed and perhaps even wiser moral agents. Morality tends to *bind* us to likeminded people, but it also tends to *blind* us to how others function morally. Christian morality often operates in both ways, that is, to reinforce group membership and to make it hard for us to empathize with the point of view of others. As we will see, this pertains as much to divisions within Catholicism as to relations with outsiders.

Mapping Conscience in Catholicism

We can now use some of moral foundations theory to highlight certain features of the Catholic debate over conscience. We need, however, to note two caveats. First, Haidt's theory is meant primarily to account for what distinguishes political conservatives from political liberals. While it doesn't apply in a simple and straightforward way to Catholic moral concepts of conscience, it can provide suggestive insights about the Catholic debate over conscience.

Second, we need to acknowledge the limitations of Haidt's liberal-conservative typology. Labels usually distract and deform more than they inform. There are many possible ways to be "liberal" as well as to be "conservative." It is not even clear how we can define these terms in ways that are conceptually clear. One person's liberal is another's conservative; whether you are one or the other depends on your perspective. Moreover, the landscape of political and moral possibilities is much more complex than the simple liberal and conservative options. Haidt doesn't even have a category named moderate.

These categories are even more problematic when it comes to moral theology. There are significant variations among Catholics identified as liberal moral theologians as well as those considered conservative. Many of the nearly 450 American bishops don't fit into either one of these two categories. Finally, there is variation in style. Two people can have the same moral stance, but one relishes polemics while the other speaks calmly with pastoral prudence.

Yet, for all these limitations, moral foundations theory does lift up certain features of the current landscape of the Catholic conscience. The differences are not primarily intellectual but emotional, social, and political. In the Catholic debate it is clear that both sides often talk past each other. This reflects, Haidt would say, the likelihood they are working with very different moral psychologies.

We can begin by comparing the two dominant Catholic conceptions of conscience in terms of Haidt's six moral systems. Conservatives emphasize the duty of the Catholic conscience in terms of the first three systems (authority, loyalty, purity): to obey authority, to be loyal to the church, and to respect the God-given sacredness of the moral order, especially when it comes to the sanctity of life, marriage, and the family. These leading values provide the hermeneutical lens through which they engage the other three moral systems (care, fairness, liberty): the kind of care we owe to one another (especially at the end of life); what counts as fairness for everyone (for example, two women cannot have a "right" to get married, and so forth); and what counts as legitimate liberty as opposed to irresponsible license (for example, Catholic healthcare facilities should be free from having to provide employees with the means to do what is intrinsically evil). The conservative theological framework insists that the conscience of a "true" Catholic obeys the church because it is the institution founded by Christ to be God's agent for the salvation of the world.

The corresponding view of the task of theology fits Haidt's account of reasoning. Theologians are supposed to give reasons that justify the church's teaching. We can map Haidt's interpretive framework onto one paragraph of *Veritatis Splendor*, indicating in brackets which of the six moral systems it triggers:

> While recognizing the possible limitations of the human arguments employed by the Magisterium [*authority*], moral theologians are called to develop a deeper understanding of the reasons underlying its teachings and to expound the validity and obligatory nature of the precepts it proposes, demonstrating their connection with one another and their relation with man's ultimate end [*sanctity*]. Moral theologians are to set forth the church's teaching [*authority*] and to give, in the exercise of their ministry, the example of a loyal assent [*loyalty*], both internal and external, to the Magisterium's teaching [*authority*] in the areas of both dogma and morality. Working together in cooperation [*loyalty*] with the hierarchical Magisterium [*authority*], theologians will be deeply concerned to clarify ever more fully the biblical foundations, the ethical significance and the anthropological concerns which underlie the moral doctrine and the vision of man [*sanctity*] set forth by the church. (VS, no. 110)

Haidt describes the "rider" as a kind of press agent or lawyer who finds reasons to support the "elephant's" behavior. In many experiments Haidt discovered that moral intuitions have a strong hold on people even when they cannot explain why they are so important to them (the state of being dumbfounded). Applied to Catholicism, conservatives see theology as useful when the magisterium is "dumbfounded" and resist theologians who uncover the inadequacies in the formulations of church teachings. When theologians cannot provide persuasive reasons for a position adopted by the magisterium, then the magisterium can appeal to divine authority: "*When people ask the Church the questions raised by their consciences . . . the*

Church's reply contains the voice of Jesus Christ, the voice of the truth about good and evil" (VS, no. 117).

We can distinguish this view from that found in Linda Hogan's *Confronting the Truth: Conscience and Catholic Tradition*. "In Christianity," she writes, "conscience refers to the individual's capacity to make autonomous and free moral decisions."[9] She wants the hierarchy to admit that Catholics remain in communion with the church even when they come conscientiously to hold beliefs at variance with the teachings of the magisterium.

Liberals seek to protect individuals from religious bullying and authoritarian domination. Hogan tries hard to maintain a balanced but progressive view of the authority of the conscience, but her language would alarm conservatives. She asks: "Is conscience about following church law or about determining for oneself what is right and wrong?"[10] While Hogan has Catholic "both/and" instincts, posing the question this way would sound to conservative ears like a rhetorical dichotomy: *either* obedience *or* autonomy. Conservatives might say she sounds more like Kant than scripture or the Catholic theological tradition.

Yet elsewhere it is clear that Hogan thinks we have to determine what is right and wrong *for* ourselves but not *by* ourselves. Hogan describes conscience as the place in which we "discover God's will" for us and insists that Christianity works with a "community-based model of ethics not with an individualistic one."[11] Christian consciences are formed in faith communities, rooted in the church's narratives and traditions; they engage in "dialogue" with scripture, doctrine, and tradition and seek to integrate the wisdom of the tradition into everyday life. She suggests that the conscientious Catholic will approach church teachings with respect and loyalty and only dissent for "serious conscientious reasons."[12]

In Haidt's terms, Hogan emphasizes the moral systems of care, fairness, and liberty. She does not dismiss authority, loyalty, and sanctity, but she gives them secondary status and interprets them in relation to the first three. She is more empathic with Catholics who feel limited by ecclesial authority than with those who worry about the erosion of the church they love. Hogan does not think it is helpful for Catholics to be told to "conform," "submit," or "assent" to church teachings. She writes, "The duty of conscience is not to *assent* to magisterial teaching but to work earnestly and courageously for the *articulation of the good* in each context" (emphasis added).[13]

---

[9] Linda Hogan, *Confronting the Truth: Conscience and Catholic Tradition* (Mahwah, NY: Paulist Press, 2000), 23.

[10] Ibid., 110.

[11] Ibid., 14.

[12] Ibid., 174.

[13] Ibid., 178.

Hogan's sensitivity to doctrinal changes in the history of the church (for example, regarding torture, usury, religious freedom, and so forth) leads her to emphasize the gradations of teaching authority (moral notes) that culture warriors usually ignore. She gives even less weight to church teachings when she describes them as "nothing more than the accumulated wisdom and insight of our forebears." From this position she draws the conclusion that "when the church teaches, it must do so with respect for the seriousness with which most people engage in ethical reflection and with a supportive attitude toward their conscientiously held beliefs."[14]

Hogan seems to have a higher estimate than Haidt of the average person's level of ethical thoughtfulness. Haidt, recall, thinks most "riders" follow their own particular "elephants" and the herd within which they move. Conservatives would appreciate his point and add that a strong church is needed if Christians are to remain steadfast in a secular world bent on its destruction. They would argue that we should not take a supportive attitude to Christians who, allowing themselves to be shaped by unchristian forces, come to conscientiously held beliefs that violate the gospel. Particular bishops were wrong in the nineteenth century to take a supportive attitude to conscientious Christian slaveowners, and the same goes for particular bishops in the twentieth century who took a supportive attitude to conscientious Eastern European Catholics who helped the Nazis slaughter Jews.

Haidt reminds us that the moral reflection of Christians, like that of everyone else, is usually not a disinterested quest for truth, but a process of coming up with reasons that justify the truth as we intuit it. When we think we are acting out of our own self-chosen principles in matters of religion and morality, we are usually merely replicating the choices of our in-groups. Because most of the people we talk with are like us (a problem made much worse by the Internet), intra-community conversation usually supports rather than challenges our commonly held intuitions.

The conservative insists that the Catholic conscience can't look like the liberal conscience because what works for liberal democratic citizenship will not work for Christian discipleship. The source of authority for the former is the consent of the people, but the latter comes from God's will. Conservatives thus tend to see the church as a sacred, divinely instituted body, and liberals tend to see it as an ancient human tradition. Hogan clearly accents the humanity of the church. She thinks we are all—the ordained as well as the laity—frail, limited, but responsible moral agents trying to live the best way we can, and that Christianity offers us resources for meeting this responsibility.

---

[14] Ibid., 180.

Conservative Catholics might claim that Hogan's fallibilist view of the church is based on a historicist view of revelation that generates a very low Christology. This is what leads her to see a significant distance between God's will and the teachings of the magisterium. Hogan might reply that her historically conscious view of the church undercuts both an overly exalted view of hierarchical wisdom and the patronizing characterization of the people of God as a "herd" that needs a "shepherd" to be kept safe from the "wolves." Her ethic suggests instead a vision of the church as a body of self-governing participants whose administration is marked by procedural fairness, transparency, and downward as well as upward accountability.

Conservatives could argue that Hogan's characterization of magisterial teaching as just another source of "insight" is more Protestant than Catholic. They might claim she wants the church to mimic the liberal state; that is, to recognize that lay people are adults who have a duty and right to exercise responsibility for their own lives, actions, and choices. To a conservative, this is "cafeteria Catholicism," in which individual Catholics decide which teachings are relevant to their lives and which are not. The fact that Catholics often act this way is beside the point—or, rather, it is the problem not the solution.

The key issue for many conservatives is ecclesiological: whether Christians acknowledge the church as the authoritative interpreter of God's will. Unless we submit to the church as the divinely sanctioned interpreter of divine revelation, everything else in Catholicism falls apart. Adhering to this authority holds the community and tradition together and resists the acid of aggressive secularism. The key issue for liberals, in contrast, is self-responsibility. We must acknowledge our responsibility to act like adults and take the trouble of deciding how we ought to lead our lives.

Haidt finds that political conservatives understand political liberals better than the other way around, because conservatives tend to take seriously all six moral systems while liberals take care, fairness, and liberty much more seriously than loyalty, authority, and purity. A conservative would not say, "That is disgusting, but that doesn't make it wrong," but liberals would. If one is a liberal, Haidt suggests, one will find it difficult to empathize with people who are strongly motivated to avoid disgust and protect purity. Conservatives, on the other hand, know that the moral systems favored by liberals are important. While liberals tend to place a greater emphasis on compassion, for example, conservative Christians give a greater percentage of their income to charity than do liberals.[15]

---

[15] See David E. Campbell and Robert D. Putnam, *American Grace: How Religion Unites and Divides Us* (New York: Simon and Schuster, 2012), chap. 13.

Conservative Catholicism provides strong religious glue that binds fellow believers. Haidt characterizes religion as a "team sport"—primarily a matter of practices and group membership rather than beliefs.[16] Conservative believers are inclined to develop strong connections to their local parishes, dioceses, and the Holy See. They see the institution as providing access to sacramental grace and eternal beatitude, and the communion of saints as the supernatural perfection of group solidarity.

Haidt's social intuitionism, though, offers a sharp challenge to the conservative Catholic's ascription of supernatural wisdom to the magisterium. Moral foundations theory suggests that the leaders of the church are just as subject to human error, ideology, and oversight as any other human beings. On this point Haidt offers strong support for Hogan's view of conscience.

Emphasis on the individual conscience, on the other hand, tends to send liberal Catholics to likeminded parishes that accent what differentiates them from their own diocese and even more from the Holy See. "Refuge parishes" that welcome cohabiting couples, divorced and remarried Catholics, and gays and lesbians have an "oasis" ethos. They offer a kind of inclusive hospitality that, ironically, makes their members acutely aware of their differences from "normal" parishes. This message can be taken to imply a liberal version of sectarianism in which "our" liberal community has to fend off the "church."

Protecting individual diversity can lead to a form of Christianity that becomes "spiritual but not religious." In one of his studies Haidt's team asked people from Brazil, India, and the United States how they would respond to this bizarre scenario: He asked them what they felt about a family that cooked and ate its pet dog after it had been killed by a car.[17] Participants from all three countries found this behavior to be disgusting and ethically unacceptable. The only dissenting subjects were American college students. Though they felt disgusted at the behavior, they believed that the family has a right to eat their dead pet as long as they don't harm anyone.

Reaction against this kind of liberalism draws some young Catholics to forms of piety that stress the distinctiveness of the Christian life. The younger generation of Catholic moral theologians find themselves put off by polemics and alienation in both the church and the public sphere. They are a mixed bunch, but they usually want to lead with what we have in common rather than with what divides us. This move often takes forms that define the "us" narrowly and in a way that writes off more liberal Catholics. Instead of supporting a truly Catholic, inclusive notion of community,

---

[16] Haidt, *The Righteous Mind*, 292.

[17] Jonathan Haidt, S. H. Koller, and M. G. Dias, "Affect, Culture, and Morality, or Is It Wrong to Eat Your Dog?" *Journal of Personality and Social Psychology* 65 (1993): 613–28.

ecclesial-identity politics divides people into faithful insiders (with obedient consciences) and the world (with autonomous consciences).

Applications to Conscience in Catholicism

Haidt believes the best way to reduce political polarization is for liberals and conservatives to listen to, form friendships with, and engage in empathic dialogue with each other. Catholics in particular should have strong religious and ethical reasons for doing so. Each side has insights that the other needs to hear. The Catholic conscience at its best is characterized by what the philosopher Gabriel Marcel called "creative fidelity."[18] Fidelity without creativity is authoritarian, but creativity without fidelity is chaos.

The social intuitionist model suggests we misunderstand the nature of the conflict if we think it mainly about interpreting religious beliefs or sacred texts. Haidt says that our emotions are the dog that wags the tail, and reason the tail. If you want to make the dog wag its tail, you have to make it happy. Just as you can't make it happy by grabbing its tail and manually waving it back and forth, so you can't change people's minds by dismantling their arguments. "If you want to change people's minds," Haidt says, "you've got to talk to their elephants."[19] This suggests that if we want to get beyond dueling accounts of the Catholic conscience, we have to understand one another's intuitions and try to communicate in ways that elicit new intuitions from one another. This means we have to listen to one another's stories and create experiences that engage the imagination and empathy of the other.

If friendship and respect do not come first, dialogue about hot-button issues quickly deteriorates to debate that produces winners and losers. Haidt tells us that elephants tend to lean toward those they perceive to be trustworthy, cooperative, and friendly. Friends are more willing to acknowledge the truth as we see it from our point of view. Friends help us see evidence that we ignored, questions we did not raise, and qualifications that have to amend our conclusions.

We mainly change our minds as a result of talking to other people who hold views different from our own. So, it is important to be able to discuss matters of great moral importance with friends who are not just fellow in-group members. When he started the Common Ground Initiative, Cardinal Bernardin understood that talking to other people only works after you have established relationships based on respect, trust, and friendship.

[18] Gabriel Marcel, *Creative Fidelity*, trans. Robert Rosthal (New York: Farrar, Strauss, and Company, 1964).

[19] Haidt, *The Righteous Mind*, 57.

Confirmation of this "primacy of friendship" approach comes from the work of the late Bishop Claverie of Oran, Algeria.[20] Claverie was the bishop of a few thousand Catholics in a population of four million Muslims. After Algeria established independence, he was ordained a bishop and had to find a way to allay Muslim fears that the church was going to be an agent of neo-colonial domination. He came to see his mission as an apostolate of friendship with Muslim Algerians.

In Claverie's experience, friendship and solidarity with Muslims are the only basis for developing real understanding. He hoped that greater understanding could stimulate a process of "reciprocal conversion" in which both Christians and Muslims would come to a deeper appropriation of the riches of their respective traditions. He knew that this apostolate takes a long time and much patience, and he gave his life trying to exercise it. His project was based on a core belief: "I believe there is a God, but I do not possess God. . . . One does not possess the truth—and I am in need of the truth that others have found."[21] If Claverie could say this about Algerian Muslims, surely liberal and conservative Catholics can say this about each other.

Liberals should aim not to convert conservatives to being liberals, or vice versa, but rather to foster friendships that open up possibilities for greater mutual understanding. To do this, we have to work harder to avoid language that alarms the other's elephants. Conservatives would do well to avoid the language of *obedience* and *submission* because to liberal elephants these words sound like tools for domination. For their part, liberals need to eschew loaded terms like *autonomy* and *authenticity*, which, no matter how qualified, make conservative elephants suspicious. Catholicism has plenty of terms that are less likely to make anyone's elephants nervous, including *dialogue, faithfulness, compassion, community, grace,* and *forgiveness.*

Timothy Radcliffe, O.P., suggests we avoid the language of liberal and conservative because both terms are used as labels and group markers that get in the way of real understanding. He suggests we use the phrases *kingdom Catholics* and *communion Catholics* because both are fundamental to the gospel and play a central role in the life of the church. Radcliffe believes that both kinds of Catholic are suffering from a form of "root shock" or feeling that they have lost their home. We can only overcome this kind of alienation, he argues, if we empathize with the other's sense of exile and

[20] See Jean-Jacques Perennes, *A Life Poured Out: Pierre Claverie of Algeria*, trans. Phyllis Jestice and Matthew Sherry (Maryknoll, NY: Orbis Books, 2007).

[21] Ibid., 261.

loss and begin to reenvision the church as "a community in which they may feel that they too belong."[22]

Haidt believes that his account of how we function morally is more consistent with virtue ethics than with either utilitarian or Kantian moral theories. Moral foundations theory stresses the primacy of perception over rational argumentation in the routine operation of our consciences, the formative significance of stories and exemplars, and the impact of community (other elephants) and its institutions on our moral sensibilities. It also alerts us to the danger of dysfunctional communities that malform their members. Explicit reasoning and conversation enable us to criticize ways in which our communities damage rather than enhance our lives; commitment to truth requires us to listen to the voices of outsiders.

Catholic education in this vein includes a dimension of social and moral formation. It must address both rider and elephant. If moral psychology is correct, elephants are always primarily influenced by the other elephants. This implies that effective moral development, formation, and education will be pursued in communal and practice-based contexts more than in primarily cognitive ways. Virtue ethics thus has to be social ethics.

An account of conscience in the context of virtue ethics informed by moral psychology faces a major challenge: we have evolved to cooperate with people in our own groups rather than with outsiders. Applied to Catholicism, many liberals feel more in common with liberal Protestants than they do with conservative Catholics. Our sense of "us" and "them" is less a matter of de facto ecclesial membership than shared ecclesial sensibility, and these differ radically. Both sides, it turns out, run the danger of Catholic sectarianism.

To be Christian is to participate in the body of Christ. To operate with a truly Christian conscience is not just to have an American or Irish or Mexican conscience plus information, insights, wisdom, and so forth, from the Christian church. If we have to choose, most Americans are Americans who happen to be Christian rather than Christians who happen to be American. Liberal Catholics run the danger of assimilation to popular cultural norms. Conservatives appreciate this danger more than do liberals. Conscience can and does lead us astray, and it may or may not be the place where we hear the voice of God.

Christian communities have a rich set of social structures, institutions, and practices that shape character. These questions are the product of complex historical processes that are always ambiguous and in need

[22] Timothy Radcliffe, O.P., *What Is the Point of Being a Christian?* (New York: Continuum, 2005), 171.

of continuing reform. Thoughtful Christians can in turn contribute to the deliberate shaping of these social structures, institutions, and practices so that they help form people to be active, adult, co-responsible members of the church instead of just passive recipients of its teachings and sacraments. Liberals appreciate this better than conservatives. If conservatives underscore the importance of character formation, liberals appreciate the responsibility of all Christians for that formation.

We all need to help the church develop structures, institutions, and practices that will enable lay people to develop consciences that accept their responsibility for the well-being of the church as well as for their own personal lives. This involves a significant cultural change within the church at the grassroots. We see this happening in some parishes and vowed religious communities, in pockets like the campus ministry programs of some colleges and universities, in Maryknoll Lay Missioners and Jesuit Volunteer Corps, and in institutions like L'Arche and the Catholic Worker.

Conclusion

Christians in the second half of the twentieth century needed to be encouraged to embrace a personalist account of conscience when they lived in contexts dominated by the church. This notion is still valuable for people who feel the power of the church bearing down upon them, but this experience seems less widespread than it did forty years ago. Christians in the future will need to cultivate adult consciences that can sustain vital faith communities that are not supported by the wider society. The church of the future will have to be one in which thoughtful Christians are free to raise questions and come to different conclusions about non-infallible teachings, not out of an attitude of disobedience, but on the contrary, out of obedience to God as one understands God's will. If Haidt is right about the power of our moral systems, the development of vital Christian communities in the future will do best if they show how the Christian conscience can be shaped to take seriously not only care, fairness, and liberty, but also loyalty, authority, and sanctity.

5.

Conscience Formation and the Challenge of Unconscious Racial Bias

Bryan N. Massingale

> *Almost as color defines vision itself, race shapes the cultural eye—what we do and do not notice, the reach of empathy and the alignment of response.*
>
> —Taylor Branch, *Parting the Waters*

As I write this essay, I am haunted by the long series of tragic killings of unarmed African Americans, especially young men, by police officers, security guards, and neighborhood vigilantes that is occurring with terrible frequency in the United States. An advocacy group, the Malcolm X Grassroots Movement, documented over 313 such extrajudicial killings of African American men in 2012 alone—a rate of one such death every twenty-eight hours.[1] Among the most recent and notorious of these killings are those of Trayvon Martin (Sanford, Florida), Michael Brown (Ferguson, Missouri), Eric Garner (Staten Island, New York), and Tamir Rice (Cleveland, Ohio). Though each death occurred in unique circumstances, there is a disturbing pattern here, one eloquently expressed by *New York Times* columnist Charles M. Blow:

> There is an eerie echo in it all—a sense of tragedy too often repeated. And yet the sheer morbid, wrenching rhythm of it belies a larger phenomenon, one obscured by its vastness, one that can be seen only when one steps back and looks from a distance and with data:

[1] Malcolm X Grassroots Movement, *Operation Ghetto Storm: 2012 Report on the Extrajudicial Killings of 313 Black People by Police, Security Guards, and Vigilantes* (April 2013), https://mxgm.org.

> *The criminalization of black and brown bodies—particularly male ones*—from the moment they are first introduced to the institutions and power structures with which they must interact.[2]

This pervasive criminalization is what disturbs me, for it is an association that is not necessarily deliberate or conscious. One researcher, studying the propensity of police officers to use deadly force more often in situations involving black people, rejects the conclusion that such officers must be either intentional bigots or completely unbiased. Rather, she notes something much more complex at work: "Racial stereotypes operate at a subconscious level to influence a police officer's decision to use deadly force. The police officer may not consciously decide to use deadly force because of the suspect's race, but the suspect's race nonetheless influences the officer. Racial stereotypes thus may alter the officer's perception of danger, threat, and resistance to authority."[3] The Malcolm X Grassroots Movement concurs, concluding that these deaths are the effects of a pervasive social "conditioning."[4]

In addition to this cycle of tragedy, I am disturbed by the official Catholic response to the events surrounding one of these deaths, that of Michael Brown in August 2014, as represented by my own Archdiocese of Milwaukee in its official newspaper, the *Catholic Herald.* In its August 21, 2014, edition, the *Catholic Herald* published a cartoon on its editorial page depicting two African American men wearing tee-shirts. No commentary accompanied the cartoon, nor was there any other mention of the events of Ferguson on the editorial page.

[2] Charles M. Blow, "Michael Brown and Black Men," *New York Times* (August 13, 2014).

[3] Cynthia Ann Lee, "'But I Thought He Had a Gun'—Race and Police Use of Deadly Force," *Hastings Race and Poverty L. J.* (2004).

[4] Malcolm X Grassroots Movement, *Operation Ghetto Storm.*

This cartoon provoked a furious outcry from the *Catholic Herald's* readership, particularly—and thankfully, not only—from the black Catholic community. I wrote a lengthy letter to the editor, copied to the archbishop as the newspaper's publisher, expressing dismay, sadness, and anger at this offensive and tasteless treatment of the events in Ferguson. I noted that the paper provided no context for the events being depicted. In fact, the shooting of the unarmed teenager, and the fact that his lifeless body was left in the middle of the street in the hot sun for over four hours before being disposed of—in other words, the catalytic events to which the cartoon refers—were unnoted. The caricatured, thug-like portrayals of the black men in the cartoon neither elicit sympathy nor engender understanding from the reader. Instead, they convey that the militarized police response to this community in the face of the protests was perhaps unavoidable and justifiable. The cartoon oversimplified current events to the point of insult by ignoring the pervasive and longstanding sense of grievance and frustration that may have led some to take the misguided actions that they have. I further noted the absence of any faith perspective or content in the cartoon itself, something contrary to the mission of an official diocesan newspaper.

In response to widespread protests and similar acts of disapproval, a series of meetings occurred with archdiocesan officials, the newspaper's editors, and community leaders from the black Catholic and other constituencies. In all of these venues the editors denied that there was any deliberate racist malice or intent in the cartoon's publication and actively resisted any suggestion to the contrary. Yet they also could not explain why an African American with another perspective and insight into these events was not consulted in the decision to publish the cartoon. In a subsequent issue the editors issued an apology—though addressed primarily, even solely to the black Catholic community, despite the fact that numerous white Catholics also expressed anger, dismay, and disappointment—and also published eight letters that eloquently, forcefully, and insightfully articulated the faith-based reflection and social context lacking in the paper's initial publication.[5]

I begin with the pervasive criminalization of black men and its depiction in this cartoon because they constitute a pertinent case study of this essay's central questions: How can one rightly form one's conscience when that conscience is blind, not through personal fault (that is, vincible ignorance) or lack of diligence (that is, invincible ignorance), but from a scotosis that is rooted in the pervasive conditioning of one's culture? How does one account for conscience formation in an atmosphere of what I call a cultured racial indifference; that is, where one's very socialization instills in one

[5] "An Apology, and Hope for a Fruitful 'Conversation,'" *Catholic Herald* (September 4, 2014).

insensitivity or social callousness toward those with darker skin? How can one rightly form conscience in a morally compromised environment when that environment is not only familial but the very culture itself?

In other words, it is too easy to focus our moral concern upon either rogue police officers and security guards or upon the *Catholic Herald's* editors or archdiocesan representatives. (I take these people at their word when they avow that they acted without deliberate racial malice.) I contend that the individual actors in the events I narrated are influenced by and are products of an underlying cultural formation system; that is, they are not aberrations but representatives of something normal and typical in US (and Western) society.

I not only want to examine in this essay the reality of social injustice—specifically the killings of unarmed African Americans and especially black men—but I also seek to highlight "culturally legitimated" unjust social situations and how cultural formation facilitates blindness and/or indifference to social injustice.[6] I posit that we need to address the *cultural* significance of a belief in black criminality that the cartoon conveys, the repeated denial of any racial motivation in the publication of the cartoon, and the systemic prevalence of such killings in diverse locations throughout the nation.

To this end I address the formative power of culture, specifically its malformative manifestations as revealed in the reality of unconscious racism. I then attend to the limited reflection on conscience formation in Catholic theological ethics and show how it inadequately accounts for the pervasive influence of culturally induced moral insensitivity. I conclude with tentative musings toward a more adequate account of conscience formation in the light of the pervasive influence of culture.

I stress that this contribution is more suggestive than definitive. No doubt there will be places needing greater clarity and refinement. I invite the reader to join this exploration of an issue that marks the frontiers of Catholic moral theology and ethical analysis.

Racism Today: A "Cultured Indifference"

In my work I strive to account for both the reality of undeniable major progress in race relations in the United States—especially as symbolized in the election of the first person of African descent as its president—with the equally undeniable reality of the continuing persistence of racial disparities and resentments. What, I wondered, is the underlying constant that endures

---

[6] Gregory Baum, *Essays in Critical Theology* (Kansas City, MO: Sheed and Ward, 1994), 196.

despite external changes in social institutions? What is the link that unites African enslavement, Jim Crow segregation, and the so-called new Jim Crow, also known as James Crow Jr. Esquire?[7]

My insight was to look beneath the visible personal and institutional manifestations of racism and to understand racism as a culture. Using Canadian philosopher Bernard Lonergan's understanding that "a culture is a set of meanings and values that informs a community's way of life,"[8] I could posit that culture is more fundamental than social institutions, policies, and customs. Culture expresses the meaning of society and the significance of the ways in which we order our communities. The pivotal insight that I took from Lonergan is that "culture stands to social order as soul to body";[9] that is, culture is the spirit that animates social institutions and customs, makes them intelligible, and expresses their meaning. This cultural set of meanings and values could endure despite changes in social institutions. Left unchallenged and unnoted, it simply adapts new social forms and expressions.

Moreover, cultures—the sets of meanings and values that inform a people's way of life—are also systems of identity formation. Cultures shape a human group's behavior and consciousness; they condition thoughts, values, actions, and awareness. They provide the matrix of meaning for answering the questions of who we are and what we stand for.

Thus, I argue for a more cultural and systemic understanding of racism. I contend that racism is a deeply entrenched symbol system of meanings and values attached to skin color that provides group identity, shapes personal consciousness, and justifies the existence of race-based economic, social, and political disparities. The specific disparities and race-based injustices change over time; the underlying symbol system, left unchallenged, assumes shifting social forms and expressions that nonetheless reflect the underlying set of meanings and values. As important as these functions are, however, racism does more. As a culture, racism is also *formative*. Racism is a symbol system, a culture operating on a preconscious level, a learned and communal frame of reference that shapes identity, consciousness, and behavior—the way social groups understand their place and worth. Race, in the Western world, tells us who we are.[10]

---

[7] Michelle Alexander, *The New Jim Crow: Mass Incarceration in the Age of Colorblindness* (New York: New Press, 2010).

[8] Bernard Lonergan, *A Second Collection*, ed. William F. J. Ryan and Bernard J. Terrell (Philadelphia: Westminster Press, 1974), 232.

[9] Ibid., 102. I discuss this in greater depth in *Racial Justice and the Catholic Church* (Maryknoll, NY: Orbis Books, 2010), 13–19.

[10] Gary L. Chamberlain, "A Model to Confront Racism," *Theology Today* 32 (January 1976): 355.

"Unconscious" Racial Bias

The influence of culture leads us to consider the reality and power of racial bias that is not conscious, which is called unconscious racism. Unconscious racism connotes how race can operate as a negative—yet not conscious, deliberate, or intentional—decision-making factor due to the pervasive cultural stigma attached to dark skin color in Western culture. Its proponents argue that the US population has been socialized, in tacit and hidden ways, to associate dark skin color with danger, stupidity, incompetence, immorality, promiscuity, and criminality.

The seminal core insight of unconscious racism is conveyed in the following paragraph:

> Americans share a common historical and cultural heritage in which racism has played and still plays a dominant role. Because of this shared experience, we also inevitably share many ideas, attitudes, and beliefs that attach significance to an individual's race and induce negative feelings and opinions about nonwhites. . . . At the same time, most of us are unaware of our racism. We do not recognize the ways in which our cultural experience has influenced our beliefs about race or the occasions on which those beliefs affect our actions. In other words, a large part of the behavior that produces racial discrimination is influenced by unconscious racial motivation.[11]

Put more simply, because a racialized set of meanings and values permeates all of our society's cultural products, through socialization in US society we learn at a preconscious level to attach negative associations with dark skin color, which induce negative feelings about nonwhites. Such associations are transmitted through unconscious socialization, the "tacit understandings" that are expressed in "what everybody knows" yet at times are not consciously aware of, for they seem thoroughly natural, reasonable, and rational:

> Culture—including, for example, the media and an individual's parents, peers, and authority figures—transmits certain beliefs and

[11] Charles L. Lawrence, "The Id, the Ego, and Equal Protection: Reckoning with Unconscious Racism," *Stanford Law Review* 39 (January 1987): 322. Note that Lawrence states that he is not using *unconscious* as it is understood in Jungian psychology. He is simply describing a "collection of widely shared individual memories, beliefs, and understandings" at a "nonreporting level" that are widespread because "individuals who live within the same culture share common developmental experiences."

> preferences. Because these beliefs are so much a part of the culture, they are not experienced as explicit lessons. *Instead, they seem part of the individual's rational ordering of her perceptions of the world.* The individual is unaware, for example, that the ubiquitous presence of a cultural stereotype has influenced her perception that blacks are lazy or unintelligent [or more prone to violence]. Because racism is so deeply ingrained in our culture, it is likely to be transmitted by *tacit understandings*: Even if a child is not told that blacks are inferior, he learns that lesson by observing the behavior of others. These tacit understandings, because they have never been articulated, are less likely to be experienced at a conscious level.[12]

What needs to be underscored and emphasized, however, is not merely the presence of such preconscious motives and beliefs in individual persons. Rather, what is pivotal is their source. They are the effects of *cultural conditioning*, that is, the effects of a culture that transmits certain beliefs and preferences through its symbolic code of meanings and values.

Cultural Conditioning and "Racially Selective Sympathy"

Yet, the fact that this conditioning occurs without conscious awareness and is acted upon without deliberate advertence does not mean that it is innocent or without harm. Indeed, one of the most pernicious effects of unconscious racism, which is directly related to "cultured indifference," is what critical race scholar Charles Lawrence calls "racially selective sympathy and indifference," that is, "the unconscious failure to extend to a minority the same recognition of humanity, and hence the same sympathy and care, given as a matter of course to one's own group."[13] Put more colloquially, racially selective sympathy addresses these questions. Who gets the break? Who gets the benefit of the doubt? Who gets the presumption of innocence . . . and assumption of guilt?

This cultured indifference, reflecting unconscious racial bias, is critically important for understanding the public discussion concerning the shootings of unarmed black young men. For example, what African Americans call racial profiling many white Americans consider reasonable behavior. For them, it is a self-evident fact that the majority of crimes are committed by black males, despite the empirical evidence to the contrary. They deny they are racists, for, they say, they do not believe that *all* black men are

---

[12] Lawrence, "The Id, the Ego, and Equal Protection," 323, emphasis added.

[13] Ibid., 323n.135.

dangerous or malevolent. But at a visceral level, many white people are convinced that most black men are—or could be—threats, and thus they are justified in acting upon that presumption until a particular black man proves otherwise.

This sentiment was expressed in the comments of the first juror to speak publicly after the acquittal of George Zimmerman for the 2012 killing of Trayvon Martin, an unarmed African American teenager, in Sanford, Florida. Identified only as Juror B37, she stated: "I think George Zimmerman is a man whose heart was in the right place, but just got displaced by the vandalism in the neighborhoods, and wanting to catch these people so badly that he went above and beyond what he really should have done. But I think his heart was in the right place. It just went terribly wrong."[14]

Note who gets the benefit of the doubt. Note how this juror states that although things "went wrong," at least Zimmerman's "heart was in the right place." He acted reasonably, simply trying to protect his neighborhood from African American vandals. Note that it was irrelevant that his barely seventeen-year-old victim was not a criminal. Nor was it relevant that Trayvon's heart may have also been "in the right place" of just trying to walk home. He becomes an unfortunate but excusable victim of a reasonable desire for safety.

This is how racism enters the picture, not in the sense of deliberate and intentional acts of meanness and cruelty. We are dealing with a more or less unconscious racial bias that is manifested in the pervasive cultural association of black with criminality, in the willingness to presume the innocence of non-blacks (or, at least, to give them the benefit of the doubt), and above all, in the inability to empathize with the plight of a black teenager confronted by an armed adult.[15] This is an illustration of racially selective sympathy and indifference.

It is important to underscore how these actions and dispositions are not necessarily the outcomes of conscious decision making, however, but rather the unnoted effects of socialization in a culture of racism. To the

---

[14] Anderson Cooper, "Exclusive Interview with Juror B-37; Defense Team Reacts to Juror Interview," *Anderson Cooper 360 Degrees* (aired July 15, 2013), transcript at http://www.cnn.com.

[15] For a fuller treatment, see Bryan N. Massingale, "When Profiling Is 'Reasonable,' Injustice Becomes Excusable," *US Catholic Blog post*, http://www.uscatholic.org. Also relevant is Charles Lawrence's insight that unconscious bias is especially prevalent and operative in chaotic or ambiguous conditions. He notes, "In ambiguous social situations, it will always be easier to find evidence supporting an individual's assumed group characteristics than to find contradictory evidence" (Lawrence, "The Id, the Ego, and Equal Protection," 338–39).

extent that individuals are influenced by the endemic racism of American life—however unwittingly or preconsciously—indifference is "cultured" and cultivated within them without moral qualms of conscience.

These considerations of racism as a culture and cultural formation demonstrate the importance of going beyond a consideration of the deliberate acts of individual actors in our moral reflection and ethical analysis. An adequate understanding of the human situation demands that we take into account the *cultural meaning* of such acts—such as George Zimmerman's shooting and Juror B37's comments—and how preconscious racial cultural conditioning can block awareness of the harm being done or, even worse, justify its harmful effects upon human persons.

The Relevance for Conscience Formation

I begin by noting the lack of scholarly attention devoted specifically to the formation of conscience. There is a common recognition of the obligation to form one's conscience. But little sustained attention has been given to the process by which one does so. More significant, there is a lack of consensus about what is meant by "forming one's conscience" or the desired goal of doing so. There appear to be at least two schools of thought. One approach views conscience formation as a process of information gathering. That is, in forming one's conscience, one strives to develop as complete a picture as possible of the moral situation, the ethical dilemmas that are present and the decisions that must be made, the ramifications of possible courses of action, the counsel and wisdom offered by responsible authorities—including, most notably, the hierarchical magisterium—all toward the end of coming to a responsible ethical decision and moral judgment on proposed courses of action.

Karl H. Peschke represents this perspective, in which conscience formation is the process of acquiring sufficient information so that the "dubious conscience" can be sufficiently informed to move beyond doubt to moral action. Peschke writes:

> Since conscience stands in need of illumination and guidance, a man is responsible for its formation. To call upon the judgments of one's conscience without having striven to inform it properly is an insulting abuse. Unwillingness to inform one's conscience, "to use the best available resources to understand the truth of the moral situation facing one, is already an unwillingness to respond to the one true God." The sources of information are the order of creation, the

word of God, man's personal communion with Christ, the living faith of the Christian community, and the findings of the ethical sciences.[16]

The second approach views conscience formation as a process of character development. Conscience formation is a kind of shorthand for fostering growth in moral virtue and ethical discernment. The focus is not on the particular judgment or decision to be made. Rather, the emphasis is upon enhancing the agent's ability to be a more effective seeker of moral truths and values. The aim of conscience formation, then, is facilitating moral maturity and integrity. Moral catechesis thus seeks more to form a well-rounded decision maker rather than an upright moral decision.

Richard Gula is a representative of this perspective. He explicitly avows that "the aim of the formation of conscience is not simply to increase a person's knowledge of acts and values, or skills for resolving a moral dilemma. It must also include the fuller texture of the person's moral character." He further declares that "moral choices are fundamentally matters of integrity: we act in character or out of character."[17] Thus, while he agrees that conscience needs to be adequately informed in order to reach upright moral judgments and decisions, he privileges the need for a more holistic ethical formation that goes beyond the acquisition of moral norms and insights. Indeed, he states that such formation would both take into account and tutor the "nonrational factors" of human decision making such as "imagination, vision, habits, affections, dispositions [and] somatic reactions."[18]

Yet, despite Gula's appreciation of the importance of "vision" for correct moral action, and his declaration that "the properly informed conscience sees rightly," he does not develop these insights in any detail.[19] Nor does he devote specific attention to the influence of "nonrational" social or cultural conditioning upon character formation. Instead, he pays far more attention to how conscience formation relates to authoritative church teaching and moral norms, and thus in practice falls back into the mode of "informing" conscience seen in Peschke.

The problem, therefore, is that neither approach, in practice, is adequate to the challenges raised by the reality of nonconscious racial bias. Both are dependent upon the conscious awareness and intentions of the moral agent.

---

[16] Karl H. Peschke, *Christian Ethics: General Moral Theology,* vol. 1, *A Presentation of General Moral Theology in the Light of Vatican II* (Dublin: C. Goodliffe Neale, 1979), 244. Conscience here is conceived as a faculty of the person that needs to be informed rather than as a dimension of the person in need of comprehensive formation.

[17] Richard Gula, *Reason Informed by Faith: Foundations of Catholic Morality* (Mahwah, NJ: Paulist Press, 1989), 137–39.

[18] Ibid., 141.

[19] Ibid.

But as we have seen, one can be a person of upright virtue and fail to see racial offense and violation. One can be a sincere seeker after moral truth and fail to consider the insights of persons of color. One's culture, including one's moral formation, can induce one to not see such omissions or to view such omissions as not being morally problematic.

In other words, neither approach is sensitive enough to the "unconscious, nonvoluntary dimensions" of social evil, that is, to the false consciousness and "blindness produced in persons by the dominant culture, blindness that prevents them from recognizing the evil dimension of their social reality."[20] (For example, one cannot be aware of the absence or omission of certain voices or perspectives if one believes that such omissions are normal, the way things ought to be.) The evil of such a situation resides not only, or even primarily, in individual hearts but is embedded in cultural patterns, social conventions, and civic institutions that endure beyond the individual. Neither existing approach to conscience formation considers how the cultural legitimation of injustice can blind us to our captivity to value systems contrary to the gospel. Such systemic manifestations of sin cannot be attacked through strategies aimed at individual conscience formation alone, whether this is conceived of as a process of information gathering or moral maturation.

Even more troubling, however, is that the focus upon what the moral agent is consciously aware of that marks both Peschke's and Gula's processes of conscience formation can *exacerbate* racial injustice through instilling a conviction of the individual's moral rectitude. Catholic ethicist Maureen O'Connell, in reflecting upon the killing of Trayvon Martin, cogently argues that the "clean white conscience" is a major impediment to a racially just society.

> But racism is not about isolated and blatantly evil acts. Rather, it is a far more subtle and pervasive way of perceiving ourselves and others that is shaped by our collective way of being together. Failing to name racism as a cultural phenomenon—a set of dispositions and perspectives on the world that are collectively learned and symbolically shared—only perpetuates white complicity in racism. Since few of us have probably ever committed conscious, intentional and deliberate acts of racial hatred, most whites can be assured of our lack of culpability with the events related to the Martin case in Florida and shirk any kind of responsibility for it that others try to foist on us. Catholic social teaching tells us that our consciences are clean.

---

[20] Gregory Baum, "Structures of Sin," in *The Logic of Solidarity,* ed. Gregory Baum and Robert Ellsberg (Maryknoll, NY: Orbis Books, 1989), 118.

> It's this clean white conscience that is the biggest impediment to racial justice. As philosopher Barbara Applebaum noted in *Being White, Being Good*: "White people can reproduce and maintain racist practices, even when, *and especially when*, they believe themselves to be morally good."[21]

In short, Catholic ethical reflection has not taken full account of the impact of culture, symbol, and false consciousness on moral action and responsibility. Laurie Cassidy helpfully and accurately names my concern: "Because of the covert nature of racism's transmission its meanings are internalized without awareness of the source and judged to be normal and normative."[22] That is, one's sense of right and wrong, one's grasp of morality, and one's very conscience become blunted and twisted by one's socialization in a culture of racism. This is not merely a matter of culpable ignorance. Nor do I believe that the issue can be satisfactorily resolved by an appeal to what the tradition calls invincible ignorance. Such an appeal can somewhat deal with individual culpability but does not attend to the deeper web of injustice that the predominant understandings of conscience formation as voluntary and conscious acts neither address nor redress but rather compound. Lisa Fullam's essay in this volume attends to the deforming effects of internalized sexism upon conscience formation in an analogous manner.

Unconscious racial motivation, implicit bias, tacit racism: these realities not only severely challenge our dominant understanding of racism but also reveal the inadequacies of our current understandings of sin, culpability, and conscience. A forthright engagement with culture as a set of meanings and value that shapes identity and consciousness—and with racism as an identity-shaping ethos—demands a more or less radical rethinking of conscience formation and human responsibility.

Toward a New Direction in Conscience Formation: Cross-Racial Solidarity

A central challenge to a serious engagement with cultural sin—that is, culturally legitimated grave social evil—is well articulated in a haunting question posed by Lonergan: "How is a mind to become conscious of its own bias when that bias springs from a communal flight from understanding and is

---

[21] Maureen O'Connell, "Catholics and Racism: From Examination of Conscience to Examination of Culture," *NCR Online* (March 30, 2012).

[22] Laurie Cassidy, "Review Symposium on *Racial Justice and the Catholic Church*," *Horizons* 37 (Spring 2010): 128.

supported by the whole texture of a civilization?"[23] What, then, can free us from culturally induced blindness? If conscience is responsible to the truth,[24] and the culture of racism blinds the racially advantaged and privileged to a full awareness of moral wrongs/harms, what needs to happen if their consciences are to overcome such an ethical handicap? To answer these questions adequately would require a major treatment of the social and cultural dimensions of conversion. For now, I suggest that a way forward lies in the cultivation of authentic interracial solidarity and transformative love (compassion). A major task of future Catholic reflection on conscience will be to articulate a process of conscience formation that would facilitate these realities.

What would authentic interracial solidarity entail? It would seem that the following would be among the essential requirements: an ability to hear and be present to black anger; the interior space to welcome perspectives that significantly differ from one's own; and the cultivation of genuinely affective relationships with persons of color. I distill these minimum requirements in part from the work of Joe Feagin, a prolific scholar on the sociology of white racism.

Feagin has discovered that in developing authentic cross-racial identification and solidarity, white Americans typically pass through three different stages: sympathy, empathy, and what he calls autopathy:

> The initial stage, sympathy, is important but limited. It typically involves a willingness to set aside some racist stereotyping and hostility and the development of a friendly if variable interest in what is happening to the racialized other. . . . Empathy is a much more advanced stage of development in that it requires a developed ability to routinely reject distancing stereotypes and a heightened and sustained capacity to see and feel some of the pain of those in the outgroup.[25]

Feagin admits that the third stage of autopathy has not been fully analyzed by social scientists. This stage, he writes, "is one in which a white person has intentionally put herself or himself, if only partially, into the racist world of the oppressed and thereby not only receives racist hostility from other whites but also personally feel some of the pain that comes from

[23] Bernard Lonergan, *Insight: A Study of Human Understanding* (London: Longmans, Green, and Co., 1957), xiv.

[24] Cf. Vatican II, *Declaration on Religious Liberty (Dignitatis Humanae),* nos. 1, 2, 3; and *Gaudium et Spes,* no. 16.

[25] Joe R. Feagin, *Racist America: Roots, Current Realities, and Future Reparations* (New York: Routledge, 2001), 254. Feagin revisits this research in a later work: Joe Feagin and Eileen O'Brien, *White Men on Race: Power, Privilege, and the Shaping of the Cultural Consciousness* (Boston: Beacon Press, 2003), 64–65.

being enmeshed in the racist conditions central to the lives of the oppressed others."[26] Here the beneficiaries of white privilege and advantage not only grieve the suffering of others through vicarious experience but themselves endure some of the same racial animus and hostility.

Feagin notes that this is often the experience of whites who are the close friends, spouses or life partners, parents, or other close relatives of those who are the direct targets of racism. This goes beyond being a "white ally," as that term is sometimes understood, for here white Americans, out of a commitment to share life with the other—indeed, to share the life of another—"intentionally place themselves in the discriminatory settings of loved ones and thus endure some of the hostility and pain of those settings."[27] Such loving and committed relationships give one the visceral outrage, courage, strength, and motivation to break free from the "rewards of conformity" that keep most whites complacent with white privilege.[28] Transformative love, or compassion, empowers them for authentic solidarity. This makes them ethical agents who are able to see, and willing to act upon, truths to which they were previously blind or impervious.

Let us apply these reflections to the tragic killings of unarmed African American young men. In the aftermath of the shootings of Trayvon Martin and Michael Brown, many black men offered moving testimonies of their own experiences with law enforcement, their trials of having constantly to contend with white fear, and the pain of educating their sons about the potentially lethal danger in encounters with the police.[29] In the face of such testimonies rightly formed consciences would hear such pain with empathy and compassion, allowing themselves to be disturbed by the accounts of pain of which they were previously unaware. They would also be shaken by the cultural callousness that allowed them to be impervious to a deep pain that was there all along. Indeed, they would be so troubled that they could not allow life to go on as it did before. Finally, such consciences would act upon and out of this discomfort. In the words of Jesuit priest Joseph Brown, "Individual acts of compassion and understanding are worthwhile only when they strengthen a person to then confront the laws that *buffer* them and *buffet* us."[30] The acid test of genuine compassion is that it moves a person to act on another's behalf out of a deep recognition and acceptance

---

[26] Feagin, *Racist America,* 254–55.

[27] Feagin and O'Brien, *White Men on Race,* 65.

[28] Ibid., 236.

[29] Cf. Bryan Massingale, "When Profiling Is 'Reasonable,' Injustice Becomes Excusable"; and the letter of Larry Ashley, an African American father and grandfather, "Cartoon 'Clumsily Insulted' Readers," in *Catholic Herald* (September 4, 2014).

[30] Joseph Brown related this insight to me in a private conversation.

of one's shared humanity. Thus such consciences, out of their compassionate discomfort, would be moved to challenge the mass incarceration of African American and Latino young men, who are sentenced more severely for crimes that white men also commit and at times in greater numbers.[31] Or to join with racial-justice activists in their public protests with the demand that "Black lives matter."[32] In other words, compassionate discomfort would enable such consciences to overcome, or at least struggle against, culturally induced ethical blindness and indifference.

These observations are more suggestive than definitive. Yet I am convinced that current Catholic reflection on conscience formation, being overly rational and abstract, lacks the appreciation of the nonrational depths needed to move people to see social reality differently and then act against their own social interests and malformed racial identities. It cannot reach deeply enough to confront and overcome unconscious racial biases.

Thus conscience formation for Christians in the United States must include the cultivation of the qualities essential for authentic interracial solidarity. Lacking these, (white) consciences will not be able to be aware of, much less overcome, their culturally induced or legitimated blindness to the suffering of racial injustice.

To conclude, the reality of unconscious racial bias—indeed, of culturally legitimated social evil—poses a significant challenge not only to Catholic ethical reflection on racism, but also to its understanding of conscience and its formation. The dominant trend of Catholic ethical discourse privileges a concern with conscious, intentional, deliberate, individual acts of racial malice. Even where there is an awareness of "social sin," official Catholic teaching sees this reality as the entrenchment of individual sinfulness.[33]

Such an analysis is not only sociologically inaccurate or naive, but it is also woefully inadequate to the task of ethical analysis and moral

---

[31] See, among other studies, Alexander, *The New Jim Crow;* and Alex Mikulich, Laurie Cassidy, and Margaret Pfeil, *The Scandal of White Complicity in US Hyper-Incarceration* (New York: Palgrave Macmillan, 2013).

[32] The origins of this rallying cry, which has become a theme of the protests against the killings of unarmed African Americans, are detailed on the *n+1* magazine website, http://www.nplusonemag.com.

[33] Pope John Paul II, in his 1987 encyclical *Sollicitudo Rei Socialis,* acknowledged "structures of sin" that are "rooted in personal sin" and "thus always linked to the *concrete acts* of individuals" who create and maintain these social structures (no. 36). This conviction reiterates what he taught in his 1984 *Reconciliatio et Paenitentia,* that "cases of social sin," that is, certain collective behavior of certain social groups, "are the result of the accumulation and concentration of many *personal sins*" (no. 16). Thus, even in this consideration of "social sin," the emphasis remains upon personal responsibility, agency, deliberation, and intentionality. The full weight of cultural constraints upon human knowledge and freedom is not considered.

scrutiny that events such as the killings of Trayvon Martin and Michael Brown—among too many others—demand. In the words of theologian Gary Chamberlain:

> Past efforts of the churches to deal with racism have been impeded by numerous misunderstandings. Generally racism was viewed as nothing more than prejudice. Thus appeals have been directed to individuals on a level of rational understanding. But *racism is an irrational, preconscious element in American society and culture, impervious to rational efforts to root it out.* Furthermore, the churches' inadequate approaches to racism rest upon a false understanding of the cause of the problem. . . . The churches' efforts to alleviate the suffering of the oppressed, as needed as they are, divert attention from the core of the problem, the oppressing agents [and I add, their distorted or false consciousness], whether individuals or institutions, in white society.[34]

It is my conviction, one that has only grown stronger with time, that until we see racism as primarily a cultural phenomenon, one with derivative personal and interpersonal effects, and develop an understanding of conscience that highlights the influence of culture as a significant formative factor, we will have neither the understanding nor the resources that are adequate for effective ethical struggle against the social evils that are prevalent in twenty-first-century America and the global community.

[34] Chamberlain, "A Model to Confront Racism," 355.

6.

Joan of Arc, Holy Resistance, and Conscience Formation in the Face of Social Sin

Lisa Fullam

You've never been to the moon
But don't you want to go
Under the sea in the volcano
You've never looked into my eyes
But don't you want to know
What the dark and the wild
And the different know

—Melissa Etheridge, "The Different"

Introduction

The goal of conscience is truth. Conscience formation involves developing the cognitive skills and moral character that allow our moral discernments to hew more and more closely to the truth that is personal, culturally situated, and objective.

In a Thomistic/Aristotelian ethics of virtue, it is prudence, the virtue of the practical intellect, that guides the moral virtues toward their ends. Virtues are perfections of natural capacities (the will and the two sense appetites) by their becoming responsive to prudence. Virtues enable us to do the right thing easily, as though by "second nature." We flourish, we grow in virtue toward a state Aristotle called *eudaimonia* ("happiness"). Since virtues perfect human capacities, virtues are only secondarily abstract ideas; they are primarily qualities of human lives that we perceive as good. Thus the practice and reflection on practice by which we acquire virtue begin with imitation of admirable people.

But what happens if our perception of who is worth imitation is fundamentally warped? At least two problems immediately arise. First, this poses a serious challenge to the adequacy of virtue ethics as a moral methodology. If the method is grounded in imitation of good people, and we cannot identify with at least preliminary confidence who is admirable, then virtue ethics can only serve the status quo, at best, or the agenda of the most powerful, at worst, and should be subject to another overarching ethical modality.

The second problem follows from the first. In an ethics of virtue, conscience formation involves holistic character formation, not only prudence: "it belongs to prudence . . . to apply right reason to action, and this is not done without a right appetite."[1] The symbiosis of prudence and the other cardinal virtues requires rectitude both of reason and appetite for well-formed character. If our perception of who is worthy of admiration is warped, then the entire array of virtues we strive to acquire is corrupted from the start.

Social sin is one cause of this corruption. Social sin is especially dangerous for virtue ethics because it seems to elude the easy rejoinder to a wrong vision of happiness that can identify other kinds of moral mistakes. For example, a student might think that cheating on an exam is an easy route to a good grade, and thus is conducive to flourishing in two ways—the student gets the good grade and also gets extra leisure time that can be spent doing something more fun than, say, memorizing Greek verb forms. But academic culture can recognize and respond to that mistake: grades are never an end in themselves, and if the work is important to the student's future life (whether or not the student recognizes it), then actually gaining the knowledge matters.

But social sin strikes deeper and is not so easily gainsaid from within a culture. Social sin obstructs human flourishing by misrepresenting what flourishing entails for a certain kind of human being: as a man or woman, as a person of a particular race, as a person of a given sexual orientation, and so on. Lisa Tessman describes the oppression of social sin as operating at two levels. First, unjust social structures directly thwart the flourishing of oppressed people. The second level of damage is more insidious: "The second way . . . oppression interferes with flourishing . . . is by creating inclinations that conflict with liberatory principles, thus barring the possibility of full

---

[1] Thomas Aquinas, *Summa Theologiae*, II-IIae, q.47.3c.

virtue."[2] Social sin tends to become internalized, so that the subject carries, even if unwillingly, a distorted vision of flourishing. All human communities are afflicted with different kinds of social sin.

Bryan Massingale describes this deeper dynamic of the social sin of racism in terms of culture in this volume. Massingale writes: "Racism is a symbol system, a culture operating on a preconscious level, a learned and communal frame of reference that shapes identity, consciousness, and behavior—the way social groups understand their place and worth. Race, in the Western world, tells us who we are."[3]

Further complicating the picture is the degree to which social sin shapes our moral intuitions, and thus the immediate and often unexamined judgments that shape our acts. Stephen Pope explains: "Most of our moral judgments are made rapidly on the basis of moral intuitions. Intuitions are "the sudden appearance in consciousness of a moral judgment, including an affective valence (good-bad, like-dislike), without any conscious awareness of having gone through steps of searching, weighing evidence, or inferring a conclusion."[4]

These immediate affective responses are thought by some moral psychologists to far outweigh moral reasoning, as an elephant outweighs the rational rider who tries to guide it:

> Our cognitive "rider" engages in a second-order, strategic activity that is strongly shaped, and usually driven, by our more determinative underlying moral emotions (the "elephant"). The basic structure of the emotion has been shaped by natural selection to deal with the challenges of survival and social cooperation. Emotions are primary because they come first, they operate very quickly (in an "affective flash"), and they provide powerful motivation for behavior.[5]

Here I want to address the social sin of sexism, which I understand as prejudice, stereotyping, and therefore unwarranted discrimination on the basis of sex, typically to the detriment of women. My aim here is to address the two questions of methodology and conscience formation: How might

---

[2] Lisa Tessman, *Burdened Virtues. Virtue Ethics for Liberatory Struggles* (Oxford: Oxford University Press, 2005), 27.

[3] Bryan N. Massingale, "Conscience Formation and the Challenge of Unconscious Racial Bias," chap. 5 in this volume. See Gary L. Chamberlain, "A Model to Confront Racism," *Theology Today* 32 (January 1976): 355.

[4] Stephen J. Pope, "Conscience, Catholicism, and the New Science of Morality," chap. 4 in this volume. The quotation is from Jonathan Haidt, *The Happiness Hypothesis: Finding Modern Truth in Ancient Wisdom* (New York: Perseus, 2006), 818.

[5] Pope, "Conscience, Catholicism, and the New Science of Morality," explaining the thought of Haidt, *The Happiness Hypothesis*, 818.

virtue ethics explain and unmask the influence of sexism (or social sin more broadly)? And what are some practices that help us to form conscience in a way that resists self-destructive deformation of our moral ideals?

I chose sexism because it has been the subject of moral analysis for decades.[6] Feminist ethical methodology has been well articulated. Because we can at least name sexism for the warping of human ideals that it is, I can use it as a methodological case study that might begin to help us find strategies for conscience formation that both resist well-known social sins like sexism, and may also help us recognize and resist those social sins that have not yet been so completely named and described. A caveat: sexism is analogous yet different in important ways from racism, homophobia, and other "isms." Social sin deforms moral anthropology, but different social sins do so differently.

We see virtue in lives. As a paradigm of resistance, I want to suggest Joan of Arc, a saint in the Roman Catholic tradition and therefore worthy, at least in a preliminary way, of receiving the benefit of the doubt as an admirable person. To call her a feminist would be an anachronism, yet she lived in dramatic tension with the ideals of femininity of her time. It was only through resistance to those ideals of femininity that she was able to be the saintly figure the tradition admires. Next, I raise some methodological points about social sin and virtue ethics, connecting them to Joan's life. Finally, I bring the question back around to us: How do we practice a kind of resistance that might help us come to know "what the dark and the wild and the different know"?

Joan of Arc

Joan of Arc was born in 1412 or 1413 to a peasant family in Domremy, France. When she was twelve or thirteen, she began hearing voices she identified as Saint Michael, Saint Catherine, and Saint Margaret, telling her to drive out the English and bring the dauphin to Reims for coronation. From this time on she vowed not to marry. (Her virginity was an important marker of female sanctity to both the French and the English; representatives of each nation examined her in the course of her career.) She did not style herself as a man but as Joan the Maid, even as she cut her hair,

---

[6] One classic text on the conventional image of femininity in American twentieth-century culture is Betty Friedan, *The Feminine Mystique* (New York: W. W. Norton, 2001 [1963]). Friedan critiques the ideal of the homebound woman devoted exclusively to care of husband, children, and home, a contrast even to career women in the United States in the 1930s. She calls the profound unhappiness of many housewives of her time "the problem that has no name" (57).

assumed male dress (a necessity for battle), wore armor, and learned to ride and fight.[7] She appealed to those who would be moved by her claim to divine aid, but also she seems to have deliberately cultivated a resemblance to the heroine of a French legend predicting that a prophetic young woman in armor would come from Lorraine.[8]

From the beginning, Joan was suspected of being a sorcerer. Charles VII convened a commission to evaluate her character and morality. In April 1429, they "declared her to be of irreproachable life, a good Christian, possessed of the virtues of humility, honesty and simplicity."[9] They did not judge her voices to be true or false, but told Charles VII that a "favorable presumption" of divine origin should be granted and put to further test. Joan promised that a sign would be forthcoming at Orleans.

The rest is legend. Joan rallied the troops at Orleans and finally broke the siege of the city. A number of successful engagements followed, including the retaking of Reims, enabling the coronation of Charles. Joan briefly turned her attention to the forced reformation of the Hussites, but then a truce with England broke down, and Joan was back in battle.

Joan was captured in May 1430, when she stayed with the rear guard following a retreat from a skirmish at Margny. A number of escape and rescue attempts failed, and Joan was put on trial for heresy in January 1431.[10] The illiterate nineteen-year-old was faced by about sixty pro-Burgundian and

---

[7] One might wonder why a teenage girl asking for an army was listened to at all. Beyond Joan's claim of supernatural aid was the tattered state of the French at this time. The Hundred Years War for control of France was eighty-five years on at the time of her birth. The twin devastations of the war and the Black Death left France demoralized and vulnerable. Charles VII inherited the throne of France in 1422, but not before Charles VI (Charles the Mad) signed the Treaty of Troyes (1420) naming England's Henry V as heir to the French throne. A civil war between the Burgundians, allied with England, and the Armanacs divided French loyalties. Stephen Richey explains it this way: "After years of one humiliating defeat after another, both the military and civil leadership of France were demoralized and discredited. When the Dauphin Charles granted Joan's urgent request to be equipped for war and placed at the head of his army, his decision must have been based in large part on the knowledge that every orthodox, every rational option had been tried and had failed. Only a regime in the final straits of desperation would pay any heed to an illiterate farm girl who claimed that the voice of God was instructing her to take charge of her country's army and lead it to victory" (Stephen W. Richey, *Joan of Arc: The Warrior Saint* [Westport, CT: Praeger Publishers, 2003], 115).

[8] Anne Llewellyn Barstow, "Joan of Arc and Female Mysticism," *Journal of Feminist Studies in Religion* 1/2 (Fall 1985): 33.

[9] M. G. A., Vale, *Charles VII* (Oakland: University of California Press, 1974), 55.

[10] In what is probably the most well-known exchange of the trial, her accusers laid a theological trap for her by asking whether she knew she was in God's grace. She replied, "If I am not, may God put me there; and if I am, may God so keep me" (W. P. Barrett, "The Trial of Jeanne D'Arc," in *Medieval Sourcebook: The Trial of Joan of Arc* [1932], 52, available at http://www.fordham.edu).

English lawyers, clerics, and academics; she was convicted of lying about hearing voices, blasphemy, wearing men's clothing, and other offenses.[11] She then signed an abjuration and was sentenced to life imprisonment.[12] In prison she resumed wearing men's clothing (perhaps to make rape more difficult,[13] or perhaps because her guards provided her with only men's clothes[14]), which was regarded as a relapse into heresy, a capital crime. She then recanted her denial of the voices and said she regretted denying them. Retried as a relapsed heretic, she was sentenced to death and burned at the stake on May 30, 1431.

What shall we make of her? Certainly her courage is remarkable. Her role in the battles at which she was present seems to have been mostly a matter of rallying the troops without killing enemy soldiers herself, but she did carry a sword[15] and was always in the thick of the fight. She was wounded at least twice in the course of her brief military career. The judgment of Charles VII's commission evaluating her lauded her humility and simplicity, which seems somewhat at odds with the fiercely assertive woman who demanded a voice in military strategy, who demanded in the name of God that the English surrender, who demanded fair representation at her trial and talked back to her accusers, and who seemed to acquire military skills, and who showed acuity in the very different arenas of military strategy and theological disputation.

Women who claimed to be guided by divine voices or visions were increasingly common in late medieval Europe.[16] What is significant about Joan is not that she heard voices, even voices telling her to do outlandish things like drive the English out of France, but that she found the resolve

---

[11] Of course, Saint Margaret, whom Joan claimed spoke to her, was another notable saintly transvestite, cutting off her hair and entering a monastery as "Brother Pelagius." The history of cross-dressing female saints was invoked in Joan's defense to no avail.

[12] The entire trial is a masterpiece of ineptitude, legal malfeasance, and deceit. See Daniel Hobbins, *The Trial of Joan of Arc* (Cambridge, MA: Harvard University Press, 2005); or Régine Pernoud, *Joan of Arc, By Herself and Her Witnesses* (New York: Scarborough House, 1994 [1962]).

[13] It appears likely that she was raped or gang raped in a British prison before her execution. "The testimony of three witnesses at her posthumous retrial, one of whom had been her court-appointed confessor, claimed that she had been sexually abused during her last days in prison. Régine Pernoud, ed., *The Retrial of Joan of Arc*, trans. J. M. Cohen (London, 1955), 182–83" (Barstow, "Joan of Arc and Female Mysticism," 42n.).

[14] She had been imprisoned in a secular, not an ecclesiastical prison. In an ecclesiastical prison her guards would have been women, not men. See Pernoud, *Joan of Arc, By Herself and Her Witnesses,* 228.

[15] At her trial she testified that she obtained it after her voices told her to dig behind the altar in the church of Sainte Catherine-de-Fierbois. She sent a letter to local clergy, and the sword was unearthed and sent to her (see http://www.archive.joan-of-arc.org).

[16] Barstow, "Joan of Arc and Female Mysticism," 29.

to listen to them. She forcefully and persistently claimed her position as military leader and strategist. Stepping into battle when she might have hung back from the active fighting required considerable courage. Further, whether adopting male dress was a matter of mere practicality, obedience to the voices she heard, a strategic appropriation of a local legend, self-defense, or some combination of these, her resolve in this matter is striking. She exhibited a boldness, self-assertion, and self-confidence that her murder by a kangaroo court cannot erase.

Joan both navigated and revised the standards of femininity of her time. She didn't simply flout those conventions—she reworked them in a way that fit her mission. Joan didn't pass as male. Instead, she made use of a popular legend that foretold the coming of a woman in armor who would rise to the defense of the nation. She was evaluated in part by extant norms for women—Joan submitted to the humiliating genital inspections that would situate her within the tradition of virginal female holiness—and was judged, however paradoxically, as a humble, simple woman. At the same time she cut her hair short, donned armor, carried arms, and led an army to rain ruin on the English. She flourished in her own way by her renegotiation of women's roles, a unique figure for her—and many other—times.

Is Joan rightly held up as a model for imitation, or is she dangerously redefining femininity in ways ultimately contrary to *eudaimonia*? Can virtue ethics help us parse the aspects of her character that might find her admirable, rather than an odd exception in Christian history?

Method

In virtue ethics virtues reflect moral anthropology. Aquinas derives his cardinal virtues in two ways, first formally, as reason moves to action, and then subjectively, in which each of the powers of the human soul pertaining to action is perfected by a cardinal virtue. Neatly, the two lists agree, and Thomas has his list of prudence, justice, temperance, and fortitude. All other true virtues (except the theological virtues) belong to one of these virtues as parts or subtypes.

In his 1995 essay "Proposing Cardinal Virtues," James Keenan suggested that a revision was in order, in part because Thomas's moral anthropology is no longer accepted, and in part because philosophers and theologians have begun to consider virtues premised on human relationality. Keenan proposes cardinal virtues constructed in light of spheres of relationship:

> As persons, we are relational in three ways: generally, specifically, and uniquely. And each of these relational ways of being demands

> a cardinal virtue. As a relational being in general, we are called to justice. As a relational being specifically, we are called to fidelity. As a relational being uniquely, we are called to self-care.[17]

Keenan construes these virtues to make equally urgent claims; none of them is subordinate or instrumental to the others. Prudence, his fourth cardinal virtue, integrates the other three, considering the demands of each.

There is much to recommend this revision of the cardinal virtues. Beyond its more adequate moral anthropology, it also attains comprehensiveness as Thomas's framework did, though comprehensiveness of a different sort. It enables the inclusion under the banner of a virtue ethics of much of relationality-responsibility ethics. Further, when applying this method diligently, the interconnection of our spheres of relationality becomes evident rapidly. A proposed course of action might rest primarily in the sphere ruled by self-care, but on reflection its ramifications extend to fidelity and the larger social concerns of justice as well.

This framework can also help us fathom Joan of Arc. Two methodological moves can shed light on the problem of moral assessment of unlikely lives. First, from within Keenan's framework, I explore the unity of the virtues. Second, I suggest that we need to reclaim Thomas's general (not specific) cardinal virtues in using Keenan's framework.

The Unity of the Virtues

Unless we are created absurdly, virtues cannot conflict with one another, but clearly *acts* of a particular virtue often conflict. Any parents of young children know their self-care can suffer in practicing fidelity to a needy infant. Yet, at the same time, none of the virtues lose their significance as aspects of a good human life. Parents who fail to practice self-care rapidly become poor parents. When the exhausted parent is hurtfully cranky, the child suffers. Further, parental self-annihilation sets a poor example for children. Prudence balances the virtues in action, but the virtues all continue to invite practice toward *eudaimonia.*

Social sin misshapes the balance of the cardinal virtues. Among the effects of sexism on women are these: First, when women are socialized into caretaker roles, they are defined as people whose value inheres in ignoring self-care in favor of fidelity to husband and children. Women are offered as a virtue a vice of insufficient self-care. Second, until recently, women

[17] James Keenan, S.J., "Proposing Cardinal Virtues," *Theological Studies* 56 (1995): 723.

in the United States were denied a role in community leadership—even gaining the right to vote required a long hard fight. Women are still underrepresented in government and in corporate leadership in the United States and most of the world. There are even Christian churches that still deny women a voice in leadership. In virtue language, women have been offered as a virtue a vice of injustice, specifically the injustice of a lack of or underrepresentation in political and social leadership. When women confront those twin forces—inadequate self-care and disregard for larger questions of justice—they deserve our attention.

In Joan of Arc we see a woman practicing self-care in the service of justice. It might seem odd to characterize someone whose public career lasted about two years and ended in judicial execution as a model of self-care. But in Joan we see a woman who claimed her mission against the prevailing model of femininity and pursued it assiduously. Self-care is not merely a matter of physical security (though that's an important value). Self-care also involves developing and using one's gifts, and valuing the satisfaction that comes with fulfilling one's mission in the world. Self-care, then, includes self-assertion. Joan acted boldly on behalf of beleaguered France—a stance attributable to justice. Fidelity? Joan stood with her fellow soldiers on the battlefield—indeed, her staying with the rear guard after others had retreated led to her capture. In Joan we see a profound, habitual resistance to the depiction of what women should be. She stood out from the crowd in that she practiced a more balanced life of the cardinal virtues than was generally permitted to those of her sex.

General Cardinal Virtues

Unity of the cardinal virtues is a helpful tool in parsing the effects of sexism on women, but it isn't sufficient. What are we to make of Joan's spectacular courage? How about the humility and simplicity attributed to her? Neither courage nor humility fits neatly into Keenan's schema of cardinal virtues. Indeed, both of those character traits cross over into all three spheres of relationality defining his cardinal virtues.

Thomas Aquinas recognized that some virtues seem to be necessary for acquiring virtue. He describes fortitude in two levels: in its specific form, it is "firmness only in bearing and withstanding those things wherein it is most difficult to be firm, namely in certain grave dangers." But in its general sense, fortitude is "a certain firmness of mind, and in this sense it is a general virtue, or rather a condition of every virtue."[18] Likewise,

[18] Thomas Aquinas, *Summa Theologiae,* II-IIae, q.123.a.2.

general temperance "signifies a certain temperance or moderation, which reason appoints to human operations and passions: and this is common to every moral virtue."[19] General justice is defined in two ways: in the *Summa Theologiae* Thomas calls it "a certain rectitude of the mind, whereby man does what he ought in any matters."[20] Later in the same work he speaks of justice in its general sense as directing the other virtues to its own end, the common good.[21]

We can use general cardinal virtues from Thomas's framework in the service of Keenan's. Justice is simple; Keenan's conception of justice in its relational form is defined in terms of the common good: "Our relationality generally is always to be directed by an ordered appreciation for the common good in which we treat all people as equal."[22] For the others, I suggest that Thomas was correct: general courage and general temperance are necessary to acquire virtue at all. In order to live out self-care, fidelity, and justice well, we need general courage and temperance. Since they operate at a level above that of focused practice of moral virtue, I call them meta-virtues, virtues of acquiring virtue.

How does this help us understand social sin and the warped moral anthropologies it presents? We see in Joan of Arc a better balance of Keenan's cardinal virtues than is often posited for women. But how do we know that women are not just different from men, that in fact for women, ideal self-care means radically privileging the needs of others? Joan showed a different integration of cardinal virtues than was typical of women of her time, but not necessarily a better one. It is when we look to the general virtues that she is also noteworthy. Joan was remarkable for her consistent and near-absolute courage in the face of opposition, battle, examination and interrogation, and trial. Each of these would be matters of specific courage. General courage is revealed in Joan's consistent firmness of purpose in her

---

[19] Ibid., q.141.a.2.

[20] Ibid., I IIae, q.61.a.4.

[21] Ibid., II IIae, q.58.a.5–7. Thomas is fairly complex on this topic, changing the terms of his discussion to that of legal justice, which is also tied to the common good. See Jean Porter, "The Virtue of Justice," in *The Ethics of Aquinas*, ed. Stephen J. Pope (Washington, DC: Georgetown University Press, 2002), 273. Prudence does not follow the same schema. Usually, virtues are distinguished by having different objects. Prudence is distinguished from the other intellectual virtues because it has a different object, because it is concerned with things done. However, it is distinguished from the other cardinal virtues formally, because it is an intellectual not a moral virtue (strictly speaking). Prudence seems to be a general virtue with respect to the moral virtues because of its special role in guiding the virtues to acts congruent with their ends, but this is a different understanding of what it means to be general than Thomas used when discussing general and specific forms of the other cardinal virtues.

[22] Keenan, "Prudence," in Pope, *The Ethics of Aquinas*, 724.

life and mission. She was undeterred overall, even though she wavered briefly in her imprisonment. Likewise, the self-discipline—the temperance—she showed testifies to that meta-virtue.

When sexist culture offers a view of women as passive, quiet, and responsive first to the needs of other before themselves, how are we to evaluate those who flout those norms?[23] First, do their relational cardinal virtues reveal a balanced or integrated way of life? Second, do they also show the traces of the virtues that allow virtues to be acquired—do they show a concern for the common good, are they disciplined by general temperance, and, perhaps most important, are they courageous, bold, and firm of purpose?[24] If so, then we posit that they represent not odd malformations of femininity but a widening of femininity's scope. Sometimes real women lead armies.

Conscience Formation

What does this mean for us? First, I doubt that many contemporaries would be shocked at the idea that women's roles include the kind of life Joan of Arc lived. We can say this now because the feminist revolution revealed the corrosive effects of sexism on the self-understanding both of women and of men. A broad and lively literature has emerged, featuring sociological endeavors, work to recapture women's history, theology encouraging a "hermeneutics of suspicion" to recover the suppressed roles of women, and even slogans on tee-shirts (such as "A woman without a man is like a fish without a bicycle") and viral memes that rocket around the Internet (like fireballing Little League pitcher Mo'ne Davis shown on a poster that

[23] This understanding of women is at work in Pope John Paul II's 1988 encyclical *Mulieris Dignitatem*. While he said women and men are equal in dignity, the difference between the sexes must not be violated: "In the name of liberation from male 'domination,' women must not appropriate to themselves male characteristics contrary to their own feminine 'originality.' There is a well-founded fear that if they take this path, women will not 'reach fulfillment,' but instead will *deform and lose what constitutes their essential richness*" (no. 10). Interestingly, he cites Joan of Arc as "an incarnation of the feminine ideal" (no. 27).

[24] Of course, the contrary holds, too. Betty Friedan cites a study of Vassar women indicating that as women felt the tension between their prescribed social role and their own identity, "they more or less consciously stop their own growth to play the feminine role. Or, to put it another way, they evade further experiences conducive to growth" (Friedan, *The Feminine Mystique*, 261). She notes as symptoms of this malaise American housewives' "emptiness, idleness, boredom, alcoholism, drug addiction, disintegration to fat, disease and despair after forty" (263). When whole groups of people deliberately halt their own psychological growth, or more or less deliberately slide into self-destruction, an issue of the balance of self-care to the other cardinal virtues, or an issue of general courage and temperance to resist those destructive forces, might be surmised.

says, "This is what it means to throw like a girl"). Sexism isn't dead, but we can call it out for what it is.

Internalized sexism is trickier. The degree to which women still feel constrained by anti-feminist ideals varies with context and generation, but it still exerts its effects in our lives, often in ways that can go unrecognized. What are our strategies for becoming people of resistance? Among the modalities of conscience formation available to us, what are some practices that might help us discern a truer image of human flourishing?

The tools of liberation ethics and feminist ethics begin to point the way; these ethical methodologies indicate some of the ways we can begin to expand our moral imaginations to help resist the corruption of social sin. Virtue ethics adds a confidence that deliberate practice to oppose social sin shapes not only our minds, but the "elephant" of moral intuitions that Pope described. Here are six practices rooted in those ethical discourses that may help us grow in the kinds of virtues and meta-virtues we look for in people worthy of emulation.

1. *Practice solidarity with the other.* Not every position that challenges dominant social norms is correct; some people make mistakes, and some people offer lifestyles that are not in fact human flourishing. Where people challenge fundamental conceptions of what a good person should be, however, we should exercise a "preferential option for the strange." The name for the virtue that seeks God at work in different ways in the world, in different kinds of lives, is humility, properly understood.[25] In the context of racism Massingale points to the necessity for authentic cross-racial solidarity and the true compassion that both enables and results from that solidarity.
2. *Regard and celebrate embodiment.* All true virtue liberates the human person for the flourishing promised by God. The fact of embodiment invites us to an awareness of the different kinds of claims that women have on societies in which women's needs are too often relegated to the realm of the private or the charitable.[26] Social sin in general defines the marginalized as aberrant, defective,

---

[25] See Lisa Fullam, "Humility and Its Moral Epistemological Implications," in *Virtue: Readings in Moral Theology* 16, ed. Charles E. Curran and Lisa A. Fullam (New York: Paulist Press, 2011), 251.

[26] Consider as an example the need women with children may have for work arrangements that can support breastfeeding. See Cristina Traina, *Feminist Ethics and Natural Law* (Washington, DC: Georgetown University Press, 1999), 331–34. Or consider the particular vulnerability of undocumented women to rape and sexual harassment. See Kristin Heyer and John Gehring, "The 'Family Values' Case for Immigration Reform," *San Jose Mercury News* (February 1, 2013).

lesser, or bestial, so deliberate attention to the ways different kinds of bodies are described and ranked as superior or inferior is a first step toward recognizing the dignity and beauty of all kinds of bodies, not only those that our culture offers as ideals.

3. *Recognize the interweaving of the personal and the social.* One early feminist slogan, "The personal *is* political," shows that solo or shared reflection on particular experience is a political act that can unmask structures of oppression and foster creative responses.
4. *Name what constrains.* Especially when faced with social sin that tells what women cannot do, it is important to name the offense and demand to be heard. Dorothee Soelle writes: "If people are not to remain unchanged in suffering, if they are not to be blind and deaf to the pain of others, if they are to move from a purely passive endurance of suffering to suffering that can humanize them in a productive way, then one of the things they need is a language."[27] One traditional form of this language is lament. Calling for a more adequate Catholic engagement with racism, Massingale calls for lament, which arises from and leads to compassion: "Laments name the pain present, and they forthrightly acknowledge that life and relationships have gone terribly wrong. They are uncivil, strident, harsh and heart-rending."[28] Lament carries with it an implicit claim—the situation is wrong and must be changed. All who hear must act.
5. *Practice cataphatic spirituality.* Apophatic spirituality emphasizes the fact that none of our ideas or images about God is sufficient. Cataphatic spirituality, while it recognizes that no one image can capture the totality of the being of God, seeks glimmers or reflections of God in all creation. Cataphatic spirituality, especially seeking feminine (or multiracial, multi-gendered, or other) images of God, can serve to dismantle the sexism and other social sins that can remain hidden and unchallenged in the shadows of apophatic spirituality.
6. *Do something.* Virtue ethics says that we become virtuous by doing virtuous things, even in small steps. Accordingly, conscience formation must shape acts. Awareness of social sin calls for resistance. Some of the activities women undertook in the early days of feminism can look silly in retrospect. Bra burning, for example, just destroys a useful undergarment. But such acts helped people to

[27] Dorothee Soelle, *Suffering* (Philadelphia: Fortress Press, 1975), 75.

[28] Bryan Massingale, *Racial Justice and the Catholic Church* (Maryknoll, NY: Orbis Books, 2010), 106–7.

begin to challenge what they had taken for granted and to see more substantive ways of claiming women's authority.

These six kinds of practice do not end the discussion, of course. Creativity and a passion for justice will show the way forward. And some saintly voices might tell us where to find a handy sword, if one is needed.

Conclusion

I started this essay with a problem in conscience formation, one that is methodologically dangerous for an ethics of virtue. Recognizing the reality of social sin, how do we form consciences to resist the influence of the warping of moral imagination that can derail *eudaimonia*? Different kinds of social sin have different if analogous effects, so I engaged one example of social sin, sexism, that has been named but not defeated. I offered Joan of Arc as an example of holy resistance. Then I returned to virtue methodology—what can Joan show us that might help us be more resistant to social sin? Finally, I offered six kinds of practice that can help make us more like Joan, more like those who resist social sin than like those who blindly reinscribe it in society and in their own lives. The goal? As Mary Daly puts it, "to call attention to the emergence of free persons whose lives communicate a kind of contagious freedom."[29] So we might be the kind of people who can, according to Melissa Etheridge's lyrics, "know what the dark and the wild and the different know" and heed their invitation:

> Come dance with me now
> We'll dance without a care
> I'm as free as a fire
> And change is in the air.[30]

---

[29] Mary Daly, *Beyond God the Father: Toward a Philosophy of Women's Liberation* (Boston: Beacon Press, 1973), 10.

[30] Melissa Etheridge, "The Different," MLE Music, 2001.

7.

Marriage Equality, Conscience, and the Catholic Tradition

LINDA HOGAN

There are few concepts more sacrosanct than conscience. Throughout the long history of philosophical and theological reflection on the nature of conscience, it has been recognized as a faculty that expresses the person's profound conviction about the importance of certain values and the rightfulness of particular judgments and actions. The stress on the personal and ultimate nature of conscience has been evident from antiquity; for example, Cicero declared "my own conscience counts for more with me than the verdict of all other people."[1] It has been reinforced through the ages, and has acquired even greater significance in the modern context, as for example in *Gaudium et Spes,* which uses the iconic statement in describing conscience as the person's "most secret core, and their sanctuary," and affirming that "deep within their consciences men and women discover a law which they have not laid upon themselves and which they must obey" (no. 16).

Within the Christian theological tradition much of the debate over conscience has focused on the relationship between the individual's subjective judgment and the person's apprehension of, or discernment of, the requirements of the moral law. Throughout Catholic history these tensions frequently emerged, particularly when the judgment of conscience was regarded to be in error or to be contrary to what the church taught on a particular matter. Within that context different schools of thought attempted to deal with this in various ways, but always with the objective of preserving the primacy of the judgment of conscience while also maintaining the position that through its teaching the church apprehends and articulates the moral law.

[1] Cicero, *Epistulae ad Atticum,* XX.28.2.

The transformation that has occurred in Catholic moral theology in the last five decades, which has seen a move away from the act-centered, legalistic, minimalistic, and casuistic enterprise of the manuals and toward more biblically based, historically conscious, context-sensitive frameworks, has had profound ramifications for the theology of conscience.[2] The immediate background to this transformation was the development of the revisionist strand of moral theology that began with Odon Lottin, Fritz Tillmann, and Klaus Demmer in the 1940s and 1950s, with Bernard Häring, Charles Curran, Margaret Farley, Lisa Cahill, James Keenan, and others adding impetus in the subsequent decades. They recast in fundamental ways how Catholic moral theology thought about the nature of the human person and his or her capacity to discern the truth, about the nature of the truth that is sought, and about the extent to which human knowledge and reason can apprehend the good.

However, this transformation has not been uncontested. Rather, it has occasioned a series of difficult and often acrimonious debates about the nature of moral truth, the primacy of conscience, the role of the social context in the formation of conscience, and the authority of the magisterium on matters of morals. I do not intend to rehearse these debates here or to intervene further in what has become a "dialogue of the deaf," as Richard McCormick called it. Rather, I wish to develop the implications of the revisionist strand further by considering more thoroughly the contextual dimension of conscience and particularly the role that the social, cultural, and religious contexts we inhabit play in shaping and structuring the discernment of conscience.

Contemporary life is replete with debates about significant moral issues, and increasingly these debates pit one individual's conscience-claims against another's or against the power of the state or other institutions. In this context the liberty of conscience is regarded as sacrosanct, and as a result these debates tend to be framed in terms of conflicts of rights, wherein the rights of individuals to act according to their respective judgments of conscience conflict with another's right or are at risk of being encroached upon by the state or other institutions. A common thread throughout these contemporary conflicts of conscience, however, is the manner in which the claims of conscience can hinder rather than facilitate dialogue and are often a catalyst for acrimony rather than for respect. Moreover, this is the case whether the conflicts of conscience occur within the church or when there are conflicts of value among different religious or other communities within

---

[2] See James Keenan, *A History of Catholic Moral Theology in the Twentieth Century: From Confession of Sins to Liberating Consciences* (New York: Continuum, 2010).

pluralist societies. I wish to suggest, however, that this contemporary framing of the conflicts of conscience fails to recognize the constructive nature of our moral understanding and to propose that we need to restore to our conceptualization of conscience the contextual dimension of its formation and some sense of the provisionality of its claims.

Insights from feminist, postcolonial, and communitarian thinking are particularly important in this regard because they have taught us a lot about how we attain moral knowledge (effectively how our consciences are shaped), in particular about the role of contexts and communities in the mediation of value. What these theorists remind us is that our consciences are formed in the context of communities, within the currents of discursive traditions, and through our interactions with the world around us. This is important not only because it articulates a more comprehensive understanding of the nature of moral truth and how human beings come to discern that truth, but also because it can allow us to have a different kind of conversation about important and disputed moral issues, a conversation in which the appeal to conscience is no longer a conversation stopper[3] but rather an occasion for a more meaningful exchange about why certain of our views are so deeply held, what fundamental values they express, and why they are of such elementary significance.

Although there are many debates in which the claims of conscience are invoked in contemporary society, few are as contested as whether gay and lesbian couples should be able to marry on the same basis as heterosexual couples. The divergent views on this issue tend to reflect people's deeply and sincerely held convictions about what is right and good. Moreover, given that this diversity of views is evident both within the church and in society more generally, and given that there has been a significant and rapid transformation in attitudes to marriage equality in the last two decades, it provides a valuable context in which to consider whether a different kind of conversation about how to handle the divergent claims of conscience in pluralist contexts (whether the pluralism is within the church or in the wider society) can be imagined.

Conscience and Context: The Context of Conscience

The Western tradition of conscience encompasses two major strands, one focused more on the interior, and the other more social and contextual.

---

[3] This is John Rawls's phrase, which he used to describe the manner in which appeals to religious and other comprehensive doctrines tend to be (improperly) invoked in political debate in pluralist liberal societies.

These two strands have existed simultaneously in the history of Western theological thinking and have informed and shaped each other. In the Greek tradition the etymology of conscience points toward a strong focus on interiority. Indeed, the earliest known fragment in which the term *synderesis* ("conscience") is used is a fifth-century-BCE saying attributed to the philosopher Democritus of Abdera, in which conscience refers to the faculty of self-reflection on moral matters.[4] While the Latinate tradition mirrored the Greek in etymological terms *(con scientia* being the Latin translation of *sunoida)*, it did emphasize that "knowing with" *(conscientia)* could be knowledge shared with other people or knowledge within oneself. Notwithstanding this dual orientation, the strongly interior and somewhat individualistic articulation of conscience developed, strengthened, and acquired particular philosophical and psychological nuances through the centuries. This dimension has been reinforced in the modern period with the heightened concern for the individual subject and the primacy of his or her autonomy. This, of course, is only one dimension of the nature of conscience, although it is the preeminent one. However, as has already been said, notwithstanding the dominance of the conceptualization of conscience as the individual's interior moral guide, there has also been a parallel and intersecting focus on the social and contextual nature of conscience in the tradition, although this has not been as prominent or influential.

This intersecting focus on the social and contextual nature of conscience is particularly evident in the Pauline writings. Indeed, the primary focus of the Pauline corpus on conscience is on understanding and explaining the relationship between its internally and externally oriented dimensions. For Paul, the discussion about the authority of conscience and its binding nature is framed precisely in the context of these two dimensions. Conscience is both an interior witness to one's past actions—"Indeed, this is our boast, the testimony of our conscience: we have behaved in the world with frankness and godly sincerity, not by earthly wisdom but by the grace of God" (2 Cor 1:12)—and an externally oriented contextual evaluator, whose judgment is based on its conformity to the objective moral law—"when Gentiles, who do not possess the law, do instinctively what the law requires, these, though not having the law, are a law to themselves. They show that what the law requires is written on their hearts, to which their own conscience also bears witness; and their conflicting thoughts will accuse or perhaps excuse them" (Rom 2:14–15).

Paul's discussion of how conscience can bind the will even when it is in error is especially important in the history of conscience, since it is the first place where we have this explicit recognition that conscience is a faculty

---

[4] Hermann Diels, *Die Fragmente der Vorsokratiker* (Berlin: Weidmannsche, 1951), 68, B, 297.

that is simultaneously interior and contextual. It is, of course, also the first place where we have an unambiguous statement about the respect due to the judgment of conscience, even when it is in error. Respect is required, moreover, not only for one's own conscience, but also for the conscientious judgments of others. Thus we must respect the judgments of conscience, not because they are necessarily correct, but because we recognize that they reflect the person's authentic understanding of what ethical behavior dictates in a particular situation.

The history of this dual orientation of conscience is not the primary concern here, although it provides an important backdrop to the discussion. What I want to consider is how a renewed focus on the social and contextual dimensions of conscience can help to clear some ground in the deeply divisive contemporary debates about same-sex marriage and create a space wherein the claims of conscience no longer function as conversation stoppers, but rather can be the place from which we can build discursive bridges across our differences.

Moral Truth and the Formation of Conscience in the Post–Vatican II Church

Vatican II marked a critical turning point in the way in which the nature of moral truth and the discernment of conscience were understood. However, although Vatican II inaugurated a paradigm shift in moral theology, this shift has been deeply contested. As a result, there has been a fault line in the church regarding the nature of moral truth, with one dimension of the tradition stressing the objectivist, exclusivist, and universalist nature of the moral truth, and the other stressing its more contextual, pluralist nature. This fault line is especially pronounced in relation to theologies of conscience, and in the papacies of John Paul II and Benedict XVI a strongly objectivist and universalist notion of moral truth began again to be promoted. Pope John Paul II's seminal encyclical *Veritatis Splendor* was especially influential in this regard, asserting as it does an objectivist and universalist account of moral truth to counter what he believed was a crisis of truth that engulfs today's world. Developing a strongly anti-relativist argument, the encyclical defends a natural-law approach to ethics in which "the universal and the permanent validity of its precepts" (no. 4) are recognized and argues that "the Church has the right always and everywhere to proclaim moral principles, even in respect of the social order, and to make judgments about any human matter" (no. 27).[5] It is within this framework that the role of the conscience is understood, although the encyclical also

[5] This is a quotation from the Code of Canon Law, canon 747.

recognizes that the judgment of the individual conscience has an imperative character, and that the maturity and responsibility of its judgments are measured by "an insistent search for truth and by allowing oneself to be guided by that truth in one's actions" (no. 61). Moreover, it contends that "the Church puts herself always and only at the *service of conscience,* helping it . . . to attain the truth with certainty and to abide in it" (no. 64).

However, the conviction that the truth can be attained with certainty, and related language that speaks of universal and permanently valid precepts, find little resonance in the contemporary world. Indeed, the very concept of universal moral truth has come under attack, as has its most influential contemporary articulations, namely, Enlightenment philosophy and Christian theology. Much of the criticism arises from the conviction that these are essentially ethnocentric, colonialist, and exclusivist narratives that are masquerading as universal ones. Feminist and postcolonial voices have been highly influential in advancing this criticism, arguing that traditional universalist frameworks, including religiously based ones, are replete with hidden assumptions about what is good and right as well as natural for human beings.

As a result, these voices are critical of the view that we can speak about and identify universal truths independently of the social matrices in which such truths are articulated. Furthermore, they point out that many of these ostensibly universal moral truths have functioned to exclude certain persons from participation in the social polity and from being able to live lives that accord with their understandings of human flourishing. Revisionist theologians, too, have reservations about this universalist conceptualization of the nature of moral truth, and for similar reasons. Charles Curran, for example, is critical of the neo-Scholastic approach to moral truth, particularly highlighting its failure to give due recognition to the formative role that the subject's historical and cultural positioning plays in how human beings come to know moral truth. Curran argues that we must recognize explicitly "the limits on truth and certitude, especially in the moral area," that we must move away from the "classicist notion of the truth as something out there," and specifically acknowledge the contextual nature of the human capacity to apprehend the truth.[6] Within such a moral framework the discernment of conscience is properly cognizant of the fact that it is shaped by context and cultural inheritance, as well as by sociopolitical and other factors. As a result, we must be prepared to subject our claims of conscience to a self-critical reflection to ensure that they are not merely the embodiment of inherited values or prejudices. Moreover, when we are involved in conflicts

[6] Charles Curran, *The Moral Theology of Pope John Paul II* (Washington, DC: Georgetown University Press, 2005), 34.

revolving around our claims of conscience, we should approach them with a degree of epistemic humility.

Situated Moral Knowledge and the Personalist Conscience[7]

The idea of a universal moral rationality, existing independently of the social matrices in which it is exercised, is rejected by many contemporary theologians and philosophers on the basis that what are taken to be the objective standards of reason are themselves the products of socially embedded assumptions about what is reasonable, logical, coherent, and self-evident. Instead of this objectivist conceptualization of moral truth and knowledge, many contemporary theologians propose a contextual, situated one. A contextualist, situated model of moral truth and knowledge recognizes that the very substance of reason is enmeshed in the historical and social contingencies of each age. For example, decisions about what counts as evidence, how evidence is evaluated, the relative merits of one piece of evidence over against another, and many other evaluative concerns shape the trajectory of reason to a considerable degree. Indeed, all moral reasoning is tradition dependent, so that there are no objective criteria that allow one to identify the norms of rationality separately from the lived traditions of inquiry. In fact, moral values and the traditions of inquiry through which they are articulated are more appropriately understood as simultaneously the products and the producers of particular moral traditions. Thus our ethical reasoning is contingent and historically shaped. We are creatures of tradition and history and our expressions of value, our accounts of the good life, our apprehension of the virtues, our practical reasoning about how to live a dignified life, these and all our other deeply held convictions emerge from the communities we inhabit and become our own through the worldviews we encounter and through the narratives we construct and reconstruct. And it is this contingent character of our understanding, especially of our moral understanding, that is at the heart of the renewed theology of conscience in Catholicism (the personalist conscience) and that provides a new platform for how we must begin to think about the judgments and claims of conscience.

The personalist theology of conscience recognizes precisely this contingent and historical character of our moral discernment and seeks to articulate more thoroughly how context influences the fundamental orientation of conscience, as well as its judgments and claims. In the personalist

[7] In this section I draw heavily on chapter 4 of my forthcoming book *Keeping Faith with Human Rights* (Washington, DC: Georgetown University Press, 2015).

framework one's conscience is more than the sum of one's actions and judgments. Indeed, the language of conscience is recalibrated to express the fundamental orientation of the person to seek and do the good, as well as the actualization of that orientation in specific decisions and judgments. The cultural and historical forces that converge to make up both the general and the proximate context of one's life inevitably shape one's worldview and therefore what one understands by 'the good,' how one conceptualizes human subjectivity, and how one sees the possibilities for action and impact in one's environment.

In short, such forces shape one's fundamental understanding of one's environment and the role of human beings in it. Within the Christian tradition this worldview is distinctive and all encompassing. It is conveyed through multiple languages (the most common being the language of moral law and often especially natural law), which articulates some of the core ethical beliefs, for example, that the difference between good and evil is a meaningful one, and that although frail and flawed, human beings have an obligation to strive to do good and to avoid evil. Moreover, when Christians consider what is required by that moral law, they refer to sacred texts and traditions; to classic narratives of moral heroism and exemplary practice; and to a repository of core principles, values, and virtues—all expressed through the languages, metaphors, and practices of distinct theological traditions.

All our moral claims emanate from and reflect this situatedness and are expressed through these indigenous languages. Moreover, when we justify (explain) our moral positions to others, and when we seek to adjudicate among competing moral positions, we do so against this backdrop. Inevitably, when we admit the contingency of our moral knowledge and therefore of our moral judgments and claims of conscience, the issue of relativism is raised. Indeed, many worry that once the contingency of moral knowledge is conceded, there will be no firm ground on which to stand and from which the claims of conscience can be established and defended. Such an anxiety is misplaced; as I shall suggest, it is possible to acknowledge that rationality is contingent and that justification is always contextual without also endorsing a relativist position in respect to truth. Rather, one can defend an ethical framework that is simultaneously realist in respect to truth while contextualist in terms of justification.[8]

---

[8] For many centuries philosophers have debated the question of justification in ethics. The fundamental question is whether ethical and value judgments can be proved or justified in any objective way similar to the way in which our factual judgments can be justified. There are many different answers to this question of how one's moral judgments may be justified, and in this essay I make the case for a contextualist answer and endorse value pluralism.

Justifications are essentially answers to "why" questions. I may hold a belief, for example, that same-sex relationships, like other sexual relationships, have the potential to be life affirming, just, and honorable, but in addition to holding that belief I must be able to justify that belief to someone else; I must be able to say why I hold this belief. The answer to the question must be intelligible to the one who asks it, if it is to have a chance of being persuasive. In this way justification is always and inevitably dependent on context.[9] In justifying our ethical positions to one another we must explain why we believe we are correct in holding the view we do, for example, on the equality of men and women, or the goodness of same-sex relationships, but we should do so in a manner that conveys something about the moral framework out of which we are speaking and acting, and which we hope will be intelligible and convincing to the other. Indeed, especially on important ethical and political issues, the justifications we give will inevitably draw heavily on the core values we espouse and on the moral worlds we inhabit. Justifications that are essentially abstract or that are focused purely on procedure are therefore unlikely to convince, since the answer to a "why" question is such that it must be a bridge between the world of the one who is asking the question and that of the one who is providing the explanation.[10]

In addition to justifying our deeply held moral beliefs and claims of conscience to one another, we must also have a way of adjudicating between these moral beliefs and claims of conscience, particularly when they are in conflict. It is important that we promote an approach that at the same time allows for recognition that these conclusions are ultimately provisional and therefore must be open to change.[11] Moralities are embedded in situated, historical communities, and moral conflicts come in many different guises; therefore, adjudication will only be possible where there is a basis

---

[9] With this approach I am indebted to the modest pragmatism of Jeffrey Stout, particularly his *Democracy and Tradition*, (Princeton, NJ: Princeton University Press, 2004). Justification is context dependent, according to Stout, "first because conversational context determines the question to which a justification counts as an answer and thus the sort of information being requested; second, because conversational context determines a justification's audience; and third, because a justification's success can be appraised only in relation to its audience, including their relevant reasons for doubting and the commitments they are entitled to accept" (235).

[10] The classic argument for the procedural approach to justification in the debate about basic justice is Rawls's idea of public reason. See John Rawls, "The Idea of Public Reason Revistied," in *The Law of Peoples* (Cambridge, MA: Harvard University Press, 2001).

[11] Stout, *Democracy and Tradition*. Stout's discussion of these distinctions draws heavily on Robert Brandom, especially his classic *Making It Explicit: Reasoning, Representing, and Discursive Commitment* (Cambridge, MA: Harvard University Press, 1994).

for believing that the terms of comparison are meaningful. However, when we are attempting to adjudicate among different moral claims, we should not be attempting to evaluate discrete moralities according to whether they conform to a set of abstract ethical norms. Rather, as Jeffrey Stout argues, adjudication in ethics functions according to a different model. In fact, it takes different forms, proceeds on an ad hoc basis, and trusts "that whatever uniformities there are will necessarily turn up locally among the similarities obtaining to the case at hand."[12] Adjudication in ethics is, in other words, cross-contextual. Stout is clear, however, that even when we can adjudicate among values or practices in particular cases of conflict, this in itself is no guarantee that adjudication will be possible in all cases. This is because the possibility of adjudication is itself dependent on a degree of kinship in respect of worldviews or of commensurability in respect of certain values or of some other form of comparability that would make the practice of adjudication meaningful.

One can acknowledge that adjudications and justifications are context dependent without adopting a relativist position in respect to moral truth. Thus, the prospect of adjudicating a moral conflict between two different groups depends, to a significant degree, on the nature of the contextual moralities and discursive practices of the different groups that are in conflict. Whether one is justified in holding a particular moral position also depends on the extent to which it is intelligible and persuasive within the moral framework within which it is articulated. In this way relativity in adjudication and in justification can coexist with moral realism, that is, with confidence that the distinction between good and evil is a meaningful one in the moral context and that we must strive to reflect and embody this in our codes and practices.

The personalist model of conscience provides a particularly sophisticated and nuanced framework in which this approach to justification and adjudication in ethics can be advanced. It understands that the conscience is a dimension of an embodied, situated person, one who is shaped by the conventions of culture, by the sensibilities of religion, and by desires both conscious and unconscious. It acknowledges that our ethical discourse, with its values and commitments, is constructed and narrated through the cultural and religious worlds that we inhabit, and it proceeds with the recognition that our claims and judgments of conscience emanate from such moral contexts. In so doing, it allows for, indeed encourages, the kind of ethical deliberation and debate for which I have been arguing in this essay.

As I have suggested throughout this discussion, this does not mean that we have to give up on the idea of the truth of our moral positions and

---

[12] Stout, *Democracy and Tradition*, 230.

of the rightfulness of our moral convictions. Nor does it mean that we must give up on the conviction that certain claims have a purchase that is wider than the contexts from which they have originated. We can indeed defend moral realism while also acknowledging the embedded character of our moral understanding. However, the moral realism on which finite human beings can depend is not such that it corresponds to some abstract and universalist set of norms or principles. Rather, this moral realism is a fractured realism. It is a realism that is based on an acknowledgment that, while our identities are shaped by the material and discursive conditions of our lives, and while the ethical judgments we make are inevitably shaped by the historical and religious contexts of our moral formation, we can nonetheless strive to embody the virtues and excellences that we have come to believe reflect the best that human beings can be. It also means that we must be prepared to explain, justify, and defend the conviction that the way we treat one another matters, that human beings have an inherent dignity, that our social order and political structures must function to promote this dignity, and that those who are especially vulnerable must be the focus of particular concern and protection.

Claims in Conflict within the Church: Marriage Equality[13]

When we situate claims of conscience within this epistemological framework, then we come to understand that the issue at stake is not ethical relativism but rather ethical pluralism.[14] And when we examine the divergent claims of conscience in respect of marriage equality or same-sex marriage, whether this is within the church or in society more generally, we can see that this is precisely the dynamic at play. Each claim expresses and reflects the core values that each individual or group believes are at stake. Those who resist same-sex marriage believe that the complementarity of the sexes is fundamental, that there is an essential relationship between the unitive and procreative dimensions of sex (albeit not necessarily in each and every sexual act), and that the social fabric and therefore stability of society is upheld by traditional family structures and by the practice of marriage between man and woman. Those who support marriage equality, by contrast, challenge traditional views on the gendered body, particularly

[13] See William O'Neill, S.J., "The Wisdom of Serpents: Conscience, Power, and Politics in the Abortion Controversy," chap. 14 in this volume.

[14] Kwok Pui-lan's characterization of religious pluralism as being "constituted and produced in different concrete situations, often with significant power differentials" is also pertinent to the nature of ethical pluralism. See Kwok Pui-lan, *Postcolonial Imagination and Feminist Theology* (Canterbury: SCM Press, 2005), 204.

the moral significance of heterogenital complementarity. They argue that both same-sex and heterosexual relationships can equally embody a just and dignified vision of sexual love and that justice and equality demand that same-sex couples be given the same opportunities as heterosexual couples to live their lives according to their values and to live in a society that supports such choices.[15]

Those of us who are passionate about this issue, and who believe that our fundamental values are at stake in this debate, find it difficult to move beyond this impasse. Each side believes that the dignity of the human person is at risk of being fatally compromised and that the prospects of creating a just society are undermined by the other's viewpoint. Even the fact of such a fundamental disagreement is viewed as regrettable. However, it is not surprising that people hold such diverse views on this issue, given the trajectory of the history of sexuality and the genealogical issues embedded therein. The manner in which societies structure and support sexual relationships has long been a contested and controversial issue, and religions have traditionally had much to say on this matter and have regarded themselves as promoters and enforcers of particular standards in this regard. Nor is it only in matters of sexuality that such pluralism exists; indeed, it exists on practically every issue of moral concern, and it is as evident within religious traditions as among them.

Within the moral landscape of Catholicism such pluralism also exists, although there is a tendency to undermine it by claiming that certain conclusions do not conform with the tradition (referring to a unitary and unified tradition). In this context, however, it is important to bring a genealogical perspective to bear on the understanding of the role of tradition in the moral framework of Catholicism. As is the case with all traditions, we need to recognize that the historical processes that have shaped the moral tradition of Catholicism have involved choices between various and varying interpretations of the community's history, power struggles over the authorization and legitimation of the community's traditions, disagreements about the criteria for belonging, divergent views about the status of particular beliefs, and arguments about where the power to define the limits of the tradition resides. It is, in short, a story of history and power, and it is essential, therefore, that all who are involved in these debates are prepared to engage in a process of self-critical reflection, to interrogate their convictions, and to subject their deeply held assumptions to scrutiny. Only in this way will we be able to pursue the kind of discursive path necessary for communication

---

[15] See Todd Salzman and Michael G. Lawler, *The Sexual Person: Towards a Renewed Catholic Anthropology* (Washington, DC: Georgetown University Press, 2008).

across difference; only then will we have the kind of dialogue that respects the integrity of the claims of conscience.

So, can we find a way through the impasse of these ostensibly incommensurable values? I suggest that any attempt to resolve this impasse must be grounded in the recognition of the contextual nature of moral discernment, must acknowledge the integrity of these distinct positions, and must seek to build a discursive bridge across the divide. No doubt to some this will seem like an evasion, a failure to bear witness to the convictions of one's conscience. However, one does not have to give up the conviction of one's conscience to acknowledge the dignity of the other's claim even if one believes that it is in error. As has been discussed earlier in this essay, the respect due to the judgment of conscience (even when it is in error) derives from the fact that it reflects the person's authentic understanding of what ethical behavior dictates in a particular situation. What we do have to give up, however, is the appeal to conscience as a conversation stopper.

If we are to have an ethical conversation about our deeply held convictions of conscience, then the manner in which we treat the other's claims is of critical importance. We cannot shy away from dissonance. Indeed, points of dissonance may over time become occasions for deep learning about human needs and desires and may be the basis on which real transformation occurs. The nature and tone of the conversation through which these discussions are pursued is as important as the substance of the dialogue itself. It is precisely when the substantive issue involves a claim about human dignity that it behooves the participants to pursue such debate through the language of respect and restraint. For example, in this volume Eric Genilo's essay plots a creative way through these contentious issues by focusing on ways in which the common good can be promoted by constructively engaging with the implementation of civil laws that some Catholics regard as contrary to God's law (in this case the Reproductive Health Act in the Philippines).[16] Regardless of how deeply held are one's views, each person has an obligation to engage in debate in a manner that upholds rather than corrodes the integrity of the polity. This is the case whether the debate is conducted within the church or in the broader societal context. All citizens have a role in ensuring that our public forums are places of civility and respect, and these values become even more important when our deeply held convictions are at stake. In these situations, therefore, it is essential that we begin to cultivate a form of virtuous public speech as we debate our claims of conscience.

[16] See Eric Marcelo O. Genilo, S.J., "Public Officers as Conscientious Objectors: Consequences to Reproductive Health in the Philippines," chap. 9 in this volume.

8.

Marriage Equality in Argentina

Catholicism, Democracy, and the Situated Conscience

EMILCE CUDA

Introduction

In the current popular, democratic, and Catholic Latin American context, conscience is built discursively. Of course, such a statement in itself arouses doubts and causes debates when it refers to the Catholic moral conscience. But this essay demonstrates in the context of the promulgation of the same-sex marriage law in Argentina how the concerns of the Catholic opposition to the law on the basis of sexual morality were a distraction from the appropriately full range of values at stake in the dispute (and especially of the values associated with social inequality). In short, the Catholic conscience that focused only on sexual morality was poorly formed. By contrast, the conscience of anyone involved in the dispute, Catholic and otherwise, was properly formed insofar as it made its judgments from the awareness that conscience itself is always situated and shaped by a process of discursive construction. In drawing on this Argentinian example, we also see how Cardinal Jorge Mario Bergoglio of Buenos Aires (now Pope Francis) not only accepted the discursive construction of the situated conscience, but also sought to find an exit from the conflict by seeking reconciliation. The Egalitarian Marriage Law was promulgated on July 21, 2010. Studying Argentina's case in particular allows us to see that the concept of conscience must be rethought from the perspective of the complexity of social and political conflict, especially when such conflict occurs in a popular, democratic, and constitutional context.

We observe that the Catholic Church in Argentina, through the voice of some of its more conservative bishops, described same-sex marriage according to its sexual, ethical values in a way that was not only narrow-minded for the context but also resulted in enabling the concealment of the deeper conflict—over social inequality—at stake in the dispute. Thus, this portion of the Argentine Catholic Church was not able to see that same-sex marriage became the "empty signifier" into which a hidden uneasiness over other social, moral problems was displaced. And, indeed, it is evident that political differences over the universal principle of equality and not moral differences over family ethics were the causes of the antagonism that divided the Argentinian social field amid the debate over the marriage law.

Since in large measure the Catholic conscience in Argentina was not sufficiently focused on the political problem of equality, the church largely assumed that the antagonism generated by the sharp dispute over the marriage law was the result of profoundly different views of sexual and family ethics. By contrast, Cardinal Bergoglio showed there was a better way for the church to participate in conscience building by paying attention to the situated nature of conscience and, especially in the Argentinian world at the time, to the popular democratic assumptions influencing the debate. The cardinal showed that in such a context the church should not lend itself to antagonism around a narrow range of values but instead should be "agonistic" and focus on the political values that lead to the accepting of difference in a more Christian and eschatological sense.

Case Introduction: Process and Promulgation of the Egalitarian Marriage Law in Argentina as an Example of the Situated Catholic Moral Conscience

Law 26,618 of the Argentine Civil Code about egalitarian marriage—that is, same-sex marriage—was promulgated on July 21, 2010. At that time Jorge Bergoglio was the primate cardinal of the Argentine church. He was known for his committed pastoral focus toward marginal sectors, and in that way he differentiated himself from the conservative profile that had characterized the Catholic Church until then in the country. The presidency of the country was in the hands of the Argentine populist party, Peronism, originated in 1945 by General Juan Domingo Perón and represented at that moment by Cristina Fernández de Kirchner and her husband, Néstor Kirchner, who were part of the party's wing more committed to the marginal sectors of society. The phenomenon of Peronism is not a minor data point in the context to be studied in this essay, since it allows us to understand why the Catholic conscience ended up being constructed in a battle that was more political than moral. Peronism is the popular party that defends the rights of workers and the unemployed while respecting republican principles of equality and freedom. The party is anti-liberal (in the Argentinian sense of liberal) in its opposition to an emphasis on individualism and free markets. But the party is also anticommunist, and instead of class struggle, favors social mobility through employment and labor-union strength. Having said this, an unavoidable question to ask is why Bergoglio—once sympathetic to Peronism and at the time of the marriage debate sharing many of the social goals of the Kirchner government—ended up being portrayed as the leader of the antagonistic opposition to gay marriage, when in truth he was not.

At the beginning of the 1990s, the Association of Gays for Civil Rights began to promote a legislative bill for civil marriage and it reintroduced it in 2002 and 2004. In 2005, already with a popular party in power called Frente para la Victoria and headed by Néstor Kirchner, the Argentine Homosexual Community (CHA, in Spanish) proposed a bill that called for civil unions and in May 2007 the bill for same sex marriage was introduced.[1] Argentina was the first country in Latin America to recognize this type of homosexual union. However, other countries in the world already had some type of legal recognition in place, and in some these unions were even recognized as marriages. After three years of lawsuits filed by the Argentine Federation of Lesbians, Gays, Bisexuals, and Transsexuals, the Senate recognized its demands and transformed them into rights, approving the bill. However, this approval was not unanimous. The arguments about the bill were threefold: "Those who defended the equality of rights as the foundation for democracy; those who publicly rejected the expansion of the civil marriage; and those who insisted that considering civil marriage did not imply discrimination."[2] The democratic argument stated that what was at stake was not homosexuality, but the universal constitutional right to equality. In this context, ruling that marriage only applied to people of different sexes was seen as a discriminatory position toward a sector of citizens. That is why the term "Egalitarian Marriage Law" was used: The law sought equality for citizens, not the rights of a homosexual minority.

In this populist context, complaints emerged over the unconstitutionality of those sections of the Civil Code that prevented the right to marriage for same sex persons. It was not until November 2009, with Cristina Fernández de Kirchner as president, that the Supreme Court of Justice acknowledged these claims and allowed the first marriage to take place in Buenos Aires. But a legal action by the Catholic Lawyers Association blocked that marriage. The Association argued that "homosexual marriage violates human rights," and "the common good must be provided through the assumption of

---

[1] Cf. "Para que el Código Civil no discrimine," *Página 12*, May 2, 2007, trans. Rossario Garriga, http://www.pagina12.com.ar.

[2] "El derecho a la igualdad llegó al matrimonio," *Página 12*, July 15, 2010, trans. Rossario Garriga, http://www.pagina12.com.ar.

the moral values contained in the Doctrine and Magisterium of the Catholic Church, and these should try to regulate the actions of individuals and society." Their argument also noted: "From ancestral times marriage has been understood as the union between man and woman." Bergoglio then made his first intervention in the debate—though in a different way from other more conservative Catholic groups. He neither emphasized moral arguments of the Catholic magisterium nor the universal idea of human rights. Instead, he framed his claim within the context of Argentinian law, saying: "The Argentine civil legislation that rules us . . . regulates marriage as a civil entity comprised of a man and a woman. Therefore, the ruling of a judge in the contentious administrative that allows a matrimonial bond between same sex persons is contrary to the aforementioned legislation."[3]

On May 5, 2010, the House of Representatives approved the bill with 125 votes in favor, 109 against, and 6 abstentions. The vote against the law was greater among lawmakers who opposed the popular government of Cristina Kirchner and who represented the elite sectors of the Argentine society: Federal Peronism (a faction of Peronism to the right of Kirchner's populism) voted 79 percent against; Union Cívica Radical voted 56 percent against; and PRO (the liberal party) voted 55 percent against. Curiously, among the minority parties the majority voted in favor of the law, supporting the government; these parties represented sectors of the population that are mainly practicing Catholics (as, indeed, are the representatives of these minority parties). In the Senate the same pattern occurred. The ruling party was in favor, along with the almost unanimous support of the minority parties. On July 15, 2010, the law passed in the Senate with 33 votes in favor, 27 against, and 3 abstentions. Catholics who supported the new marriage law said that being Catholic did not prevent them from supporting democracy. They also argued that the practice of conscientious objection pertained to the period during which a controversial law is debated, but not to the time after a law has been duly approved; conscientious objection should not be invoked to prevent enforcement of the law.

During the debate over the bill, three positions emerged: (1) the democratic popular position in favor of the law, through arguments supported by the constitutional principle of equality (the Kirchner position); (2) the conservative position against the law, supported by moral arguments (the position of conservative Catholics and the liberal and antipopular parties); and (3) the intermediate position of civil union as an alternative to the extreme viewpoint of same-sex marriage (represented by many progressive

---

[3] *La Nacion*, "Apelaron el fallo que autorizó la boda gay en la Capital," February 24, 2010, trans. Rossario Garriga, http://www.lanacion.com.ar.

Catholics and by Bergoglio).[4] As the debate progressed, the third position was obliged to radicalize itself; this radicalized position provided the political moment of populism. Such a moment takes place when the social field is divided into two. Thus a field that in fact contains thousands of parts representing infinite demands is reduced to merely two, so that one part can recognize the identity of the other. This reorganization into two is made possible through the political phenomenon of an "empty signifier"—often a visceral issue of personal or sexual morality that in fact conceals the actual normative challenge present in a contentious political debate.

Political and Philosophical Framework: Conscience as an Empty Signifier of Social Antagonism

As James Keenan states in Chapter 1, it is necessary to see the ways in which conscience develops in each context. The European moral conscience is not the same as the American moral conscience, a difference made especially evident after World War II. In turn, neither the European nor the American conscience is the same as the conscience built within the context of a Latin America permeated by a participative democratic culture of popular characteristics. Linda Hogan makes special reference in Chapter 7 to the significance of cultural and political context for a discussion of conscience. She states that conscience is individual and contextual at the same time, where the personal dimension of conscience reflects the freedom to judge a concrete case but where such a personal dimension does not stand outside political and social determinations that permeate it and affect it. Hogan also expresses the view of many theologians and philosophers who currently doubt whether there can be a pure Catholic moral conscience existing outside the cultural, social and political factors.

Indeed, I argue that conscience is built through a process of discernment that emerges from conflict in a specific moment of history and in a concrete cultural context. Therefore, conscience-building processes are not all the same and vary from one context to another. But it is always a process because humanity is humanity-in-history and only in history does conscience take shape. Moreover, conscience receives different names according to how the process takes place. If the conscience-building process is considered as an individual process, we are not talking about conscience

[4] "El derecho a la igualdad llegó al matrimonio," *Página 12*, July 15, 2010, trans. Rossario Garriga, http://www.pagina12.com.ar; and Marcelo Larraquy, *Recen por él: La historia jamás contada del hombre que desafía los secretos del Vaticano* (Buenos Aires: Sudamericana, 2010), 222.

but about subjectivity—as it is common to say in the French school of thought. If the process is considered collectively, we are talking about class—as in the Marxist school. But there is also a third position that is neither individual nor collective, but is instead reflective of the integrated individual and collective dynamisms characteristic of populism. It is also important to note that conscience-building in democratic contexts is not the same as in dictatorial contexts. Moreover, even within the democratic contexts, the conscience-building process differs in industrial, developed, and technologically advanced countries with guarantees for property and the rights of workers and professionals compared to the process in societies with economies based on labor exploitation or on service markets where jobs are precarious. I submit that in the popular democratic models of governance—models that develop in countries with high levels of social exclusion and poverty sustained through time—the political is especially well understood as a moment constitutive of conscience or identity. In other words, the political appears only for a moment—when the social field divides into two due to a necessity that has been manifested in conflict.

For Ernesto Laclau, in social contexts of exclusion the division of the social field into two is due to the contingent process of collective identity building. Laclau finds in words—that is, in public discourse—the answer to the question of unity and to the possibility of bringing together differences during times of crisis.[5] Thus the popular collective identity or conscience is the result of a strategic movement between antagonistic discursive positions and an individual subject's discursive position.[6] For liberalism, conscience is the result of an individual process from which the subject emerges. For Marxism, conscience emerges from class behavior. In populism, when we talk about conscience we are talking about a contingent position of the subject in discourse, at a certain moment, behind an empty signifier, which is able to give hegemonic sense and achieve a new unity.[7] Conscience-building in contexts of inequality, exploitation, and poverty occurs from the moment in which antagonistic positions are taken. Moreover, antagonistic moments are necessary for the creation of the conscience. And antagonistic moments occur when needs are expressed or manifested as demands. Otherwise, there is no constitutive political moment of conscience nor a moment that legitimizes decisions.

But what is antagonism? It is neither contradiction nor opposition. Lucio Colletti differentiates between "logical contradiction" and "real

[5] Ernesto Laclau and Chantal Mouffe, *Hegemonía y Estrategia* (Buenos Aires: Fondo de Cultura, 2010), 31.

[6] Ibid., 129–41.

[7] Ibid., 160.

opposition"—the former is Hegelian, the latter physical and annihilating.[8] According to Laclau and Mouffe, in the social field it is not possible to talk about contradiction as in logic or about opposition as in physics but about antagonism, which replaces the notion of opposing forces with the more extreme notion of enemy forces.[9] Antagonism does not allow a tertium quid. It requires a social field divided into two, where one side presents the positive identity and the other the negative one. For example, one says that heterosexuals are good and that homosexuals are not.

The aforementioned becomes almost indispensable to understand the way a conscience is built regarding the homosexual marriage law in popular democratic contexts like Argentina, with a population that is 80 percent Catholic. It turns out that while in industrialized, developed countries there is a democratic position in which the subject has an individual conscience, in poor countries there is a popular position in which the subject participates in a momentary collective conscience. Conscience is produced through a political struggle in the cultural field, which seeks to articulate discursively demands from different sectors of society (in this case, for instance, from the homosexual sector as well as from the poor, marginalized sectors, both sectors of which were allied with the Kirchner government). Such a struggle then antagonizes and creates separate collective identities through a particular demand that becomes hegemonic. This is the empty signifier: a demand that has been emptied of its original meaning to represent all the unsatisfied demands of an unequal society.[10] In the Argentine case, the empty signifier that divided the field in two was the demand for an egalitarian marriage. But the empty signifier could have been any other demand able to articulate the differences that are the crucial unsatisfied demands of a society with democratic structures and enduring poverty. What was at stake in the Argentine social field was not Catholic sexual doctrine but the claim of social equality. Indeed, Catholic sexual doctrine became the empty signifier.

Theological Framework: God's War, Eschatology, and Social Inequality

As noted above, I suspect that the interpretative argument focused on the equality principle is the real root of the social conflict that disguised itself behind the egalitarian marriage signifier in Argentina. Nonetheless, the

---

[8] Luigi Colletti, *Tramonto della ideologia* (Rome: Laterza, 1980), Cap. II.

[9] Laclau and Mouffe, *Hegemonía y Estrategia*, 165.

[10] Ibid., 170–79.

legalization of homosexual marriage does not stop being an issue for the Catholic moral conscience. On the contrary, the way the issue played out in Argentina reveals to the Catholic conscience that the true moral problem cannot be dealt with in a narrow, particular manner, since social inequality is a problem of universal interest that always moves and hides behind particular demands.

On the one hand, to be sure, the conservative Catholic opposition to the law remained within the narrow confines of a moral purity fixed on a particular demand located outside the field of history. Thus the leader of this opposition dismissed the relevance of universal concerns to the debate by saying, "Homosexuals are not being discriminated because they cannot get married since it is not a universal right."[11]

On the other hand, Cardinal Bergoglio understood from the perspective of a situated conscience that what was at stake was a universal political problem. To deal with such a problem, he relocated it to the eschatological sphere: "Let's not be naive, it is not a simple political battle; it is the ambition to destroy God's plan . . . the work of the devil." His words about God's war prompted Kirchner's vice-chief of staff to accuse him of being a fundamentalist and of "bursting into the democratic deliberation sphere with unusual violence and calling Argentines to hatred." The vice-chief of staff added, "The one who should be preaching peace and tolerance is invoking a holy war and political acts in the streets to pressure the Senate of the nation."[12] However, Bergoglio did not belong to the stricter conservative wing but to a moderate third position that admitted civil unions between homosexuals for those who were not Catholic. For Bergoglio, it was indeed a politically antagonistic moment, but with different characteristics. The articulating subjects were neither conservatives nor populists but God and Satan.

Since 1974, Bergoglio had seen the unity of the people in terms other than those of class.[13] This early turn away from the materialist imperatives of class helps us to understand why he called for a spiritual battle, both against the temptations of the traditionalists—whom he called ostriches because they hid their heads from social drama—and the utopians who called for being "in the forefront."[14] The unity of the people—for Bergoglio then and now for Francis—implies the solution to the problems that social difference generates and that, after being generated, stand at risk of being discounted by the false unity of uniformity. In *Evangelii Gaudium* he writes:

---

[11] "La ciencia de monseñor," *Página 12*, July 7, 2007, http://www.pagina12.com.ar.

[12] Larraquy, *Recen por él,* 182.

[13] Jorge Bergoglio, "Una institución que vive su carisma," *Boletín de espiritualidad* 55 (1978): 31.

[14] Ibid., 35.

> Differences between persons and communities can sometimes prove uncomfortable, but the Holy Spirit, who is the source of that diversity, can bring forth something good from all things and turn it into an attractive means of evangelization. Diversity must always be reconciled by the help of the Holy Spirit; he alone can raise up diversity, plurality and multiplicity which at the same time bringing about unity. When we, for our part, aspire to diversity, we become self-enclosed, exclusive and divisive; similarly, whenever we attempt to create unity on the basis of our human calculations, we end up imposing a monolithic uniformity. This is not helpful for the Church's mission. (no. 131)

Moreover, Francis speaks of the disunifying power of enduring social inequality:

> The toleration of evil, which is injustice, tends to expand its baneful influence and quietly to undermine any political and social system, no matter how solid it may appear. If every action has its consequences, an evil embedded in the structures of a society has a constant potential for disintegration and death. It is evil crystallized in unjust social structures, which cannot be the basis of hope for a better future. We are far from the so-called "end of history," since the conditions for a sustainable and peaceful development have not yet been adequately articulated and realized. (no. 59)

It would seem that inequality, which endures and persists in contexts of poverty, is made possible and facilitated by consciences built on a constitutive division of the social. One of the sectors of the Argentine hierarchy insisted that the conflict was over sexual morality and thus created the antagonistic division of the social that perpetuated inequalities. Bergoglio, however, took a different position—one that bears the language of antagonism but that in fact aims at the achievements of equality and unity only made possible by the action of the Holy Spirit. For Christianity and for the cardinal, history is the dramatic stage of a war where God and human beings—as God's collaborators—must permanently defeat the destructive, disunifying works of Satan.

Such an idea sounds very Gramscian to political theorists. It involves a search for salvation that is not individual but cosmic—of each person and of the entire world at the same time. But this eschatological antagonism for Christianity is not between good and evil as in liberalism, or between left and right as in socialism, but between God and Satan. Souls are captured by the seduction of the mendacious, conflictual discourse of the devil and are only redeemed into a real unity by the unmasking words of God's children. The devil uses the deception of empty signifiers. The Holy Spirit unmasks such lies and empowers people to address inequality and achieve true unity.

I propose, therefore, to read Bergoglio's words about God's war in the framework of the Jesuit theology in which he was formed. Saint Ignatius of Loyola, a soldier at one time himself, reconceives the language of militancy and antagonism in terms of Christian salvation: "The human being is a soldier of Christ at the service of the Church militant and therefore in war against Satan, who with diabolic tactics incessantly attacks the Church and casts nets over souls."[15] Similarly, for Jesuit theologian Hugo Rahner, the apparently antagonistic images of Ignatian spirituality allow us to see men and women in service to others and "created to establish through the Church militant the battle against Satan undertaken through reverent service to the triple Majesty of God and through resemblance to Jesus, the crucified one; and by this to enter into the glory of the Father."[16] In this reconception of antagonism, Saint Ignatius rejects a Neoplatonic retreat into purity and detachment and instead invites men and women to the concrete historical commitments of rectifying injustice and fostering unity. Bergoglio's use of eschatological language was hardly fundamentalist. Instead, it reflected his insight into the ultimate challenges to justice and reconciliation at stake in the marriage debate.

Toward the Unity-in-Difference of the Situated Conscience: Antagonism and Agonism in the Construction of Popular Identities

It is important to understand Bergoglio's words more clearly. The social debate about the egalitarian marriage law ruptured the church-state relationship in Argentina between 2009 and 2013. But the debate also reconfigured the political stage regarding a theme of conscience that, emptying itself

---

[15] Hugo Rahner, *Ignacio de Loyola y su histórica formación espiritual* (Santander: Sal Terraer, 1955), 13. In original Spanish: "El hombre es soldado de Cristo, está al servicio de la Iglesia militante, y por lo mismo en guerra contra Satanás, que con táctica diabólica ataca sin cesar a la Iglesia y hecha sin cesar sus redes sobre las almas." Translated into English by Rossario Garriga from the Spanish translation of the original German.

[16] Ibid., 55. In Spanish: "Creado para entablar en la Iglesia militante el combate contra Satanás con un servicio reverente a la triple Majestad de Dios, mediante una semejanza con el hombre crucificado, Jesús, y así entrar en la gloria del Padre." Translated into English by Rossario Garriga from the Spanish translation of the original German.

of its ethical and religious meaning, became the new signifier of the pre-existent social conflict. Once more in history religious conflict was just an empty signifier in which social conflict manifested itself. This logic has been explained by different authors, such as Charles Tilly writing about Catholic Irish immigrants in the United States; William Cavanaugh writing on the religious wars in modernity; and Michael Walzer regarding Calvinist Protestant militancy.[17]

During his tenure as cardinal, Bergoglio differentiated himself from Argentinian conservative thought both in the religious and political spheres. As cardinal, he voiced his commitment to social issues—often in his Te Deum homilies. The homily of May 25, 2000, is especially important. There he said to President Fernando de la Rúa (1999–2000) that "nobody picks up the dead," referring to the poor.[18] On December 19, 2001, he spoke in support of the *cacerolazos* ("pot-banging protests") against the government. He also spoke publicly against global neoliberalism, accusing it of being a "system that produces poor people." And he strongly disagreed with the idea that to get out of the Argentine financial crisis it was necessary to get into debt to international organizations.[19] Everything indicated that the cardinal's positions on such social matters were close to those of the Kirchner government. Moreover, even on the issue of legalizing homosexual marriage, he remained on the margins of the public debate. Nevertheless, a struggle for power began between Bergoglio and Kirchner, and in 2004 the government identified the cardinal as the spiritual leader of the opposition.[20]

But neither the Kirchner government, nor the conservative Catholic faction in Argentina, nor those in Argentina averse to being allied with a fundamentalist view have understood the actual significance of Bergoglio's spiritual and eschatological concerns. In a speech given at Néstor Kirchner's funeral, Bergoglio used the category of antagonism and asked that it be left aside.[21] Recent work in political theory provides a way to understand the significance of Bergoglio's request. In this theoretical view antagonism is understood as a nonpolitical way of solving social conflict by pretending to eliminate differences not by addressing the actual cause of conflict but by

---

[17] William Cavanaugh, *The Myth of Religious Violence: Secular Ideology and the Roots of Modern Conflict* (New York: Oxford University Press, 2009); Michael Walzer, *The Revolution of the Saints: A Study in the Origins of Radical Politics* (Cambridge, MA: Harvard University Press, 1982); Charles Tilly, *Durable Inequality* (Berkeley and Los Angeles: University of California Press, 1998).

[18] Larraquy, *Recen por él*, 182–83.

[19] Ibid., 182–85.

[20] Ibid., 191.

[21] Ibid., 243.

using moral accusations of good/evil to sharpen divisions in society. Thus, in antagonism the social border is drawn from a moral perspective—not a political one—and every different position is considered illegitimate and susceptible to annihilation. To the contrary, differences properly set in political categories allow what we can call agonistic positions. In an agonistic political position, differences are classified around the categories of friend and "just enemy," as Carl Schmitt argues.[22] The evil one is annihilated as a criminal; the just enemy is not. Theorist Chantal Mouffe argues that the agonistic mode is one in which resolution of conflict is not the result of annihilation but the outcome of debate in parliament; moreover, the moment of decision is neither death nor silence but the vote as a means toward victory. In the agonistic model, dissent allows unity-in-difference. According to Mouffe, for the agonistic model to be possible, it is necessary that adversaries share at least the same symbolic world—in this case the world of the Christian and liberal principles of equality and freedom.[23]

Of course, in the conflict over the egalitarian marriage law, the main parties differed in how they interpreted the principle of equality. Those in support of the marriage law thought equality was universal and applied to all cases; those against the law thought that the equality did not apply to homosexual couples because they were not eligible to marry. Each side, in turn, resorted to moral arguments and accused the other side of being illegitimate. The cardinal's position when describing the conflict as God's war tried to displace this conflict from the social field to the theological field and, in doing so, is best understood as an agonistic attempt to preserve unity. From an agonistic perspective, when facing difference there ought to be an attempt to build social conscience from within the framework of identity as constitutively relational; we really are related to everyone else and have to work out our identity in the context of such an inescapable and inclusive social matrix.[24] Also, from an agonistic perspective there ought to be an attempt to burst asunder the hegemonically established meaning that creates antagonism in order to find ways to guarantee the unity of political society. At first, the construction of such identities is driven by passions—ethnic, religious, or national—but little by little the construction can be driven by common social interests through the mediation of political parties.[25] And here it is helpful to connect such political theorizing with the

---

[22] Carl Schmitt, *The Concept of the Political* (New Brunswick, NJ: Rutgers University Press, 1976), 54; idem, *The Nomos of the Earth in the International Law of the Jus Publicum Europeatum* (New York: Telos Press, 2003), 231.

[23] Chantal Mouffe, *En torno a lo político* (Buenos Aires: Fondo de Cultura Económica, 2011), 29–31; 10, 18, 31, 76, 96, 129.

[24] Ibid., 22–23.

[25] Ibid., 13, 31.

theological imperatives behind Bergoglio's intervention in the same-sex marriage debate—imperatives that allow us to consider more deeply the role of the Catholic conscience in the entire affair.

In particular, Bergoglio never lost sight of the underlying issues of poverty and inequality, even while he promoted (as Pope Francis still does today) the "theology of encounter" as a model for how a society moves from antagonism to agonism. Such a model is premised on the theological categories of mission and conversion:[26] to go out of oneself in order to meet others as they are and to allow oneself along the way to be converted to a deeper sense of the good and to the possibilities of social unity. In such a process there is a deep spiritual dynamism at work—from antagonism to agonism; from conflict to unity; and from the fundamentalism that solidifies division to the ultimate, eschatological longing that provides the basis for lasting unity.[27] In other words, the conversion that follows encounter turns a fundamentalist missionary into a partisan of God's war to reconcile the world. In such a process Catholics can find a new and better way of thinking about conscience.

Conclusion

Speech about conscience building indicates in itself that conscience is the result of a process permeated by culture but not determined by it. The situated conscience suffers from the systemic distortions of cultural hegemonic models. The more aware that Catholics become that their judgments—that is, the results of the discernment within the interior of their conscience—are influenced not only by grace but also by culture, the more balanced and just their conclusions and actions will be. The episcopal and pontifical magisterium is, without a doubt, a criterion of authority and an integral aspect of the Catholic tradition. But a conscience shaped by the magisterium is always also a situated conscience permeated by culture and in need of construction, as Bergoglio demonstrated in taking his position with respect to egalitarian marriage in Argentina. A situated conscience is a conscience that in each case must discern, knowing that terms are not always translatable from one culture to another. A moral theologian is called to categorize and redefine each concept within the specific context of the debate, not to judge each concept based on the universal magisterium without sufficiently taking into account the local context and culture as well.

---

[26] Bernard Lonergan, *Método* (Salamanza: Sigueme, 2006), 164, 292.

[27] Víctor Manuel Fernández, *Conversión pastoral y nuevas estructuras. ¿Lo tomamos en serio?* (Buenos Aires: Agape, 2010).

9.

Public Officers as Conscientious Objectors

Consequences to Reproductive Health in the Philippines

Eric Marcelo O. Genilo, S.J.

In the Philippines in recent years the passage of the Responsible Parenthood and Reproductive Health Act of 2012 by the National Legislature has been alternately a cause for celebration and a cause for concern for various sectors of Philippine society. While contraceptives and sterilization have always been legally available in the country, reproductive supplies and services have been inaccessible for many poor Filipinos. The new law empowers the state to guarantee "universal access to medically-safe, non-abortifacient, effective, legal, affordable, and quality reproductive health care services, methods, devices, supplies which do not prevent the implantation of a fertilized ovum as determined by the Food and Drug Administration (FDA)."[1] The law also mandates an age-appropriate and development-appropriate reproductive health education for youth in all private and public schools. In view of the country's high rates of maternal deaths, unplanned pregnancies, HIV infection, and clandestine abortions, the law is praised by its supporters as a significant contribution to the improvement of the lives of Filipinos.

The bishops' conference, however, has consistently opposed the passage of a reproductive health law. The bishops believe that providing wider access to contraceptives, sterilization, and sexuality education would compromise

[1] Republic of the Philippines, The Responsible Parenthood and Reproductive Health Act of 2012, December 21, 2012, http://www.doh.gov.ph.

the sanctity of life of the unborn, the health of women, the morals of the youth, and the welfare of the family.[2] The bishops have also argued that the law violates the consciences of Catholics and that it will encourage unacceptable sexual behavior.

After the law was signed by President Benigno Aquino III in December 2012, a case was filed at the Supreme Court challenging its constitutionality. In April 2014, the Supreme Court ruled that the law in general was constitutional except for eight provisions, which were struck down by the court. This essay focuses on one deleted provision, which imposed penalties on public officers who refused to implement the law. While the Supreme Court's decision to remove this provision was hailed by the church as a victory in defense of the right to conscientious objection, this essay argues that the removal of this provision opens the possibility for the violation of consciences of both Catholics and non-Catholics and the diminishment of the common good.

I also discuss a case where a public officer acted according to his conscience with regard to public policy on family planning, leading to serious effects on the health and well-being of women in the city of Manila. This case is the starting point for a discussion on the exercise of the right to conscientious objection by public officers and the pursuit of the common good in a pluralistic society. This essay offers proposals to guide Catholic public officers in their discernment of how to implement such laws.

A Case Study

In 2000, Lito Ateinza, a devout Catholic and the mayor of the capital city of Manila, issued an executive order (EO 003) to implement a policy to promote natural family planning in city-funded public hospitals and health centers. Atienza's rationale for the policy was to uphold "natural family planning not just as a method but as a way of self-awareness in promoting the culture of life while discouraging the use of artificial methods of contraception."[3] While the wording of EO 003 did not explicitly prohibit contraceptives and sterilization, city government employees interpreted the policy as a ban on any government support for artificial birth control. Manila City Hall ceased funding for contraceptive supplies in city hospitals and health centers. Vasectomy and tubal ligation services also ceased to be offered in these facilities.

---

[2] Catholic Bishops Conference of the Philippines (CBCP), "Standing Up for the Gospel of Life," November 14, 2008, http://www.cbcpnews.com.

[3] Philippa Fogarty, "Manila Women Fight Contraceptive Ban," BBC Online, February 11, 2008. http://www.bbc.com.

The mayor was very clear about his opposition to artificial birth control. He has been quoted as saying that "sex must always be related to procreation."[4] Ateinza also believed that contraception has a direct causal link to abortion, which is illegal in the country. At the time EO 003 was issued, Atienza was the president of Pro-Life Philippines, an anti-contraception advocacy group that subscribed to the belief that a contraceptive mentality leads to abortions. This view is also held by the Catholic Bishops' Conference of the Philippines. In its pastoral letter "Choose Life, Reject the RH (Reproductive Health) Bill," the conference argued that "the very name contraceptive already reveals the anti-life nature of the means that the RH Bill promotes. These artificial means are fatal to human life, either preventing it from fruition or actually destroying it."[5] In another statement, "Contraception Is Corruption," the bishops claimed that "a contraceptive mentality is the mother of an abortion mentality."[6] It is from this perspective linking contraception with abortion that EO 003 was enforced by Atienza.

In line with his anti-contraception stance the mayor refused to implement a national program of the Department of Health aimed at promoting safe pregnancies. The program, called Ligtas Buntis (safe pregnancy), provides information to women, especially expectant mothers, about maternal and reproductive health in order to ensure safe childbirth and lower maternal deaths. In addition to information about natural and artificial family planning methods, the program also distributes contraceptives to couples. Mayor Atienza helped organized a rally, supported by the Catholic Church, against the Ligtas Buntis program and prevented the Department of Health from implementing it in Manila.[7]

As a 2007 report from the Center for Reproductive Rights noted, a study of the effects of EO 003 on the reproductive health of women in Manila revealed disturbing results. It stated:

> [EO 003] has contributed to high rates of unplanned pregnancy, with all its attendant socioeconomic and health consequences, and affected poor women most severely. In addition to resulting in an effective ban on services in city facilities, the vague wording of the EO and the lack of clear policy guidance from Manila City Hall has also led some facilities and providers to refuse to provide even information or refer-

---

[4] Jialeen Jimeno, "In Manila, Pills and Condoms Go Underground," Philippine Center for Investigative Journalism, May 2, 2005.

[5] Catholic Bishops' Conference of the Philippines (CBCP), "Choosing Life, Rejecting the RH Bill," CBCP News, January 20, 2011.

[6] CBCP, "Contraception Is Corruption," December 15, 2012.

[7] Jimeno, "In Manila, Pills and Condoms Go Underground."

rals for family planning to women. Non-governmental organizations (NGOs) and private providers of family planning services have also felt the chilling effects of the policy and in some cases been harassed and intimidated into ceasing to provide services. . . .

Women's physical health has suffered under the EO as well. Even in cases where women were advised that another pregnancy would threaten their life or health, health personnel in Manila city hospitals could not provide for the necessary medical intervention because of the EO. They made only isolated verbal referrals for surgical family planning or ligation.

In the case of one woman with eight children, her doctor had cautioned her not to get pregnant again after her fourth child because of her poor health.

I had a difficult labor with my fourth child. I got dehydrated and was told that I had to undergo caesarean section but could not for lack of money. Aware of my fragile condition, all I could do was pray. I believe I had a difficult labor because I would always starve even while pregnant.

The doctor at OM [Ospital ng Maynila—Hospital of Manila] advised me not to get pregnant anymore because of my rheumatic heart condition. I wanted to have ligation but OM hasn't been providing FP [family planning] services. I was referred to Fabella Hospital (a maternity hospital not funded by the city) but I couldn't afford the 2,000 peso fee.

I suffered a miscarriage in my ninth pregnancy due to my medication for tuberculosis, which I contracted after my husband had the illness. Kaya ako ganito kapayat. [That's why I am this thin.] . . .

Unsafe abortion is another dangerous consequence of limiting women's ability to control the number and spacing of their children. Nationwide, approximately one-third of women who experience an unintended pregnancy have an abortion. . . .

A doctor at Fabella Hospital thought the EO was one reason for the increase of post-abortion patients she's seeing at Fabella: "Mostly it's political. The mayor of Manila doesn't approve of providing family planning services in Manila. They're not providing FP [family planning] services, [women] are getting pregnant, they resort to abortion. [I'm] not saying it happens that way with all our PAC [post-abortion care] clients, but it is one factor."

As a way of coping with lack of access to family planning, women interviewed would often try to refuse sex with their partner to avoid pregnancy. Fear of getting pregnant because of lack of protection during sex is the primary reason why they refuse sex with their partners.

> Women described how this puts a strain on their relationships and has led to heated altercations, temporary separation and even sexual violence. More often than not, women yield to their partners' wishes rather than create a shameful situation where the neighbors learn they fight because of sex.[8]

The study concludes that EO 003 "has contributed to a situation in which women have more children than they want, with grave economic, social, physical and psychological consequences for women and their families."[9] In 2008, a class action suit was filed against the city government, seeking to revoke the executive order. The case was dismissed in court. It was only in 2011, under a new city mayor, that another executive order was passed (EO 30) that gave couples wider options for family planning.[10]

Conscientious Objection in the Responsible Parenthood and Reproductive Health Act

When the reproductive health law was being drafted, legislators anticipated the possibility that a public officer like Atienza would refuse to implement the law for reasons of conscientious objection. Limits to the exercise of conscientious objection were thus inserted into the law.

The initial law allowed for conscientious objection only by private health practitioners and facilities as long as arrangements were made for referral to other reproductive healthcare providers. Public officers charged with applying the law were prohibited from being conscientious objectors. Penalties for violating this provision included imprisonment, fines, suspension, and forfeiture of retirement benefits.[11]

The Supreme Court struck down this provision as unconstitutional. The bishops' conference issued a statement after the court decision stating that "although the Supreme Court has upheld the constitutionality of the RH law, it has truly watered down the law and consequently upheld the

[8] Center for Reproductive Rights, "Imposing Misery: The Impact of Manila's Contraceptive Ban on Women and Families" (Quezon City: Linangan ng Kababaihan, 2007), 24, 28–29, 30, 31.

[9] Ibid., 54.

[10] Ana P. Santos, "'Imposing Misery' among Manila Residents," *Rappler,* February 20, 2012.

[11] Republic of the Philippines, *Implementing Rules and Regulations on R.A. 10354*, March 18, 2013.

importance of adhering to an informed religious conscience even among government workers."[12]

Conscientious Objection and the Exercise of Political Authority

Referring to the reproductive health law, the bishops' conference declared that "the Church can continue its mission even with such unjust laws."[13] The question then arises whether a Catholic public officer can resist a law that the church considers unjust. The *Compendium of the Social Doctrine of the Church*[14] presents the following teaching on the right to conscientious objection:

> Citizens are not obligated in conscience to follow the prescriptions of civil authorities if their precepts are contrary to the demands of the moral order, to the fundamental rights of persons, or to the teachings of the Gospel. Unjust laws pose dramatic problems of conscience for morally upright people: when they are called to cooperate in morally evil acts they must refuse. Besides being a moral duty, such a refusal is a basic human right which, precisely as such, civil law itself is obliged to protect. "Those who have recourse to conscientious objection must be protected not only from civil penalties but also from any negative effects on the legal, disciplinary, financial and professional plane."[15] It is a grave duty of conscience not to cooperate, not even formally, in practice which, although permitted by civil legislation, is contrary to the law of God. Such cooperation in fact can never be justified, not by invoking respect for the freedom of others nor by appealing to the fact that it is foreseen and required by civil law. No one can escape moral responsibility for actions taken and all will be judged by God himself based on this responsibility. (no. 399)

The *Compendium* also justifies acts of resistance to any law that violates principles of natural law:

---

[12] CBCP, "CBCP Statement on the RH Law," April 8, 2014.

[13] Ibid.

[14] Pontifical Council for Justice and Peace, United States Conference of Catholic Bishops, *Compendium of the Social Doctrine of the Church* (English translation copyright © 2004 Libreria Editrice Vaticana).

[15] John Paul II, *Evangelium Vitae*, no. 74.

> Recognizing that natural law is the basis for and places limits on positive law means admitting that it is legitimate to resist authority should it violate in a serious or repeated manner the essential principles of natural law. Saint Thomas Aquinas writes that "one is obliged to obey . . . insofar as it is required by the order of justice."[16] Natural law is therefore the basis of the right to resistance. (no. 400)

These church teachings can provide justification for Catholic public officers to resist the law and prevent access to contraceptives and sterilization in public health institutions.

Respecting Freedom of Conscience and Freedom of Religion

While there are church teachings that defend the right to conscientious objection, there are also church teachings that caution against violating the rights and freedoms of others in the exercise of ecclesiastical or political authority.

The Second Plenary Council of the Philippines (PCP II), a landmark gathering of the local church in 1991, has in its documents a reminder for pastors and church leaders about respecting the right of religious freedom of various members of society:

> It needs emphasizing, that, although pastors have the liberty to participate in policy debate and formulation, that liberty must not be exercised to the detriment of the religious freedom of non-communicants, or even of dissenting communicants. This is a clear implication of Vatican II's *Dignitatis humanae.* This is not just a matter of prudence; it is a matter of justice. (no. 358)
>
> There may even be some Catholic believers who in all honesty do not see the truth the way the Church's magisterium discerns, interprets, and teaches it. In such a situation, the Church must clearly and firmly teach what it believes is the truth and require its members to form their consciences accordingly. Yet the church must also, with all charity and justice, hold on to its doctrine on religious freedom—that the human person is bound to follow his or her conscience faithfully, and must not be forced to act contrary to it. (nos. 362–63)[17]

---

[16] Saint Thomas Aquinas, *Summa Theologiae*, II-II, q.104.a.6.

[17] Second Plenary Council of the Philippines, *Acts and Decrees of the Second Plenary Council of the Philippines* (Manila: CBCP Secretariat, 1992), 123–25.

The council defends the right of Catholics to act according to their sincere conscience even if they disagree with the teaching of the magisterium. The council also asks pastors to respect the individual Catholic's right to follow his or her conscience as an expression of religious freedom. Such an instruction to pastors can also apply to Catholic public officers whose conscience decisions can have an impact on the exercise of conscience of people under their authority.

Dignitatis Humanae also warns against any discrimination toward religious minorities by dominant religious traditions: "Because of its historical and cultural ties to a nation, a religious community might be given special recognition on the part of the State. Such recognition must in no way create discrimination within the civil or social order for other religious groups" (no. 6). This statement serves as a warning to the Philippine church not to use its political influence to impose Catholic norms on members of other religious traditions.

Benedict XVI, speaking on the proper role of faith in politics, also cautioned against imposing Catholic norms on non-Catholics:

> Faith enables reason to do its work more effectively and to see its proper object more clearly. This is where Catholic social doctrine has its place: it has no intention of giving the Church power over the State. Even less is it an attempt to impose on those who do not share the faith ways of thinking and modes of conduct proper to faith. Its aim is simply to help purify reason and to contribute, here and now, to the acknowledgment and attainment of what is just. (*Deus Caritas Est,* no. 28)

When trying to resolve a conflict between the right to conscientious objection of public officers and the right of citizens to act according to their conscience and religious beliefs, the *Compendium* proposes a balanced approach that calls for political prudence:

> The just limits of the exercise of religious freedom must be determined in each social situation with political prudence, according to the requirements of the common good, and ratified by the civil authority through legal norms consistent with the objective moral order. Such norms are required by "the need for the effective safeguarding of the rights of all citizens and for the peaceful settlement of conflicts of rights, also by the need for an adequate care of genuine public peace, which comes about when men live together in good order and in true justice, and finally by the need for a proper guardianship of public morality. (no. 422)

The discernment of a politically prudent approach to implementation of the reproductive health law requires a careful consideration of the common good in the context of a pluralistic and multi-religious society. The next section looks at how various stakeholders in the Philippines view the effect of the reproductive health law on the common good.

Interpreting the Common Good

The Philippine bishops, in their pastoral statement "Contraception Is Corruption," clearly expressed their position that the law was detrimental to the common good:

> The Reproductive Health Bill, if passed into law in its present form, will put the moral fibre of our nation at risk. As we your bishops have said in the past, a contraceptive mentality is the mother of an abortion mentality. The wide and free accessibility of contraceptives, even to the youth, will result in the destruction of family life and in greater violence against women.[18]

While the majority of Filipinos are Catholic (80 percent of the total population), their positions on the reproductive health law do not reflect the position of the bishops. Those who strongly oppose the reproductive health law, though very vocal in the news media, are a minority in terms of the total population. A survey taken in 2008 showed that 71 percent of Filipino Catholics supported the law when it was being discussed in the legislature.[19] A similar survey conducted in 2011 showed 69 percent of all Filipinos agreed with the proposed law.[20] Most Filipinos disregard church teaching on contraception and natural family planning. A 2011 family health survey by the government showed that 51.1 percent of currently married women of reproductive age (15–49 years old) do not use any family planning method, whether artificial or natural; 34.9 percent use modern means of contraception or sterilization; and less than 4 percent use natural family planning as recommended by the church.[21]

---

[18] CBCP, "Contraception Is Corruption."

[19] Social Weather Station, "Third Quarter 2008 Social Weather Survey: 76% Want Family Planning Education in Public Schools; 71% Favor Passage of the Reproductive Health Bill," *SWS,* October 16, 2008.

[20] GMA News Online, November 30, 2010.

[21] National Statistics Office, *2011 Family Health Survey*, http://www.census.gov.ph.

Various voices, both secular and religious, have made the claim that the law will contribute to the improvement of the lives of Filipinos. Some members of the Catholic academic community have argued that the reproductive health law was consistent with the promotion of the common good. Fourteen faculty members of Ateneo de Manila University, an institution administered by the Society of Jesus, signed a position paper in 2008 entitled "Catholics Can Support the RH Bill in Good Conscience."[22] They explained in their paper that the law improves the lives of Filipinos by providing the means to address serious health and gender issues related to reproductive health. Forty-five faculty members of De La Salle University, an institution run by the Christian Brothers, also released a statement entitled "The RH Bill Is Pro-Life." Their statement argued that the law would "strengthen the capacity of the State to assist women and their partners to make informed choices, thereby helping them to become healthy and responsible parents and attain a life of quality for themselves and their families."[23]

Twenty-three healthcare professional organizations representing 100,000 doctors and nurses and 167,000 midwives have also signed a manifesto in support of the passage of the reproductive health law. Their manifesto emphasized that the law will effectively save lives. The organizations supported the law's provisions that protected an individual's right to choose what family planning method to use while at the same time they urged that the religious convictions of healthcare providers should be respected.[24]

The National Council of Churches of the Philippines (NCCP), whose member churches include various mainline Protestant denominations, has also declared support for the law. The NCCP secretary general stated that the law "would be one way of promoting responsible parenthood and a means for the government to ensure that each Filipino live a decent life."[25]

Despite the support for the reproductive health law from a plurality of voices in the church and Philippine society, the bishops have chosen not to engage these voices. The bishops claimed that those who supported the law were influenced by secularism, materialism, and postmodern thinking.[26]

From the foregoing there appears to be an irreconcilable gap between the perceptions of the bishops and most Filipinos regarding the effect of the reproductive health law on the common good. Formal attempts to

---

[22] Ruperto Alonso et al., "Catholics Can Support the RH Bill in Good Conscience," October 15, 2008, http://www.rhbillresourcepage.wordpress.com.

[23] GMA News Online, September 4, 2012.

[24] Philip C. Tubeza, "23 Medical Groups Urge Congress to Pass RH Bill," *Philippine Daily Inquirer*, December 12, 2012.

[25] *Philippine Daily Inquirer*, "Protestant, Christian Churches Back RH Bill," December 5, 2010.

[26] CBCP, "Choosing Life, Rejecting the RH Bill."

establish dialogue between the bishops and the supporters of the law have failed because of the refusal of the bishops' conference to compromise on its position.[27] The conference chose to take a hardline approach and called for the total rejection of the law. The bishops' arguments, however, were not sufficiently compelling to convince the majority of the population or the different branches of government that the law was harmful or unnecessary. The state passed the Responsible Parenthood and Reproductive Health Act of 2012 as a necessary law for the promotion of the common good of Filipinos.

The Public Officer's Conscience and the Implementation of the Law

The church teaches that it is a grave duty of conscience not to cooperate with a civil law that is contrary to God's law. Such cooperation cannot be justified even by invoking respect for freedom of others (cf. Rom 2:6; 14:12). But what if the act of not cooperating will lead to grave harm to others? This is the dilemma that Catholic public officers will face with regard to the reproductive health law. While they will not be penalized for exercising conscientious objection to the law by refusing or limiting its implementation in their area of responsibility, such acts of civil disobedience would have serious consequences on vulnerable persons in society, as seen from the study of the effects of EO 003 on women and families in Manila.

The *Catechism of the Catholic Church* teaches that "it is important for every person to be present to himself in order to hear and follow the voice of his conscience" (no. 1779). I believe that "being present" to one's self before God requires an acknowledgment and integration of all the dimensions of one's self, including the social dimension. The Catholic public officer discerning in conscience how to implement the law stands before God not as an isolated person but as a person with a duty to protect and promote the common good of the community. The officer's action will affect not only his or her life but also the lives of others. What can help an officer to discern in a manner that integrates following one's conscience and respecting the conscience of others?

Surprisingly, one possible source of guidance for Catholic public officers on this matter is the church's just-war tradition. This tradition, ordinarily applied to situations of military conflict, is deeply committed to preventing harm from occurring or escalating. The just-war tradition recognizes

[27] GMA News Online, "CBCP Suspends Dialogues with Palace on RH Bill," February 21, 2011.

that even a sincere exercise of legitimate authority can lead to grave harm to others if the person acting is not aware or mindful of the total effects of his or her actions. The *jus in bello* principle of noncombatant immunity can serve as a strong reminder that any potential harm to the innocent and vulnerable must be avoided as much as possible. Applying this principle to the reproductive health law, it is important that public officers listen to vulnerable persons regarding their concrete situations and how the law's implementation (or non-implementation) would affect their lives and their families. The *jus ad bellum* requirement of a right intention provides a warning to public officers about improper intentions.[28] A public officer, for example, can have an unconscious intention of imposing his or her own religious beliefs on others. Listening to objective feedback can help an officer overcome his or her blind spots and purify his or her intentions. The *jus post bellum* concern about the kind of society formed after a conflict can urge ecclesiastical and public authorities to reflect on whether they should continue to engage in divisive debates or move their discourse toward healing, reconciliation, and mutual cooperation.

Another source of insight for discernment is David DeCosse's article on conscience.[29] Addressing the healthcare debate between the US bishops and the Obama administration, DeCosse appeals for a retrieval of the important role of practical reason in conscience discernment that is emphasized by Aquinas in his writings. A prudent and practical conscience seeks to achieve the proper balance between doing good and avoiding harm in concrete and often imperfect situations using all the resources of the moral tradition.

It would be helpful for Catholic public officers to consider several cases where church leaders, using practical reason and moral principles, tolerated situations involving contraceptive use to avoid worsening an already grave problem.

1. In its 1987 statement "The Many Faces of AIDS: A Gospel Response" the US Conference of Catholic Bishops chose to take a tolerant stance toward AIDS-education programs, which include the teaching of safe-sex methods, in order not to hinder the dissemination of information that could protect vulnerable persons

[28] The just-war condition of right intention can also apply to the marriage-equality debate in Argentina discussed in Emilce Cuda's essay in this volume. The political dynamics underlying the ethical and religious arguments in the debate need to be identified and exposed in order for informed discernment and formation of conscience in Argentine society to take place.

[29] David DeCosse, "Bishop's Conscience Model Makes Light of Practical Reason," January 23, 2012. A version of this article is reprinted in the Appendix to this volume.

from HIV infections. This is an example of an application of the principle of tolerance.[30]

2. The US bishops, in "Ethical and Religious Directives for Catholic Health Care Services," allowed non-abortifacient emergency contraception in case of rape (no. 36).[31]
3. Pope Benedict XVI, in *Light of the World,* spoke about the use of condoms by a prostitute as "a first step in the direction of a moralization" that would eventually contribute to a more responsible and humanizing way of living.[32] This can be considered an application of the principle of tolerance and gradualness.
4. The Vatican granted permission to nuns exposed to the risk of rape in wartime in the 1960s to use contraceptives to avoid pregnancy in case of rape.[33]

These examples illustrate the pastoral concern of the church for persons who, in their extraordinary circumstances, are incapable of faithfully following the church's teachings on sexual relations. For the person threatened or affected by rape, prostitution, and HIV infection, the church seeks to protect them from greater harm. In the situation of persons in the Philippines, whose poverty, health conditions, or relationships make them incapable of making family planning decisions as the church recommends, a well-discerned implementation of the reproductive health law can help prevent more serious conditions such as life-threatening pregnancies, domestic violence, and unsustainable family size.

Catholic public officers also need to use their practical reason to implement the law in situations where persons have different perspectives and religious beliefs on family planning and reproductive health. Below are three examples of possible ways this can be done:

1. A Catholic public officer implementing the reproductive health education curriculum in public schools can ensure that accurate and balanced information about natural and artificial family planning is presented in the context of an integral vision of the human person and a humanizing approach to sexual relations. The officer's efforts

[30] James F. Keenan, "The Principle of Tolerance," in *The New Dictionary of Catholic Social Thought*, ed. Judith Dwyer (Collegeville, MN: Liturgical Press, 1994), 951.

[31] United States Conference of Catholic Bishops, "Ethical and Religious Directives for Catholic Health Care Services," November 17, 2009.

[32] Benedict XVI, *Light of the World* (San Francisco, CA: Ignatius Press, 2010), 119.

[33] John Allen, "Exception to Birth Control Ban Raises Questions," *National Catholic Reporter Online,* February 16, 2001, http://www.natcath.org website.

will counter the ignorance and misinformation among the youth that lead to wrongful and harmful sexual attitudes and behavior (such as casual sex, use of pornography, and so forth), while at the same time facilitating character and conscience formation.

2. A Catholic public officer in charge of approving, disbursing, or monitoring government funds for reproductive health programs can exercise vigilance to make sure that only safe and non-abortifacient contraceptives are procured. The officer should make certain that natural family planning programs have sufficient financial support and personnel to enable them to have the same promotion and accessibility as artificial family planning programs. This would enable couples to have access to family planning methods appropriate to their religious and personal convictions as well as their health, marital, and family circumstances.
3. A Catholic director of a public hospital providing reproductive health services can institute a system that allows doctors and nurses to opt out of procedures that violate their consciences and provide substitutes or referrals for patients seeking these services. The director can ensure that balanced and medically accurate information about natural and artificial means of family planning are provided to patients seeking information in order to preserve and promote the patient's right to an informed choice.

In the above examples the Catholic public officer creatively applies the law rather than impedes it. By helping others make careful and informed conscience decisions, the officer exercises his or her proper role as an agent for the common good. The Catholic officer's conscience is less inwardly focused on self-preservation and maintaining "clean hands" and more outwardly directed toward forming the consciences of others in order that they make reproductive health decisions that lead to integral human development even in difficult situations.

To conclude, the option of conscientious objection remains available for public officers in the context of the Philippine reproductive health law. The exercise of this option, however, must not be at the expense of important elements of the common good such as maternal health, poverty alleviation, prevention of diseases, and the protection of vulnerable persons. The church's moral tradition and pastoral approaches can provide guidance for a Catholic public officer to implement the law in a manner that promotes values such as freedom of religion, freedom of conscience, informed choice, and the sanctity of life, while at the same time enabling the officer to fulfill his or her public duty to promote the general welfare of all persons, regardless of religion.

Epilogue

The bishops' conference has adopted a more careful and dialogical approach to the reproductive health issue since the election of Pope Francis in 2013. The bishops' conference expressed a desire to move beyond the conflicts generated by the reproductive health debate: "We cannot see eye-to-eye with our pro-RH brethren on this divisive issue but we can work hand-in-hand for the good of the country. . . . Let us [referring to the church] move on from being an RH-law-reactionary-group to [being] truly Spirit empowered disciples of the Gospel of life and love. We have a positive message to proclaim."[34] Consultative meetings between bishops and theologians have been organized to discuss appropriate pastoral responses to reproductive health issues raised by the law. Just as Francis's example of compassion for the marginalized led to a change in approach among the bishops, my hope is that his example will also influence Catholic public officers to discern carefully how they can implement the law with special concern for the vulnerable.

[34] CBCP, "CBCP Statement on the RH Law."

10.

Conscience, the Locus of our Being, and Anti-Conversion Laws in India

EUGINE RODRIGUES, B.S.

Introduction

Conscience is the locus of our freedom and of our very being. It is the scene of an interplay among a person's intellect, will, and total personality.[1] As one's moral sense of right and wrong, it is the most secret core and the sanctuary of the human person. It is here that one is alone with God and that God's voice echoes in the depths of one's heart (*Gaudium et Spes*, no. 16). *Conscience* is an equivalent term for *moral assessment;* it is acknowledged in all cultures. As an inner sacred core and sanctuary, it is an inner alarm clock that sounds at the right moment. As a faculty of responsibility it asks an account of our actions. Catholic teaching about conscience is that it is essential for the life of faith. It enables a person to live a moral life. A basic Catholic moral teaching is that one should follow one's conscience.

Vatican II makes it clear that "in fidelity to conscience, Christians join with the rest of humankind in the search for truth, and for the genuine solution to the numerous problems which arise in the life of individual and from social relationships" (GS, no. 16). Catholics are part of a community with a rich heritage that helps us consider the challenges in public life and contribute to greater justice, peace, and the common good. Part of this rich heritage is found in *Dignitatis Humanae,* the document on religious freedom from the Second Vatican Council that states, "The citizens will be really in a position to exercise their religious rights and fulfil their religious duties and so that society itself may enjoy the benefits of justice and peace

[1] Bernard Häring, *Free and Faithful in Christ,* vol. 1, *Theology for Clergy and Laity* (Middlegreen, UK: St. Paul's, 1978), 234.

which results from person's faithfulness to God and His holy will" (no. 6). This assertion highlights the role of the church in the formation of conscience and the corresponding moral responsibility of each Catholic to act upon the church's teaching.[2] Freedom of conscience is a necessary condition for seeking the truth, as people are "impelled by their nature and bound by a moral obligation to seek truth, especially religious truth" (DH, no. 2).

Neither the state nor any other individual nor the church has the authority to coerce the conscience of a person in any way. What is at question here is whether a person may be forced to believe or act contrary to his or her conscience by any human law or authority. In other words the choice of religion and its exercise, within strict limits, should never be subject to compulsion. In spite of this assertion seven states in India have passed anti-conversion laws. Moreover, the calls for forceful conversions to Hinduism by elements of Indian Prime Minister Narendra Modi's Bharatiya Janata Party (Modi became prime minister in May 2014) have raised related concerns about the use of state power to compel freedom of conscience.[3] Such Hindu nationalist efforts arise in tandem with controversial concerns about India's colonial and Muslim-ruled past as well as about its ancient traditions of religious diversity.[4] In this essay we explore the basis of the understanding of conscience behind the Catholic opposition to anti-conversion laws in contemporary India.

Enactment of Anti-Conversion Laws in India

Anti-conversion laws or freedom of religion acts—in Sanskrit, *Dharma Swantantraya Vidheyas*—have a long history in India. It was the predominantly Hindu-led princely state of Raigarh that enacted the first anti-conversion law, the Raigarh State Conversion Act of 1936, in order to prevent the lower castes and the tribals from joining or adopting other religions of their choice. The subsequent Udaipur State Anti-Conversion Act of 1946 decreed that all conversions from Hinduism needed official registration. States in India that have passed anti-conversion laws are Orissa in 1967, Madhya Pradesh in 1968, Arunachal Pradesh in 1978, Gujarat in 2003,

---

[2] United States Conference of Catholic Bishops, "Forming Consciences for Faithful Citizenship: A Call to Political Responsibility from the Catholic Bishops of the United States with Introductory Note," http://www.usccb.org.

[3] See, for instance, Aditya Kalra, "Indian PM Modi's Party Distances Itself from Religious Conversions," Reuters, December 20, 2014; see also Nida Najar and Suhasini Raj, "Catholics Fear Campaign of Church Attacks in India," *The New York Times*, February 2, 2015.

[4] See, for instance, "Modi's Idea of India," *The New York Times*, October 24, 2014.

Chhattisgarh in 2006, Rajasthan in 2006, and Himachal Pradesh in 2006.[5] Such laws regulate the right to convert.[6] Such legislation at the state level, denying an individual's religious freedom, is an obvious derogation from the Indian Constitution and a direct infringement of individual conscience.

According to the 1967 anti-conversion law in the state of Orissa, no person shall convert or attempt to convert, either directly or otherwise;[7] no person should convert from one religious faith to another by the use of force or by inducement or by any deceptive means, nor shall any person abet any such conversion.[8] In so framing such laws, the state government has made it clear that whoever wants to pursue a religious faith of one's own free choice will have to get prior permission from the government. Although the laws aim at banning conversions per se, they end up proposing to regulate conversions. It is made mandatory to secure the district magistrate's prior permission for any religious conversion in the state, with effective penalties for not doing so. The anti-conversion laws, critics argue, merely open the way for prejudiced local officers virtually to deny freedom of conscience and freedom to change one's religion.[9]

Within India debate has not sufficiently occurred either at the political level or at the judicial level to challenge and question such subtle attempts to vitiate the secular fabric of the nation and its neutrality in religious affairs. Independently of this absence of debate, there have been many incidences of religious intolerance, organized violence, inhuman acts, and atrocities against minorities, especially Christians. Article 25(1) of the Indian Constitution specifies that the state can intervene and limit the exercise of the right to religious freedom only on the permissible grounds of "public order" and "morality." But if a person acts without violating such grounds, then such a person by law is to enjoy the freedom to profess, practice, and propagate the religion of his or her choice and also the freedom to choose another religion.[10]

---

[5] Saadiya Suleman, "Freedom of Religion and Anti-Conversion Laws: An Overview," *ILI Law Review* 1/1 (2010): 106–28.

[6] Praful Bidwai, "India's Anti-Conversion Laws Loaded in Favour of Majority Hindu Religion," *South Asian Journal* (January 16, 2007): 10–11.

[7] Angela Wu Howard, "Leveraging Legal Protection for Religious Liberty," in *The Future of Religious Freedom: Global Challenges*, ed. Allen D. Hertzke (Oxford: Oxford University Press, 2013), 71–72.

[8] John Saldanha, "Legal Barriers to Conversion," *Indian Missiological Review* 5 (1990): 16–17.

[9] Goldie Osuri, *Religious Freedom in India: Sovereignty and (Anti) Conversion Laws* (New York: Routledge, 2013), 10–25.

[10] Laura Dudley Jenkins, "Legal Limits on Religious Conversion in India," *Law and Contemporary Problems* 71 (2008): 109–27.

The Universal Declaration of Human Rights on Freedom of Conscience: A Basis for the Indian Constitution

The Universal Declaration of Human Rights (UDHR) adopted by the United Nations is undoubtedly the most important document ever produced in the history of the endless struggle for the assertion of human liberties. The UDHR conceptualizes human rights as inherent to humans and therefore universal, that is, held equally by all. Article 1 proclaims that all human beings "are endowed with reason and conscience and should act towards one another in a spirit of brotherhood." Maurice Cranston elaborates this idea by stating that universality is part of the very definition of human rights: "A human right by definition is a universal moral right, something which all humanity, everywhere, at all times ought to have, and something of which no one may be deprived without a grave affront to justice, something which is owing to every human being simply because one is human."[11]

A glance at the Indian Constitution shows that the country has declared its adherence to the UDHR, which contains also the rights that guarantee freedom of conscience.[12] Article 51 of the Indian Constitution states that India will foster respect for international law and treaty obligations.[13] Article 18 of the UDHR deals specifically with freedom of conscience. It states, "Everyone has the right to freedom of thought, conscience, and religion; this right includes freedom to change one's religion or belief, and freedom, either alone or in community with others and in private or public, to manifest one's religion or belief in teaching, practice, worship and observance." While elucidating this Article, Nehemiah Robinson states that the freedom of religion and freedom of conscience are included under freedom of thought.[14] However noble the aspirations of the UDHR, however, Hindu fundamentalists have expressed concern that groups supportive of the efforts of religious missionaries lobbied those shaping the UDHR to make conversion more possible by being legal. Sita Ram Goel states:

> Thanks to the powerful missionary lobby in the United Nations, there is the Universal Declaration of Human Rights which states that everyone has a right to embrace religion of one's choice. But where

---

[11] Maurice Cranston, *What Are Human Rights?* (London: Bodley Head, 1973), 36.

[12] Sita Ram Goel, "The Hoax of Human Rights," in *Hindu-Christian Encounters* (New Delhi: Voice of India, 1996), 252–55.

[13] Susan L. Karamanian, *India and International Law* (Leiden: Martinus Nijhoff, 2005), 101.

[14] Nehemiah Robinson, *Universal Declaration of Human Rights: Its Origin, Significance, Application, and Interpretation* (New York: Institute of Jewish Affairs, 1958), 128.

is the similar Declaration which says that tolerant philosophies and cultures have a right to protect themselves against aggressive, systematic proselytising?[15]

Anti-Conversion Laws and Catholic Theological and Conciliar Arguments for Freedom of Conscience

It will be helpful next to review the concept of freedom of conscience in Catholic theology and in the documents of the Second Vatican Council. A careful reflection on the writings of Louis Janssens provides an integral understanding of freedom of conscience. For Janssens, the basic valuation of the moral activity of the subject is conscience. Freedom of conscience is manifested in the choice of ends toward which one strives. Janssens is concerned about the dignity of the human person wherein the freedom of conscience is at the core. The human person is understood to be conscious, free, unique, and responsible. It is freedom of conscience that determines the subjective culture, what one will ultimately become or not become. Janssens insists on the subjective culture of each person, which includes personal convictions, freedom of conscience, choice of vocation, and the right to a proper life. He affirms freedom of conscience as an inalienable right of the human being. The relationship of union with God is also a free choice.[16]

Furthermore, Janssens maintains that religious freedom is only a matter of applying freedom of conscience and deserves special consideration because the religious conviction of the human person contains what is most essential for the fundamental choice that the person is called upon to make. He does not deny the obligation of our conscience to the requirements of objective truth. Janssens does not altogether abandon the norms in the society but, for him, the responsibility and autonomy of the human person rank above moral laws insofar as religious freedom is concerned. Hence, religious freedom is not based on any objective right inherent in error, but on a subjective right of the human person to follow the dictates of his or her conscience in matters of faith.[17] "Freedom of conscience is the absolute and sacred core of religious freedom," writes Rene Coste.[18] The foundation of all religious freedom is twofold: a natural right to investigate moral and religious truth and a natural right to follow it according to the dictates of conscience.

---

[15] Goel, "The Hoax of Human Rights," 254–55.

[16] Louis Janssens, *Freedom of Conscience and Religious Freedom*, trans. Brother Lorenzo (New York: Alba, 1966), 19, 108.

[17] Floyd Anderson, ed., *Council Daybook: Vatican II, Session 3* (Washington, DC: National Catholic Welfare Conference, 1964), 45.

[18] Rene Coste, *Theologie de la liberte religieuse: Liberte de conscience, liberte de religion* (Gembloux: J. Duculot, 1969), 9.

Conscience also is the mediation of a dialogue between a person and God.[19] If a person judges that he or she is obliged to worship God socially, the person has a right to social worship. Moreover, conscience manifests the drive of the personal subject toward the authenticity of self-transcendence that is realized in every instance of creative understanding, genuine love, and responsible decision in religious matters.[20] Every person has a strict duty to follow his or her conscience; therefore, one has a right to fulfill one's duty. This duty is based on an imperative of the objective moral order (that is, truth as apprehended by conscience). When the duty concerns an object so intimately related to the integrity of the person such as religious choice, practice, worship, and witness through action, the person has the right to the freedom necessary to fulfill this duty.[21] Hence, the inaccessibility of the interior act of conscience to human authority requires that the government respect God's jurisdiction.[22] Freedom of conscience must be enabled and protected by church, state, and society.[23]

American Jesuit theologian John Courtney Murray helped to specify the limits of freedom of conscience and religious freedom in the context of the state and society. Murray held that the state has a certain moral power from God over the human person as a member of the political community, but that while this power extends to external actions of a person, it does not extend to the intimate sphere of conscience. Thus, the human person remains totally under the power of God, both as a member of the political community and as a unique spiritual being. In other words the person is at the same time subject to the moral law and to the public authority. When public authority is in conflict with the authority of God, the conflict is necessarily felt in the conscience of the citizen, who is at the same time a religious person and a political person.[24] According to his view the state or the government has no competence to make judgments on a person's religious belief.[25] At most, Murray argues, the exercise of religious freedom may be limited by a sense of personal responsibility. And, he adds,

---

[19] F. Russell Hittinger, "The Declaration of Religious Liberty, *Dignitatis Humanae*," in *Vatican II: Renewal within Tradition* (Oxford: Oxford University Press, 2008), 367.

[20] Walter E. Conn, *Conscience: Development and Self-Transcendence* (Birmingham: Religious Education Press, 1977), 23–27.

[21] Janssens, *Freedom of Conscience and Religious Freedom,* 119.

[22] Pietro Pavan, "Introduction and Commentary to the Declaration on Religious Freedom," in *Commentary on the Documents of Vatican II*, vol. 4, ed. Herbert Vorgrimler (New York: Herder and Herder, 1969), 66.

[23] Janssens, *Freedom of Conscience and Religious Freedom*, 117, 119.

[24] John Courtney Murray, "Freedom of Religion I: The Ethical Problem," *Theological Studies* 6 (1945): 267.

[25] John Courtney Murray, *The Problem of Religious Freedom* (London: Geoffrey Chapman, 1965), 7.

the exercise also may be limited by the state for the sake of upholding three goods that together constitute what Murray calls "public order": (1) Public peace or the political good, which will only be authentic when it is built on justice. He emphasizes that peace is the work of justice and not of violence. (2) Justice, which secures for people what is due to them, that is, their fundamental human and civil rights. (3) Public morality or the moral good, the minimum standards of public behavior on which consensus exists in society.[26]

It will also be helpful to consider theological arguments specifically related to freedom of conscience and religious freedom in light of coercion and the common good. No religion, not even the Catholic Church for its own self-interest, can ignore or override the universal right to religious freedom.[27] Coercion goes against the freedom and dignity of the human person.[28] Immunity of the human person from coercion in the exercise of religious faith or belief is the object of a genuine human right.[29] In other words the object of the right to religious freedom in *Dignitatis Humanae* has a negative content, a *non-agire* according to theologian Pietro Pavan, that is, a prevention of the use of forceful means.[30] Religious freedom is thus understood as twofold immunity from coercion, whether of restraint (that is, no one can be prevented from acting according to his or her convictions) or of constraint (that is, no one can be forced to act when this is not in accord with his or her convictions).[31] Murray did not see the individual's claim of immunity as totally inviolable. But the claim of immunity in the religious sphere was so strong that the state had to present overwhelming evidence that society was truly at risk before it could interfere with the person's religious beliefs or practices.[32]

---

[26] Ibid., 29–30.

[27] Daniel M. Cowdin, "Religious Liberty, Religious Dissent, and Catholic Tradition," *The Heythrop Journal* 32/1 (1991): 26.

[28] See, for example, David Hollenbach, "Religion, Morality, and Politics," in *Readings in Moral Theology, No. 12: The Catholic Church, Morality, and Politics*, ed. Charles E. Curran and Leslie Griffin (New York: Paulist Press, 2001), 71.

[29] Gerard V. Bradley, "Moral Truth, the Common Good, and Judicial Review," in *Catholicism, Liberalism, and Communitarianism. The Catholic Intellectual Tradition and the Moral Foundations of Democracy*, ed. Kenneth L. Grasso et al. (Lanham, MD: Rowman and Littlefield, 1995), 124.

[30] Pietro Pavan, "The Right to Religious Freedom in the Conciliar Declaration," *Concilium* 8/2 (1966): 21.

[31] See, for example, John Courtney Murray, "The Declaration on Religious Freedom: A Moment in Its Legislative History," in *Religious Liberty: An End and a Beginning*, ed. John Courtney Murray (New York: Macmillan, 1966), 31.

[32] John Courtney Murray, "The Issues of Church and State at Vatican Council II," *Theological Studies* 27/4 (1966): 593.

Thus far we have considered anti-conversion laws in light of freedom of conscience and religious freedom as attributes of individuals and of religious organizations like churches. But it is also important to consider how anti-conversion laws can inhibit the ways in which a society achieves a greater sense of cohesion and peace. Here the language of the common good can help. The common good regarding freedom of conscience is achieved when all persons and communities fully attain freedom of religion, which includes and goes beyond freedom of worship. Christians in India are obligated to participate in the process of making decisions in and for the whole society. They cannot limit their views to discussing questions of God and church, thus refusing to express strong views on right and wrong behaviors in the society in which they live and to which they belong. While a vague pluralism or pragmatism that leads to relativism in religious faith, morality, and values would be understandably unacceptable, a set of proposed ethical principles that are viewed as common to all (and the church believes it is offering such principles) may assist people to find a common moral ground.[33]

It is rightly pointed out by Murray that "whether we like it or not, we are living in a religiously pluralist society at a time of spiritual crisis, and the alternatives are the discovery of social unity, or destruction."[34] Murray was right when he opined that the common good requires that the right to the free exercise of religion be wholly protected. Here one cannot but refer to Aquinas, who states that the intention of the legislator should bear principally on the common good,[35] that is, on the obligation of giving each individual his or her due and of refraining from injustices and of working toward harmony and friendship among the members of society.[36]

Louis Janssens elaborates three fundamental aspects of the common good to which freedom of conscience and the right to religious freedom can be correlated: coexistence, collaboration, and co-participation. Peaceful coexistence on a global level in today's world, according to Janssens, "is a question of life and death."[37] For Janssens, the moral basis of all human coexistence is dialogue with others.[38] With regard to collaboration, Janssens calls upon his model of the dialectic relationship between subjective and objective culture or between one's own deepest convictions—like one's religious convictions—and the surrounding culture outside oneself.

[33] William Schweiker, *The Blackwell Companion to Religious EthicsI* (Malden: Blackwell, 2008), 135.

[34] John Courtney Murray, "Intercreedal Co-operation: Its Theory and Its Organization," *Theological Studies* 4 (1943): 271.

[35] Saint Thomas Aquinas, *Summa Theologica*, I-II, q.100.a.8.

[36] Ibid., I-II, q.99.a.2.

[37] Janssens, *Freedom of Conscience and Religious Freedom*, 84.

[38] Louis Janssens, "The Christian Concern for Society: A Roman Catholic View," in *Christian Social Ethics in a Changing World: An Ecumenical Theological Inquiry*, ed. John C. Bennett (New York: Association Press, 1966), 167.

Collaboration is a constitutive element of the common good, which must be imposed, even if for that purpose some restrictions in the exercise of freedom of conscience may prove to be necessary. Moreover, it is on the basis of common aspirations and moral norms that collaboration is rendered possible.[39] Co-participation, on the other hand, says Janssens, is working out the values of the objective culture. However, it should be oriented toward a more ultimate goal, that is, personal development of every member of a society.[40] In a multi-religious society, the goal of collaboration is to arrive at a consensus with respect to policy and action through an active exchange of views and discussion, even though each religious group finds inspiration and justification for it in its own religious tradition.[41]

In closing this section, it is helpful also to consider discussions and decisions from the Second Vatican Council. Many of the theological arguments I have just noted found their way into conciliar documents. Of course, *Dignitatis Humanae* affirmed clearly the universal human right to religious freedom. Elsewhere in the document the state is warned not to impose upon its people the profession or repudiation of any religion by force or by any other means; not to hinder people from joining or leaving a religious community; and especially not to destroy or repress religion, either in the whole of humankind, or in a particular country, or in a certain community (no. 6). The first two warnings are necessary to guarantee the importance of the freedom of true individual faith. The third warning is necessary to reinforce, on the one hand, the right to religious freedom as a collective right, and on the other, the importance of institutional religion for exercising a particular faith. These warnings should be most urgently and actively heeded in all places, but especially where statutory laws against religious freedom are enacted in spite of the constitutional provisions in favor of religious freedom. More recently, Pope Benedict XVI strongly reaffirmed the decisions of the Second Vatican Council when he called upon governments to respect religious freedom precisely because it touches the constitutive dimension of the human person and his or her relation with the creator.[42] Moreover, he unequivocally stated that religious freedom is "an essential element of a Constitutional state," an element that cannot be denied to the individuals by unjust laws.[43]

---

[39] Janssens, *Freedom of Conscience and Religious Freedom*, 90–91, 105.

[40] Janssens, "The Christian Concern for Society," 176.

[41] Michael Amaladoss, "The Church's Engagement in Civil Society: A New Way of Being Christians in India Today," *Vidyajyoti Journal of Theological Reflection* 72/8 (2008): 603.

[42] Benedict XVI, "Address to Members of the Diplomatic Corps," *L'Osservatore Romano* (January 12, 2011), 4.

[43] Benedict XVI, "Message for World Day of Peace," *L'Osservatore Romano* (December 16, 2010), 4.

Anti-Conversion Laws and the Catholic Church in India

Conversion to Christianity has become a serious concern in India. How can the Catholic Church in India respond to existing anti-conversion laws and to suggestions for further legal intrusion into the process of religious conversion? I have shown the clear basis for the opposition to such laws in international law, in the Indian Constitution, and in theological and doctrinal resources of Catholicism. Here I briefly review the Catholic history in India of opposition to such laws and suggest some ways for the Catholic Church today to engage the Indian state and society on this issue.

Mother Teresa of Calcutta agitated against this unwarranted limitation of personal freedom in her 1979 letter of protest to the government, in which she stated her conviction that "religion is not something that you and I can touch. Religion is the worship of God, therefore a matter of conscience."[44] She further argued that anti-conversion laws were false because there is no freedom if a person cannot choose according to his or her conscience. Having stated her fundamental argument, Mother Teresa pointed out that anti-conversion laws, specifically the freedom of religion bill that was passed in the state of Arunachal Pradesh on November 21, 1978, had disturbed peace and social harmony.[45]

Also at that time Archbishop Angelo Fernandez of Delhi, who was one of the participants in the Second Vatican Council, condemned anti-conversion laws as an encroachment on basic human rights, an affront to human dignity, and a threat to the freedom of conscience.[46] Speaking then against the state's interference in religious matters through the issuance and implementation of anti-conversion laws, Cardinal Joseph Höffner, of Germany, who presided over a meeting of the Catholic Bishops' Conference of India at New Delhi, urged the state to respect the freedom of individual citizens in religious matters to uphold religious values and to preserve the religious traditions of the nation.[47] Having known about the existence of anti-conversion laws in India, in his meeting with all the religious leaders of India in 1999, John Paul II stressed the importance of religious freedom by stating: "Let the right to freedom of belief and worship be respected in every part of this continent! For if this most basic of rights is denied, then the whole edifice of human dignity and freedom is shaken."[48] Cardinal

---

[44] Mother Teresa, "An Open Letter Delivered in Person to Morarji Desai, the Prime Minister of India, on 25 March 1979," *The Examiner* (March 31, 1979), 193.

[45] Ibid., 194.

[46] Angelo Fernandez "Text of the Memorandum to the Prime Minister, New Delhi," *The Examiner* (May 31, 1979), 242.

[47] Catholic Bishops Conference of India, "Report of the General Meeting of the CBCI, Delhi 1982" (New Delhi: CBCI Center, 1982), 69–70.

[48] John Paul II, "Homily: New Delhi," November 6, 1999, http://www.vatican.va.

Oswald Gracias of the Archdiocese of Mumbai in 2009 defended the freedom of religion, including conversion, as a human right and a sacred right, recognized by the Indian Constitution. In resistance to anti-conversion laws, he writes: "No civil authority has the right to enter the shrine which is the conscience of every single person, let alone to decide what a conscience should say. No government can come into my soul and stop my conscience saying 'you can not change your religion.'"[49]

Though the issue of religious conversion has been central to the rhetoric of Hindu fundamentalist attacks on the church in India, it needs to be stated again that their attacks are contrary to the law of the nation. The Indian Constitution specifies the principles and general directives for building a civil society that dynamically protects the rights of all citizens irrespective of their religious affiliations. In light of this constitutional position and allied provisions, anti-conversion laws unjustly pave the way for the oppression of minority religions in the country. They subject the right to freedom of religion to the scrutiny of society at large, thus causing individuals to lose the right to change their religion.[50] Moreover, such laws also undermine the church's social ministries in India. The church's concern and involvement in charitable acts are fundamental to Christian living and to the church's life. In the creedal schema of Christianity, witness and service are integral parts of faith. Nevertheless, in some states in India the educational facilities, medical care, and any form of service to the poor provided by the church are viewed by Hindu fundamentalists as allurements intended to produce conversions to Christianity.

In this situation the church in India as a whole has the duty, first, to remind the state that it cannot underestimate the intelligence and free will of the individual who willingly makes a choice of his or her religion, and second, to pronounce without hesitation the self-evident fact that whenever the state imposes an unjust law on its citizenry, it does great harm to the dignity of the human person and a disservice to society and people. Since the state has to be strictly neutral in dealing with religious matters, it should not set itself up as the judge for assessing particular religious behavior as proper or improper.[51] The Catholic Church in India, in the context of the violation of freedom of conscience, should take the lead in bringing together various communities of people and public authorities for a dialogue

---

[49] Nirmala Carvalho, "Cardinal Gracias: The Church Wants to Serve India, Freedom of Conversion Is a Right," *Asia News,* October 19, 2009.

[50] Margaret O. Thomas, "Changing One's Religion: A Supported Right?" in *Christianity and Human Rights: Influence and Issues*, ed. Frances S. Adeney and Arvind Sharma (Albany: State University of New York Press, 2007), 172.

[51] Julian Saldanha, "Conversion in the Context of Fundamentalism," in *The Church in India in the Emerging Third Millennium*, ed. Thomas D'Sa (Bangalore: NBCLC, 2005), 243–44.

and discussion on questions of life and human dignity. The basic aim of this discussion must be to find ways to live together harmoniously without religious violence and to promote the common good of the people.[52]

In the midst of religious conflicts the one important alternative the church has in its power is to set "Christian priorities in the politics of peace." It is "only by integrating gospel credo with political responsibility [that] Christians, together with non-Christians, [can] construct a society that is inhabitable in peace."[53] Focusing on the task of the church in state and society, Paul Mikat writes: "The Church is the conscience of the public to awaken both the society members and the state to their role in making the common good a reality. It is to awaken the conscience of all people, proclaiming that they must always observe justice and love in their doings."[54] Therefore, the duty and responsibility of Christians is to collaborate with the followers of other faiths and public authorities to search for ways and solutions to problems, both sporadic and perennial, so that all citizens may grow morally and spiritually.[55] The church, on its part, should always uphold the gospel ideals of truth, love, peace, nonviolence, freedom, and justice, and its teaching will definitely contribute to the refinement of the moral conscience of the person and society.[56] The way of sharing the truth can never be the way of fanaticism, fundamentalist extremism, or force. An imposition of religious truth is a self-contradiction. Only in solidarity, in dialogical relationship, and with respect for the conscience and the dignity of human persons created in the image and likeness of God can we propose and share religious truth.

---

[52] Thomas Cherian, *Hindutva Agenda and Minority Rights: A Christian Response* (Bangalore: Centre for Contemporary Christianity, 2007), 310–11.

[53] Johan Verstraeten, "Christian Priorities in the Politics of Peace," in *Swords into Plowshares: Theological Reflections on Peace*, ed. Roger Burggraeve and Marc Vervenne (Louvain: Peeters, 1991), 195.

[54] Paul Mikat, "Church and State," in *Encyclopedia of Theology: Concise Sacramentum Mundi,* ed. Karl Rahner (New York: Seabury, 1975), 233.

[55] Catholic Bishops' Conference of India, "Report of the General Meeting of the CBCI," in S. Arulsamy and S. Singaroyan, *Guide to the CBCI, 1974–2000* (New Delhi: CBCI, 2000), 15–16.

[56] Vincent Kundukulam, "Church Responding to Religious Extremisms," in *Church's Role for a Better India: Catholic Council of India, XI General Body Meeting* (Kochi, November 24–27, 2011), ed. Paul Pulikkan (Thrissur: Marymatha, 2012), 73.

11.

From Catholic Healthcare West to Dignity Health

Conflicts of Conscience in American Catholic Health Care

Carol Bayley

The formation of our conscience comes about through the constant struggle to become good. We may first experience this as we learn our parents' ideas of good and naughty and then internalize those ideas as the superego develops. But gradually the formation of the moral conscience takes place, distinct from the voice of the subconscious, as we enter the complicating challenges of adulthood and find that moral problems worth the name are rarely black or white; as we live our lives of real moral choices; as we confront the systemic failures of our society to bear forward the kingdom of God. In the Catholic tradition the formation of one's conscience must also include a careful listening to the accumulated wisdom of the church, as the Holy Spirit guides it in love to the union with God that is humanity's end.

But knowing each and every word of magisterial teaching from the last thousand years, even if that were possible, does not equip a person to exercise his or her conscience in any given situation. Such a situation would be full of contingent particulars, requiring the prudential application of the principles to the actual case in all its human grit, messiness, and uncertainty. Although far from the insights of *Gaudium et Spes* in other ways, the manualist tradition, in which confessors had lists of the many ways persons can offend God and used them to calculate relative culpability, gravity, and punishment, recognized the importance of the complexity and near-uniqueness of any situation.[1] Simply knowing the principles is not enough. One cannot read oneself into a well-formed conscience.

In the years following the Second Vatican Council, theologians explored the implications of the council's understanding of the interiority of conscience and its relation to and distinction from psychological concepts such as the "self" and the "superego." One such theologian, John W. Glaser, writes that while in the superego there is the subconscious drive of the person to reestablish belonging in the community from which he has become isolated by his bad action, conscience is an entirely different reality. Glaser writes that while a "good conscience" may be described as harmony between God and the self co-created by a person's free act, conscience can also well call one to an extremely isolated position. He writes that conscience is an insight into love and a "call issued by the ultimate value and promise of love."[2]

In this essay I describe two contemporary situations, full of contingent particulars, in which the decision of conscience was relatively straightforward.[3] If conscience is like a muscle, getting stronger with use, these decisions were like the muscles the mother needs to throw the truck off her child to save its life—it is a muscle far stronger than anyone knew, and the decision is made almost without thought, because the requirements of conscience, the response to the call of love, are so absolutely and immediately clear. In both situations, one individual and one institutional, the challenge was not in the conscience determining the requirements of love, but in accepting the consequences of acting on them. In Glaser's framework, the harmony was there, but so was the isolation.

---

[1] Albert R. Jonsen and Stephen Toulmin, *The Abuse of Casuistry: A History of Moral Reasoning* (Los Angeles and Berkeley: University of California Press, 1988); see also James F. Keenan, "Vatican II and Theological Ethics," *Theological Studies* 74 (2013): 162–90.

[2] John W. Glaser, S.J., "Conscience and Superego: A Key Distinction," *Theological Studies* 32 (1971): 31.

[3] I was the system ethicist at the time the events in these stories occurred. I was part of the original conversations with the bishops when non-Catholic hospitals joined Catholic Healthcare West (CHW) and at the time CHW became Dignity Health; I wrote the revised "Statement of Common Values"; and in the first story, I was the person who dealt directly with the sister and her canon lawyer, wrote the initial opinion for the bishop, secured an independent theologian's formal moral opinion, consulted with our board and other system ethicists to assess the moral appropriateness of our position, and worked with our communications team in order both to honestly represent our position as well as to preserve what might be left of a relationship with the bishop.

Two Cases

This is the story of two decisions of conscience, two acts of love, both very much resembling the mother and the truck. The first involved a hospital's approval of a life-saving termination of pregnancy for a woman in pregnancy-induced heart failure and the acceptance of the consequences of that when the local bishop, after the fact, disagreed. The second involved a Catholic organization's decision to maintain its integrity in the face of changing ecclesial priorities. Both decisions, and the actions subsequent to them, sprang from deeply held convictions, informed by fidelity to Catholic teaching, to manifest the healing love of God in the context of twenty-first-century healthcare in the United States.

Healthcare and the Limits of Magisterial Authority: Conscience within the Catholic Church

This case illustrates the question of exactly what sort of discernment the Catholic engages in when he or she invokes conscience. Is conscience, in the language of *Gaudium et Spes,* "the most secret core and sanctuary of a man" (no. 16)? Is it a listening in faith to the law in one's heart written by God? Or must a Catholic, in order to be Catholic, submit to a hierarchical authority outside of self? Does conscience manifest primarily in obedience or in love?

In October 2010, a woman with primary pulmonary hypertension discovered that her birth control had failed and she was seven weeks pregnant. Pulmonary hypertension presents on a continuum of severity. The condition in pregnancy carries a 25 percent risk of death overall, but in those with milder disease the risk is lower and in those with severe disease the risk is much higher. To understand pulmonary hypertension in pregnancy, think of a defective sump pump in a damp basement. For the ordinary rainstorm, the debilitated pump works hard and manages the job. But when the hundred-year flood comes, the pump is inadequate to the task. It burns out and stops.

A woman before she is pregnant has a certain volume of blood; by the end of her pregnancy that volume has increased by 50 percent—for a woman with severe pulmonary disease, the hundred-year flood. The heart of someone with pulmonary hypertension may manage with the standard volume of blood, but when the volume increases, the heart may be overwhelmed, inadequate to the task—and it simply fails. This is why her doctor, knowing the severity of the woman's disease before pregnancy, counseled her, at seven weeks, to end the pregnancy. She did not.

Four weeks later her blood volume had predictably increased and, despite medication, her heart had begun to fail. She was admitted to the ICU of the local Catholic hospital, where her physicians now warned her that if she did not end the pregnancy immediately, she would die. With four other children at home and her own mother encouraging her to terminate the pregnancy, she finally agreed.

Because this was a Catholic hospital, its ethics committee was consulted about the permissibility of terminating this pregnancy. Abortion is not permitted in a Catholic hospital, according to the *Ethical and Religious Directives for Catholic Health Care Services (ERDs). ERDs* defines abortion as the directly intended termination of pregnancy before viability, or the directly intended destruction of a viable fetus, and further specify that "every procedure whose sole immediate effect is the termination of pregnancy before viability" is an abortion.[4] However, according to Directive 47, "Operations, treatments and medications that have as their direct purpose the cure of a proportionately serious pathological condition of a pregnant woman are permitted when they cannot be safely postponed until the unborn child is viable, even if they will result in the death of the unborn child." The ethics committee decided that the termination of pregnancy was justified under Directive 47. At eleven weeks the only procedure to end a pregnancy is a dilation and curettage (D&C). The aim of the procedure in this case was to save the mother's life by removing the placenta, which was producing the blood-volume-increasing hormone. The intention was not to end the fetus's life, but it was an inevitable and foreseen side effect. The termination occurred, and the woman survived.

After the fact, during the moral theological analysis, categories such as the "intention," "the object of the act," and "what they were really doing" became relevant.[5] In the practical world of emergency medicine, those theological points are not the focus. If one had asked those on the woman's medical team what they were doing, they would have said they were saving the one life they could save. They were not performing an abortion, terminating a pregnancy, removing the placenta, or even performing "an operation that has as its direct purpose the proportionately serious pathological condition" of the woman. They were saving a life.

Several months later the hospital administrator and the Sister of Mercy who had communicated the ethics committee's decision to the physician

---

[4] United States Conference of Catholic Bishops, *The Ethical and Religious Directives for Catholic Health Care Services*, 5th ed. (Washington, DC: USCCB, 2009), 26.

[5] See Cathleen Kaveny, "What Is 'Abortion,' Anyway," *dotCommonweal* (May 20, 2010), http://www. commonwealmagazine.org; see also Therese Lysaught, "Moral Analysis of a Procedure at Phoenix Hospital," *Origins* 40/33 (January 27, 2011): 537–47.

were summoned to the local bishop's office. Having heard (from a priest whose mother worked at the hospital) of the termination, the bishop accused the two of authorizing an abortion. No amount of explanation, even after the bishop's version of the medically relevant facts had been corrected, dissuaded him from the position that the hospital had acted contrary to the *ERDs* and that by authorizing an abortion that she knew was against church teaching, the sister had excommunicated herself. The administrator was told that unless the hospital and the system that sponsored it publicly admitted its wrongdoing and promised never to do it again, the bishop would cease to recognize the hospital as a Catholic hospital. After sustained conversation with the bishop and meetings at the highest level of the Catholic organization that owns the hospital where the case occurred—and four days before Christmas—the bishop publicly announced that he had withdrawn his recognition of the Catholic identity of the hospital and refused to allow mass to be celebrated in its chapel.

During negotiations with the bishop as the board and the Sister of Mercy sponsors evaluated their options, I consulted a number of moral theologians by telephone and email. They included theologians in universities and seminaries as well as those working for Catholic health systems in the role of ethicist. I cast a very wide net, consulting those with whom I have disagreed professionally in the past on a range of ethical issues in Catholic healthcare, although never on this subject. I also discussed the issue with several bishops.

Every bishop or theologian I consulted agreed that the hospital had done the only reasonable thing it could have done. When I asked them why that was so, their responses fell into three categories. One theologian said that the church's position is "cruel but it's clear." By this he meant that, regardless of intention to do good, the act to end a pregnancy necessitating the destruction of a fetus counts as an unjustified abortion and is deemed immoral in Catholic teaching. He also believed that under the circumstances, saving the woman's life was a stronger requirement than following the church's (cruel) teaching.

The second view, by far the most widely held among theologians employed as ethicists in Catholic healthcare systems, was that under the rule of double effect, the termination of the woman's pregnancy was entirely justified. In the traditional formulation, to be justified by double effect an action must satisfy four conditions: (1) the act itself must be good or at least neutral, (2) the good effect (and not the evil one) must be intended, (3) the good effect must not be attained by means of the evil effect, and (4) there must be a proportionate reason for permitting the evil effect.

These theologians held that the single act of ending the pregnancy had two effects, to save the woman's life and to end the fetus's, and it was only the first that was actually intended as the object of the act. They argued that the act was not wrong in itself; ending a pregnancy by removing a cancerous, though gravid, uterus, for example, is one of the standard cases in the teaching about double effect. The third requirement in the traditional application of the rule of double effect is that the bad effect may not be the means by which the good effect is attained. Satisfying this third condition, the good effect was not secured by means of the ending of the fetus's life; if there had been a way to end the production of the hormone by the placenta without damaging the fetus, it would have been done. The destruction of the fetus was not necessary, but it was inevitable. Finally, the gravity necessary to the calculus of double effect was certainly present. If the termination were not performed, the woman and her fetus would both die. In fact, fetal death was assured in any case.

The third response was from a theologian who said cases like this one show the limits of Catholic teaching. The *ERDs* itself recognizes that it does not address in detail all the complex issues that face Catholic healthcare today.[6] In such cases prudential decisions must be made in light of the whole of Catholic teaching.

These opinions were rendered in the immediate aftermath of the bishop's pronouncement in the case. Afterward, because the case drew so much attention in both the secular press and the theological literature, several theologians, including Kevin O'Rourke, Bernard Prusak, and Gerald Magill, used the case both to opine on the case itself and to explore the limits of those theological doctrines used to analyze it.[7] Good arguments were made for looking at the case not simply through the lens of double effect, to which medical ethics often defaults, but also through the lens of choosing the lesser of two evils and the right to self-defense.

This case, and the decisions of conscience it required, took place at several levels. At the most basic this Catholic woman resisted ending her pregnancy, because she was Catholic, until the time when her own life was at stake. She did not rely on the likelihood, which was high, that her own

---

[6] United States Conference of Catholic Bishops, *The Ethical and Religious Directives for Catholic Health Care Services*, 4.

[7] See Kevin O'Rourke, O.P., "What Happened in Phoenix? The Complicated Reasons behind an Abortion at a Catholic Hospital," *America* (June 21, 2010); idem, "Complications: A Catholic Hospital, a Pregnant Mother, and a Questionable Excommunication," *America* (August 2, 2010); idem, "From Intuition to Moral Principle: Examining the Phoenix Case in Light of Church Tradition," *America* (November 15, 2010); idem, "Rights of Conscience Responding to a Bishop's Disciplinary Decisions," *America* (August 1, 2011); Bernard Prusak, "Double Effect, All Over Again: The Case of Sister Margaret McBride," *Theoretical Medicine and Bioethics* 32/4 (August 2011): 271–83; and Gerald Magill, "Threat of Imminent Death in Pregnancy: A Role for Double-Effect Reasoning," *Theological Studies* 72/4 (December 2011): 848–78.

life would *become* threatened. It was only when it was *actually* threatened that she agreed to end the pregnancy. Clearly her conscience was at work, first in resisting the abortion and then, in light of her responsibilities to her other children, agreeing to it.

At the level of the administrator and the sister who headed the ethics committee, the requirements of conscience were somewhat different. As a Catholic hospital, identified as a formal ministry of the Catholic Church, the hospital had a responsibility to uphold Catholic teaching. This is why, rather than just approving a life-saving abortion for a pregnant woman, the ethics committee reviewed the case and concluded that Catholic teaching, explicitly in the *ERDs* and more generally in the moral tradition of the rule of double effect, would support the ending of the pregnancy for the proportionate good of saving the woman's life.

As the consequences of that decision played out—after the bishop's ultimatum—the administrator and the board and the sister-sponsors of the parent organization looked not only at Catholic teaching, which they believed justified their action, but also at the requirements of conducting a healthcare enterprise in a pluralistic society with its own standards and regulations for operating in the public interest. In order to continue to provide the services to all the people in their local community who relied on them, the parent company refused to tell women that if the only way to save their life was to end their pregnancy, Catholic teaching required the woman's death.

This case illustrates the exercise of conscience, at all three levels, that has been formed in light of the requirements of love and in fidelity to Catholic teaching. The woman knew that abortion was wrong. Leadership at the hospital understood the implications of the *ERDs*. The parent company's reason for being—to continue to be the healing ministry of Jesus in a broken world—was precisely why it lost recognition by the bishop of the hospital as Catholic. These decisions were not the exercise of conscience requiring departure from Catholic teaching. These were decisions requiring the interpretation of that teaching to the contingent circumstances of an actual case.

Healthcare and the Limits of Magisterial Authority: Conscience, Church, and the Pluralist World

To understand the second case, some background is necessary. Established in 1986, Catholic Healthcare West (CHW) began as a small, twelve-hospital organization formed for the mutual support and effective stewardship of resources by two communities of Sisters of Mercy. Although a majority of the hospitals owned by these sisters were actually named Mercy Hospital, when they named the new system, they chose what they thought would be a more inclusive name: Catholic Healthcare West. In the twenty-first century, multi-hospital systems are the norm. In 1986, the hope was that other religious congregations whose numbers were becoming too small to sustain their Catholic hospitals would join CHW when local conditions began to threaten hospitals as stand-alone, community-based, not-for-profit ventures. Sisters were, and continue to be, deployed as board members, mission leaders, chaplains, and in some cases as nurses and patient advocates, but functions such as administration, finance, planning, purchasing, and legal (where few sisters traditionally served) were entrusted to lay people. These collaborators were professionals who understood both the business of healthcare as well as its identity as a social responsibility and human right. Indeed, the vision of the Mercy founders became a reality, and the system attracted the sponsorship of five more religious congregations, who contributed their hospitals to the system and their leadership to the governance of the organization.

By the mid-1990s, CHW was strong enough to attract even non-Catholic hospitals, whose boards and leadership shared the values fundamental to the mission, especially in geographies where CHW already had a presence. In the face of shrinking reimbursement and capital challenges that were difficult to meet as an isolated borrower on Wall Street, these hospitals looked for a way to preserve both their not-for-profit status and their responsibilities to their local communities. Their choices were few, particularly as this was also a time of great consolidation and acquisition among for-profit healthcare systems like Tenet and HCA Columbia. As a way to preserve and strengthen Catholic healthcare and advance the mission of the organization to serve the healthcare needs of all, CHW undertook a process to bring these hospitals in as full members. That process resulted in the development of the "Statement of Common Values," a kind of a moral bottom line for partnership. Its first iteration was a reflection of the *ERDs* with an important difference. Whereas the *ERDs* forbid sterilization, this document was silent on the issue of permanent or temporary contraception, since it was not a value that CHW held in common with these hospitals.

Some of the hospitals had performed abortions in the past, and the "Statement of Common Values" assured that this would stop. Nor would a hospital in the network ever perform physician-assisted suicide or euthanasia, in the event that those became legal in CHW jurisdictions. Furthermore, the hospitals agreed to meet CHW's very high standards for community benefit; to implement standards for palliative care that were among the strongest in the nation; to attend to the care of the whole person by hiring professional, not volunteer, chaplains; and to give employees a voice in the conditions of their work. The bishops seemed to agree that being part of CHW was a way for these non-Catholic hospitals to advance the mission of Catholic healthcare without actually becoming a ministry of the church.

In every case, in every area where the non-Catholic hospital asked CHW for membership, the local bishop was consulted and the "Statement of Common Values" was discussed, with the provision that the hospital would continue to provide sterilization services made explicit. Since the hospitals were not going to become Catholic, the threat of scandal was minimal. The bishops who approved these mergers never did so in writing and never issued a *nihil obstat*. But they did make clear to CHW their thinking in meetings with system representatives in anticipation of the mergers. They were convinced by what the non-Catholic hospitals agreed positively to do (in the "Statement of Common Values"); the evil of sterilization, in the prudential judgment of the bishops, seemed to be outweighed by the good these hospitals would do. One bishop called it an "opportunity for evangelization."

CHW Is Dissolved

That was the state of affairs in 2010, some years after the last acquisition of a non-Catholic hospital by CHW. Several years before, a bishop new to a diocese in which CHW had a non-Catholic hospital (and therefore, not the bishop who understood and agreed to the arrangement) told CHW that he did not approve of the relationship and said it must discontinue. For seven years CHW's administrators, sister-sponsors, and their legal department met with the bishop to explain the contractual relationship with the hospital, that it was not a Catholic hospital, that the prior bishop and many other bishops in CHW had agreed to such arrangements, and that it was not possible to force the hospital to stop performing contraceptive sterilization without breaking CHW's word, violating its contract, and being liable for it in court. Important in the original negotiations—during which the non-Catholic hospitals agreed, among other things, to stop performing abortion—was the recognition by CHW that the provision of contraceptive services to their communities was, in a very real if not theologically nuanced sense, a matter of conscience for them. They considered it a fundamental part of their responsibility to their communities to maintain a service that many women, in conscience, believe is the appropriate moral choice for themselves and their families.

Unable to accomplish his goal directly with CHW, in 2010 the bishop contacted the United States Conference of Catholic Bishops (USCCB) and asked a simple question: Should a hospital in a Catholic system abide by every provision in the *ERDs*? Sometime later all the Catholic bishops in the United States received a three-paragraph letter, answering in the affirmative.

Not only was this letter prepared and sent without answering the mail or telephone calls of CHW to explain how it had arrived at the arrangements or what motivated them, but the USCCB also reached its conclusion without the benefit of any consultation with other bishops who had agreed to the inclusion of non-Catholic hospitals in CHW's ministry in the first place. Certainly the USCCB bishops must have talked among themselves, but their action displayed a profound disrespect for any outside dialogue, including the seven years of dialogue CHW had with the bishop who brought his question to them. There was no conversation with CHW leadership, none with any member of a community in which these hospitals operate, none with anyone about the legal requirements involved in the making of a secular hospital into a Catholic one, and no dialogue at all about the impact of such a decision, not only on CHW, but on the future of the Catholic healthcare apostolate in the United States. There seems to have been a complete absence of the kind of dialogue with the modern world for which Vatican II called.

Clearly, the ecclesial landscape had changed. Now concerned more with purity of Catholic teaching and clarity of witness than with what prior bishops saw as evangelization and preservation of Catholic values in secular American healthcare, the bishops of California, Arizona, and Nevada gathered and gave CHW three choices. The first was to make all the non-Catholic hospitals Catholic. This was not possible, for all the reasons described above; by legal contract, the hospitals abided by the "Statement of Common Values," preserving their non-Catholic status, and were not prepared to "convert." The second choice offered by the bishops was that CHW should simply sell off the non-Catholic hospitals. CHW by then had forty hospitals; fifteen of them were not Catholic. These forty hospitals relied on one another for favorable contracts with third-party payers, for borrowing money for capital improvements, and for shared services at the system level; they were entwined with one another in many other ways. Selling off more than one-third of them, if buyers could even be found, would leave the rest of the system in a state of collapse. This option displayed either a profound ignorance of the economy and operations of healthcare or a profound apathy toward it.

The last option, and the one that the sister-sponsors and governance of CHW eventually chose, was to stop using the name Catholic and to reorganize the governance so that the pontifical religious congregations were no longer at the head of the organization that they had founded.[8] Especially for the sisters, but also for the lay members of the governing board, it was painful to realize that in order to preserve a ministry with fifty-five thousand employees and forty hospitals, many of which are the medical safety net in their communities, they would have to give up that ministry's association with the Catholic Church, in which they were founded, on the basis of the bishops' desire to be faithful to Catholic teaching on sterilization.

One is reminded of the story of the wise King Solomon in the Old Testament. Two women come before him with a baby, each claiming to be the baby's mother. The king calls for his sword—one baby and two mothers is a math problem that he purports to solve by slicing the baby in two and giving half to each woman. What happens, of course, is precisely what Solomon counted on to reveal the true mother. The one whose child it is cries, "Give the baby to her!"

In the CHW story the sister-sponsors and the bishops each claimed to be the "real" parent. The sisters gave birth to CHW, but the bishops insisted, in a way, that it was named after them. When the proposal was to split the baby, the true mothers did what was necessary to save CHW. Painful as it was, they let CHW go.

Especially in the case of the sisters, steeped in Catholic teachings and having lived lives where many choices have been voluntarily constrained by their vows and by their commitment to church and community, it would be absurd to say that their consciences were not well formed. Their decision to "save the baby" was the result of a deep and thorough understanding of the healthcare reality in the United States today, where millions of people still have no access to healthcare other than an emergency room and where the business values of efficiency and cost containment often undermine the human values of compassion and service.

The end of these stories completes the picture. The woman whose abortion saved her life is raising her four children. The sister who had "excommunicated herself" remains in good standing in her religious community and continues in a leadership role in the administration of the hospital. The hospital, although not recognized by the bishop as Catholic, is in fact recognized by everyone else as such—it still abides by the *ERDs,* it is still

---

[8] Agbonkhianmeghe E. Orobator, S.J., notes that the same perverse threat experienced by the sponsoring congregations of CHW is felt by religious sisters in Uganda, Tanzania, and Kenya, who, trying to stem the spread of HIV/AIDS, feel the tension between the church's official teaching against the use of condoms and their compassionate duty to educate people and advise their use. The religious communities "of pontifical right" are recognized by Rome; the withdrawal of this recognition effectively destroys the religious community ("'To Pardon What Conscience Dreads': Navigating the Contours and Precepts and the Contexts of Life," chap. 12 in this volume).

dedicated ecclesial property that has not been alienated by Rome, and it is still sponsored by its religious founders. It walks like a duck and quacks like a duck.

Although it is still painful to its religious founders that CHW was dissolved as a corporation and its successor is no longer a formal ministry of the Catholic Church, that successor organization, Dignity Health, continues to educate its leaders in the tradition of Catholic social thought, continues the ministry of healing the whole person, continues to lift up the importance of the worker's voice in the workplace, and continues to dedicate millions of dollars in charity care and services for the benefit of the community. The consequences of these decisions of conscience were heavy, but in Glaser's words they were an answer to the call of love.

Conclusion

Taken together, these two cases prompt an interesting observation about the Catholic view of conscience. Brian Patrick Green suggests that there is a tension in Catholic teaching between the necessity to follow one's conscience, on the one hand, and the expectation that a rightly formed conscience will concur with the teachings of the church, on the other.[9]

That tension is witnessed by the number of Catholics who, for example, believe that using birth control is morally appropriate. Is that what is going on here? As we have seen above, it strains credibility to suggest that the sisters—the individual who approved the pregnancy termination and those who founded CHW—have consciences that are not well formed. Certainly in the first case both the sister and the hospital thought that they were abiding by a careful interpretation of the *ERDs,* as did many commentators afterward. In the second case, in founding CHW and engaging in the negotiation with the world that Vatican II invited, the sister-sponsors and the bishops who approved of the original deals also believed they were concurring with the teachings of the church. Although I agree with Green that this tension exists, it does not explain what happened in the first case.

There may be another way to view the tension, one that recognizes that just as an individual person (or institution) must listen to the voice of God within as well as the teachings of the church, no one bishop's opinion exhaustively represents the magisterium. Perhaps a bishop, or a group of bishops, can be wrong at a given time in history about what the church teaches, as can any individual. Like the rest of the faithful, a bishop may

---

[9] Brian Patrick Green, "Catholicism and Conscience," Santa Clara University, Markkula Center for Applied Ethics (May 2013), http://www.scu.edu.

follow his conscience and still be in error. His conscience, like all others, is formed by family, politics, religious experience, the law, and his own previous moral choices. This may explain the clash that occurred in the first case.

The clash in the second case is more concerned with the interpretation of church teaching, and here Green's dichotomy may explain more. It cannot be ignored that the subject of the teaching in question is one that has plagued the church since the early 1960s: contraception (in this case permanent contraception for women as it is practiced in an institutional ministry of the church). The institutional ministry is held by the hierarchy to stricter standards than any individual person might be, because it is seen as part of the teaching function of the church. That question—whether an apostolic work *should* be characterized as part of the teaching function of the church—is one currently being debated, but the parties to the debate are unequally matched. Catholic hospitals in the United States were founded and run mainly by women religious. But the owners of the Catholic brand, so to speak, are the ordained and consecrated bishops. They hold the power to allow an organization to call itself Catholic. This is the same tension that Orobator identifies as the pull between rhetoric and practice.[10]

This does not contradict the view that over time the Holy Spirit will get it right. As John Noonan writes: "Development [of moral doctrine] proceeds directed by this rule. The love of God generates, reinforces, and seals the love of neighbor. What is required is found in the community's experience as it tests what is vital. On the surface, contradictions appear. At the deepest level, the course is clear."[11] The wisdom of the church is the wisdom of a community in dialogue, persons who come together as moral equals even if they come from different perspectives or different positions—or no position—in the hierarchy. This sort of dialogue was missing in the cases above.

This is the fundamental reorienting insight of Vatican II, that the church is, in a real way, the whole people of God.

---

[10] Orobator, "To Pardon What Conscience Dreads."

[11] John T. Noonan, Jr., *A Church That Can and Cannot Change: The Development of Catholic Moral Teaching* (Notre Dame, IN: University of Notre Dame Press, 2005), 222.

12.

“To Pardon What Conscience Dreads”

Navigating the Contours of Precepts and the Contexts of Life

Agbonkhianmeghe E. Orobator, S.J.

Introduction

> *Almighty ever-living God, who in the abundance of your kindness surpass the merits and the desires of those who entreat you, pour out your mercy upon us to pardon what conscience dreads and to give what prayer does not dare to ask.*
>
> —Collect, Twenty-Seventh Sunday in Ordinary Time

This essay aims to cast fresh light on the understanding of the role of conscience in Catholic theological ethics by focusing on a two-sided question. On the one hand, I consider the position, rhetoric, and pronouncement of hierarchical ecclesial leadership, routinely labeled church teaching, regarding conscience; on the other, I inquire about how people on the frontlines of HIV/AIDS ministry understand and engage in conscience formation while aware of the dread and threat of sanctions for positions that could be construed as contrary to church teaching. This question is posed in the specific context of HIV/AIDS in Africa, a subject which has provoked a lively and heated debate about conscience and the role of conscience in morality.

On numerous occasions I have encountered conscientious Catholics who desire to act according to conscience but dread contravening ecclesiastical precepts. I illustrate this moral dilemma, first, by undertaking a documentary review of pastoral letters, statements, and communiqués produced by the Catholic hierarchy in Africa over a ten-year period (2001–10) exploring the narratives of some Christians living and ministering in the context of HIV/AIDS in Eastern Africa; and second, by analyzing their strategies for resolving the tension between the demands of institutional precepts and challenges of complex life situations. Although I introduce only three ministers, they are representative of a much larger group of ministers who continue to respond with compassion and mercy to the needs of people infected and affected by HIV/AIDS.

The Background and the Context

The year is 1999. In the sleepy rural town of Masaka, deep in southern Uganda and close to Lake Victoria, HIV/AIDS is decimating impoverished rural communities. Further down, along the southern bend of the expansive lake, in the town of Mwanza, Tanzania, the fiery fury of AIDS lays bare one neighborhood after another. A similar tale unfolds in the squalid slums of Korogocho on the northeastern fringes of Kenya's capital city, Nairobi. In these three contexts I encountered three women of faith, all members of religious communities and a representative minority of a vast warren of nurses, doctors, teachers, counselors, community health workers, and volunteers who have dedicated their lives to the care of people living with HIV/AIDS. It is this community that I term "ministers of care" and "practitioners of compassion."

The distance that separates the three women is enormous, but they are connected by a common purpose: to care with compassion and mercy for the casualties of this dreadful disease. One is a physician; the other two are social workers. All three women profess ardent faith in "the one, holy, catholic, and apostolic church." They have consecrated their lives to faith in this church.

The avowed objective of their ministry of care and compassion is to save lives and help stem the raging tide of HIV/AIDS. Notwithstanding the unfavorable sociocultural and political milieus of their ministry, they are buoyed by an unspoken resolution to do whatever is necessary, effective, and possible to prevent the further spread of the disease. But a different kind of tide rises and rages against them: the prohibition of the prophylactic method of disease prevention. As members of religious communities of pontifical right, they are cautious about contravening the precepts of the church on this matter, at least explicitly or publicly. Yet, as believing Christians and disciples of the risen Christ, they consider education and formation for life as an integral part of their duty of care, encouraging their patients to take effective "precautions" (a euphemism for prophylactic devices) against HIV infection. Their ministry lies in the interstices of rigid demands of institutional precepts and complex challenges of lived experience in the constantly shifting and unpredictable moral terrain of the AIDS pandemic, fraught with tension and controversy, and haunted by fear of being barred from continuing their ministry of care and compassion.

"This We Teach": HIV/AIDS and the Rhetoric of Conscience

Christian theology, anthropology, and ethics consider axiomatic the constitutive role of conscience in conceptualizing the human person as a moral being. The centrality of conscience in theological ethics and moral theology lies beyond doubt. Although a variety of formulations of this axiom exists, none, to my mind, rivals the depth, clarity, and poignancy with which Vatican II expounded the supremacy of conscience:

> Deep within their consciences men and women discover a law which they have not laid upon themselves and which they must obey. Its voice, ever calling them to love and to do what is good and to avoid evil, tells them inwardly at the right moment: do this, shun that. For they have in their hearts a law inscribed by God. Their dignity rests in observing this law, and by it they will be judged. Their conscience is people's most secret core, and their sanctuary. There they are alone with God whose voice echoes in their depths. By conscience, in a wonderful way, that law is made known which is fulfilled in the love of God and of one's neighbor. Through loyalty to conscience, Christians are joined to others in the search for truth and for the right solution to so many moral problems (*Gaudium et Spes,* no. 16).[1]

Viewed from the perspective of the ethics of prevention of HIV and care of people living with AIDS, the understanding of conscience and its formation reveals a dissonance between rhetoric and practice. This disconnect places official pronouncement on what constitutes "Catholic teaching" in opposition to the urgency, exigency, and emergency conditions faced by frontline, grassroots ministers of care and practitioners of compassion for people infected and affected by HIV/AIDS. The contested question of the use of prophylactic devices in the prevention of transmission of the virus

[1] This formulation resonates strikingly with Joseph Ratzinger's (later Pope Benedict XVI) assertion that "above the Pope as an expression of the binding claim of Church authority stands one's own conscience, which has to be obeyed first of all, if need be against the demands of Church authority" (*Commentary on the Documents of Vatican II,* ed. Herbert Vorgrimler [Freiberg: Herder and Herder, 1968], 134).

that causes AIDS and in the specific situation of discordant couples reignited intense debate and controversy in theological ethics bordering on the understanding and formation of conscience. Besides, the disproportionate burden of infection borne by sub-Saharan Africa during the peak decades (1980s and 1990s) of the AIDS pandemic propelled the subcontinent to the fore of this moral contestation. While ecclesiastical authorities have persisted in their condemnation of the use of such devices, they have extolled the importance of a well-formed conscience as an antidote to a practice summarily branded a "culture of death."

On August 5, 2006, Pope Benedict XVI summarized the response of the church in Africa to HIV/AIDS in the following terms: "Throughout Africa . . . we have a vast network of every level of school where people can learn, form a true conscience and acquire professional skills which give them autonomy and freedom."[2] Benedict thus restated a key component of official responses of the Catholic hierarchy in Africa, namely, conscience formation (variously rendered as "human formation" or "education") in view of autonomy and freedom of choice and action. This well-rehearsed line is repeated at many local, regional, and continental levels in official pronouncements of the African hierarchy, as illustrated by the following samples:

> To HEALTH SERVICES PERSONNEL . . . Remember especially that you must educate those who consult you by drawing their attention to the moral dimension of the problem. . . . Do not content yourselves with passively distributing condoms! . . . More deeply, be able to call on the higher values of man, on his dignity, his responsibility, on the greatness of chaste and faithful love. . . . The nation counts on your professional conscience, on your devotion to the care of the sick and on your respect for the spiritual and religious values of the Malagasy people.[3]
>
> Consequently, in the campaign against AIDS and sexually transmitted diseases, the Catholic Church insists that one not speak uniquely of a purely technical means, the condom, but that one appeal to what is most human and most dynamic in the human person: his conscience.[4]

---

[2] Quoted in Bénézet Bujo and Michael Czerny, eds., *AIDS in Africa: Theological Reflections* (Nairobi, Kenya: Paulines Publications Africa, 2007), 16.

[3] Episcopal Conference of Madagascar, *Catholic Bishops of Africa and Madagascar Speak Out on HIV and AIDS: "Our Prayer Is Always Full of Hope": A Collection of Excerpts 1987–2005*, rev. ed. (Nairobi, Kenya: Paulines Publications Africa, 2007), 31.

[4] Bishop Maurice E. Piat of Port-Louis, in ibid., 70.

> Instead, we have to take responsibility for our actions before God. This involves listening to God's word and to the teaching of the church so that we can have informed and mature consciences.[5]
>
> The ultimate moral rule is our conscience. It is up to each and every one of us to train one's conscience and to assume one's responsibility according to the situation in which one finds oneself. Because "no one is bound to do the impossible," spouses cannot be asked to abstain from sexual intercourse; we therefore understand that a person, through love, may be led to use the condom to protect himself/herself or to protect his or her partner. But everybody must understand that the condom does not provide 100 percent prevention and that it does not ultimately solve the real problem raised by AIDS.[6]

This magisterial approach may fall short of satisfying the objective of providing new insight on the understanding of conscience and formation of conscience, precisely because it does not always discriminate between what is prescribed and the conditions, contexts, and circumstances where it is applied and lived.

Understanding What Conscience Dreads

In exploring ecclesiastical pronouncements, such as those sampled above, several observations can be made regarding, first, the understanding of conscience formation, and second, the precise even if disputed content and process of this exercise. Regrettably, oftentimes official pronouncements fail to take into account the experience of frontline ministers of care and compassion.

In the first place, the view is strong that the hierarchically constituted community called church is the privileged instrument or subject initiating and imparting constituent principles and precepts of the process and content of conscience formation: "To all, the Church offers moral formation and encouragement. This includes forming moral conscience so that each one, in considering how to behave, can distinguish between what is good and what is sinful."[7] Although this position presupposes and upholds the independence and autonomy of the individual moral agent relative to the choice "between what is good and what is sinful," in perception and reality, to be deemed right or good the concomitant decision is implicitly and explicitly

---

[5] Ibid., 84.

[6] Catholic Bishops of Chad, in ibid., 93.

[7] Kenya Episcopal Conference, *This We Teach and Do: Catholic Church and AIDS in Kenya,* vol. 2, *Policy* (Nairobi, Kenya: Paulines Publications Africa, 2006), 25–26.

presumed to be that which is in harmony with the position of the church's hierarchy. Reviewing the evolution of ecclesiastical declarations since the onset of the AIDS pandemic, it is hard to miss a strong tendency to exert ecclesiastical control over what constitutes right or wrong decisions in the actions of people infected and affected by this disease.

Second, the hierarchy places the burden of conscience formation that aligns its teaching on prevention with the moral precepts of Catholic ethics on professional and nonprofessional frontline ministers. This creates a situation of ecclesiastical outsourcing of the responsibility for conscience formation that agrees with a predetermined position or understanding of conscience. For example, according to the Kenya Episcopal Conference (KEC): "All those involved in the Church's ministry—pastorally, in education and in healthcare—should help people at every stage of life to develop a well-formed conscience. This includes the Church's moral teaching as well as solid information about HIV and AIDS."[8] KEC issued a similar directive in the case of discordant couples: "We encourage priests, sisters and other pastoral agents to assist discordant and infected couples to form their consciences with regard to how they will live out their marital relationship, and make decisions that are life-enhancing and faithful." Although the reference to "solid information about HIV and AIDS" and "decisions that are life-enhancing and faithful" suggests a measure of freedom and autonomy, little doubt exists about the scope of the information that ministers of care are allowed to give or the decisions they can help to make in the process of assisting in the formation of conscience. The bishops' policy emphatically rules out one obvious specific option: "Therefore, the Church does not promote the use of condoms as protection against AIDS because sexual intercourse is for the married alone, and using a condom does not make it right in other situations."[9]

As the Symposium of Episcopal Conferences of Africa and Madagascar (SECAM), the continent-wide body of bishops, declared: "This type of education can only be undertaken effectively with the active collaboration of lay men and women who not only speak about principles of morality but also, as youth and as couples, give living testimony that fidelity to these moral principles yields a humanising and fulfilling affective and sexual life."[10] It is worth noting that the scope and impact of such injunctions can

[8] Ibid, 28.

[9] Ibid.

[10] Symposium of Episcopal Conferences of Africa and Madagascar, "The Church in Africa in the Face of the HIV/AIDS Pandemic: Our Prayer Is Always Full of Hope," in *AIDS and the Church in Africa: To Shepherd the Church, Family of God in Africa, in the Age of AIDS*, ed. Michael Czerny (Nairobi, Kenya: Paulines Publications Africa, 2005), 85.

be extensive in a context where Catholic health services in Africa account for up to 60 percent of accessible healthcare provision on the continent.[11] This context is characterized by another equally significant factor: the reality of HIV/AIDS consists of an elevated, double-sided gender quotient, precisely because "the situation in Africa has shown definitively that AIDS flourishes most demonstrably in a society where women are particularly vulnerable"[12] and the quality of response is determined by the situation where "thousands of caregivers—almost all of them women!—are caring for thousands of patients."[13]

Third, as mentioned above, the ethical contention has turned on the neuralgic issue of the use of condoms, considered by the majority of the hierarchy as "seriously immoral in itself"[14]; "condoms may even be one of the main reasons for the spread of HIV/AIDS."[15] Yet, there are dissenting and contradicting voices among ecclesiastical hierarchies that invalidate the presumed uniformity of a "Catholic" teaching on the morality of HIV/AIDS prevention. In the case of the bishops of Southern Africa (South Africa, Botswana, and Lesotho), such divergence has been evident for a very long time: "The [Southern Africa Catholic Bishops' Conference] concedes that in the case where a husband and wife have different HIV-status, it is acceptable for them to use a condom as a barrier to prevent the infection of the HIV-negative spouse."[16] In the absence of adequate nuancing of the message of the church, official pronouncements have, at best, simplified a very complex situation and, at worst, generated confusion. Here, the view of veteran South African HIV/AIDS expert Alison Munro, is instructive: "People at grassroots often did not have the tools to deal with the conflicting messages. It sometimes felt as though work around prevention was

---

[11] Sr. Dr. Raphaela Händler, "Advocacy for Care Access to Treatment," in Czerny, *AIDS and the Church in Africa*, 23; see also the impressive inventory of health facilities and programs run by the Catholic Church in Kenya for HIV/AIDS in Kenya Episcopal Conference, *This We Teach and Do: Catholic Church and AIDS in Kenya*, vol. 2, *Inventory* (Nairobi, Kenya: Paulines Publications Africa, 2006), 51.

[12] Anton A. van Niekerk, "Moral and Social Complexities of AIDS in Africa," in *Ethics and AIDS in Africa: The Challenge to Our Thinking*, ed. Anton A. Van Niekerk and Loretta M. Kopelman (Walnut Creek, CA: Left Coast Press, n.d.), 62.

[13] Händler, "Advocacy for Care Access to Treatment," 21.

[14] Episcopal Conference of Madagascar, in *Catholic Bishops of Africa and Madagascar Speak Out on HIV and AIDS*, 69. Archbishop Peter K. Sarpong of Kumasi, Ghana, describes the condom as "a licence to sin" ("Cultural Practices Influencing the Spread of HIV/AIDS," in Czerny, *AIDS and the Church in Africa*, 46).

[15] "A Message of Hope: From the Catholic Bishops to the People of God in South Africa, Botswana and Swaziland: St. Peter's Seminary, Pretoria, South Africa, 30 July 2001," available online.

[16] Peter Knox, *AIDS, Ancestors, and Salvation* (Nairobi, Kenya: Paulines Publications Africa, 2008), 215.

an Achilles' heel of the Church's response at a time when so much good was being done in the area of home-based care, and later in the field of treatment."[17] In many respects such conflicting messages unduly create anxiety for frontline ministers of care and people infected and affected by HIV/AIDS when it comes to forming and liberating consciences for moral choice and action in real-life situations.

"This We Do": Complexity of Conscience Formation

Although official rhetoric on well-formed conscience rings with familiar certainty and clarity, it has become evident that on this matter the AIDS pandemic has generated a moral complexity that strains traditional categories. I use the term *complexity* deliberately to mean "a kind of problem that not only has no clear-cut or self-evident answer but is also often thus constituted that an analytical approach wherein we distinguish parts and whole, often with the expectation that addressing the parts will fix the whole, is not always successful either."[18] By implication, therefore, the mono-causal approach adopted by some in the Catholic hierarchy falls short of offering an adequate solution to the moral complexity engendered by HIV/AIDS. Listening to the voices, strategies, and practices of frontline ministers of care and practitioners of compassion expands the discourse on the meaning of conscience formation, autonomy, freedom, and human dignity. I devote the rest of this essay to the discussion of aspects of this complexity in the understanding of conscience and conscience formation.

In the discourse on the application of precepts on conscience in concrete situations, two considerations seem important in order to delineate the focus of the conversation. The first is the need to avoid treating conscience in relation to HIV/AIDS in an exclusively analytical or disincarnate manner. The disease constitutes a violent invasion of the privacy and intimacy of human (sexual) relationship.[19] And, second, considering that responses so far have reinforced a perceived ecclesiastical obsession with sex and sexuality and with controlling it, the concomitant discourse, if poorly conducted, could inflict a greater violence on human dignity in the name of conscience formation. It is worth reiterating that conscience is primarily about people—how they relate and love, believe and act, and live and die.

---

[17] Alison Munro, "Response of the Catholic Church to AIDS: An SACBC AIDS Office Perspective," in *Catholic Responses to AIDS in Southern Africa,* ed. Stuart Bate and Alison Munro (Pretoria: Southern Africa Catholic Bishops' Conference in collaboration with Grace and Truth St. Joseph's Theological Institute, 2014), 31.

[18] Van Niekerk, "Moral and Social Complexities of AIDS in Africa," 55.

[19] See Händler, "Advocacy for Care Access to Treatment," 64–66.

This discussion does not focus on the primacy of conscience in moral decision making, but rather on the agents and ministers who assist in conscience formation and the conditions and circumstances that shape the milieu in which they exercise their life-affirming ministry.[20] While the former is an established touchstone of ethics, the latter is the locus of claims and contestations involving a variety of actors: the magisterium,[21] "the counsellors, the catechists, the nurses and doctors and social workers, the teachers, the preachers, the confessors who guide God's people, inform them, assist and support them and, most importantly, help each form his/her own conscience."[22] This contestation reveals a deep tension identified by Carol Bayley, quoting Brian Patrick Green: while all concede the necessity to follow one's conscience, there is an equally strong expectation that a rightly formed conscience will necessarily conform to the teaching of the church.[23] Oftentimes, orthodoxy is measured by the degree to which such conformity is enforced or demonstrated. Herein lies the core of the issue.

On this question of formation of conscience, the approach of ministers of care and practitioners of compassion offers a powerful narrative that evokes the delicate balance between what is prescribed and what is practiced. Aware of the many precepts and injunctions regarding what is and is not ethically permissible, they opt for an approach that takes into account the context, circumstances, and situations of the sick, vulnerable, and marginalized people living with HIV/AIDS. Their role rarely consists exclusively in providing leaflets or repeating slogans. On the basis of my observations in Eastern Africa, in apparent contradiction to received precepts, frontline ministers of care and practitioners of compassion—like the three nuns in Masaka, Mwanza, and Korogocho—advise on the use of condoms for the sake of protection of life as a key component of education and conscience formation. As Bishop Kevin Dowling puts it, "We do not distribute condoms. We give people the information they need to make an informed decision in conscience about what they are going to do with their lives."[24]

---

[20] See Robert J. Vitillo, "Ethical Issues Related to Preventing the Further Spread of HIV: Teachings and Actions of the Catholic Church," in *AIDS Thirty Years Down the Line: Faith-Based Reflections about the Epidemic in Africa,* ed. Paterne A. Mombé, Agbonkhianmeghe E. Orobator, and Danielle Vella (Nairobi, Kenya: Paulines Publications Africa, 2012), 353–54.

[21] James Keenan, *A History of Catholic Moral Theology in the Twentieth Century: From Confessing Sins to Liberation Consciences* (London: Continuum, 2010), 120.

[22] Kenya Episcopal Conference, *This We Teach and Do*, 2:30.

[23] Brian Patrick Green, "Catholicism and Conscience," Santa Clara University, Markkula Center for Applied Ethics (May 2013), http://www.scu.edu.

[24] Quoted in Charles Ryan, "Condoms and Conscience in the Context of HIV and AIDS Pandemic," in Bate and Munro, *Catholic Responses to AIDS in Southern Africa*, 251.

What shapes the content and influences the process of education and formation relates more to the lived experience and contexts of those infected and affected by HIV/AIDS than to codified precepts of sexual morality.

Dowling, who has considerable experience on this matter from his several years of direct contact with and ministry to vulnerable mine workers in his diocese of Rustenburg, South Africa, describes one such socioeconomic context and situation of women trapped in a dehumanizing spiral of poverty, survival sex, HIV/AIDS, and death:

> The woman was dying not because she had had any choice about being infected with HIV; she had been subjected to unspeakable brutality and injustice. She, like hundreds of thousands of rural women in South Africa and countries north of South Africa, had been forced to leave her rural home because of extreme poverty, no work, and nothing on which to survive. She had ended up in this shack settlement next to a mine in the vain hope she could somehow find a job and survive. She found quickly she was in an even worse poverty trap. There were no jobs for anyone like her. Her only way to survive for even just a day was to sell herself for sex with men who had money, the miners, who themselves had left their homes and wives far away for employment at the mine.
>
> I quickly termed her only possibility of putting some bread on the table as "survival sex." She would get paid for sex—all she had—to come up with enough for twenty-four hours, and then she would have to do that again and again and again. What utter, despicable, systemic injustice and degradation. The inevitable results were HIV infection, TB, pneumonia, cancer, other infections, pregnancy, birth of an HIV-positive baby—utter misery, and finally death.[25]

"In the face of such horror," Dowling queries, "what does it mean to be pro-life? . . . Is the teaching of the magisterium sufficient for me to respond to that situation, or does it perhaps appear to be irrelevant to that situation in terms of being a message of hope to the suffering and poor of our continent?"[26] This emphasis on conditions, situations, and circumstances of people living with AIDS almost invariably challenges a moral reductionism that would confine conscience formation to a vacuous exercise in

---

[25] Kevin Dowling, "Bishops as Theologians: Listening, Discerning, and Dialogue," in *Theological Reimagination: Conversations on Church, Religion, and Society in Africa,* ed. Agbonkhianmeghe E. Orobator (Nairobi, Kenya: Paulines Publications Africa, 2014), 143–44; see also Ryan, "Condoms and Conscience in the Context of HIV and AIDS Pandemic," 259–60.

[26] Dowling, "Bishops as Theologians," 144.

prescriptive legalism in advance or in lieu of serious attention to or consideration for contextual realities. It refocuses attention away from concerns about upholding injunctions and precepts toward the lived experience, contexts, and needs of people relegated to the margins of societal concerns. This understanding confirms the insight that James Keenan stresses in his essay in this volume: conscience formation is first about living, that is, becoming and living as better people.

More important, perhaps, Dowling's experience draws attention to another aspect of conscience formation that is often neglected, namely, the criterion of justice. Oftentimes, precepts seem to emerge from thin air, repeated with dogmatic certitude and hovering above the chaotic circumstances of human life. Dowling best illustrates the critical dimension of justice in the debate regarding conscience formation in the age of HIV/AIDS. Ultimately, conscience—as noted above in *Gaudium et Spes*—is about being fully human, albeit a broken humanity mired in suffering. HIV/AIDS represents a particular form of suffering and its concomitant consequences of marginalization, exclusion, stigmatization, and ostracism. Thus, when it comes to applying precepts on the formation of conscience, as Maria Cimperman points out, "the starting point for any discussion of AIDS must be the experience and reality of suffering. If theological anthropology explores the meaning of human existence, it must encounter the reality, the voices, and the faces of human suffering. . . . Such suffering exists in the midst of and stems from experiences of poverty, violence, repression, and oppression."[27] Dowling makes the same point and alerts us to the capability of the voices and faces of human suffering to refocus the lens through which we perceive the body of precepts that regulates the task of conscience formation and the attendant humility that must characterize any attempt to police this "aboriginal Vicar of Christ," as John Henry Cardinal Newman famously described it.

As Linda Hogan's case study titled "An Irish Nun Living with Contradiction" demonstrates, frontline ministers of care and practitioners of compassion routinely face accusations of disobedience and indifference "to church teaching on HIV/AIDS prevention."[28] Yet, judging by my encounter with the three nuns in Masaka, Mwanza, and Korogocho, a significant dimension of what they "teach" and "do"—to allude to the title of the Kenya Episcopal Conference's booklets of policy and inventory on church response to HIV/AIDS—regarding conscience and formation of conscience demonstrates that conscience is not an isolated reality or "a free-floating and independent ethical sense."[29] Nor is it an empty receptacle waiting to

[27] Maria Cimperman, *When God's People Have HIV/AIDS: An Approach to Ethics* (Maryknoll, NY: Orbis Books, 2005), 21.

[28] Linda Hogan, "An Irish Nun Living with Contradiction," in *Catholic Ethicists on HIV/AIDS Prevention*, ed. James F. Keenan (New York: Continuum, 2000), 43.

[29] Ibid., 44.

be filled with previously constructed teachings and doctrines. In the view advanced here, conscience formation constitutes an active, ongoing process that pays attention to circumstances, contexts, and intentions as vital determinants of morality. Sensitivity to context is a central ingredient to conscience formation, to which the rigidity of a moral monomania stands as an antithesis. This approach of sensitivity to context has played a key role in the response to HIV/AIDS by ministers of care and practitioners of compassion and enabled them to navigate the contours of precepts invoked and imposed authoritatively by a punctilious clergy and hierarchy.

Besides circumstances, contexts, and intentions, Bénézet Bujo introduces an African dimension into the discourse. "Conscience," he insists, "is a living creative *memoria*. This conscience has both a communitarian and an individual character."[30] Consequently, as Bujo further demonstrates, conscience formation is dialogical. Understood as such, two extremes are ruled out regarding the process of conscience formation. On the one hand, it avoids the dictatorship of a privatized ethics: "The African view has no place for a more or less 'dictatorial' conscience that could appeal (in the manner of situation ethics) to an inner illumination or place its trust exclusively in its own insight."[31] Nor, on the other hand, is conscience enslaved to the monopoly of an external, exclusively constituted authority, whether hierarchical or magisterial. Thus African ethics, as Bujo understands it, offers a middle ground that allows us to appreciate the moral responsibility involved in processes such as conscience formation as a shared task. In this dialogical process several factors come into play: lived experience of the individual, communal memory, anthropological constitution of the community (ancestral community), the goal of preserving and increasing the life of the community, and the common good of the community.[32]

Like Dowling, Bujo's approach reinforces an important point relative to conscience: the need to resist the temptation of an exclusivist appeal to law and precepts. It is important to pay attention to other criteria, for example, life understood more widely as a moral good and the attendant responsibility to protect and enhance its quality. Furthermore, as Osamu Takeuchi, S.J., demonstrates in his essay in this volume, forming or liberating consciences is a dialogical process and a spiritual experience that carries a high social or communal premium. This approach yields an understanding of the discourse on conscience as a process embedded in context *and* embodied in real lives—it is about people!

---

30 Bénézet Bujo, *Foundations of an African Ethic: Beyond the Universal Claims of Western Morality* (Nairobi, Kenya: Paulines Publications Africa, 2003), 141.

31 Ibid., 156.

32 Ibid., 155–61.

As evident in the foregoing analysis, the question of ecclesiology looms large. Although the church has an important teaching function in regard to the formation of conscience, it matters how we define church. A closer look at the debate reveals a preponderant emphasis on "church teaching" derived from a particular theological understanding or model of church that prioritizes the role of the institution. This approach draws on a clericalist and juridical tradition and prefers clarity, submission to, and authoritativeness of dogma over the questions, complexity, and uncertainty that the situation of HIV/AIDS may generate for Catholic discourse. While the former may successfully delineate the official boundaries of moral discourse, it risks overlooking, even compromising, the dignity of people in specific contexts (of HIV/AIDS) and seems in tension with a capability approach that pays attention to conditions, contexts, and circumstances.

Judging by my observation in Eastern Africa, for millions of people infected and affected by AIDS, the face of the church comes into relief not in the moralizing magisterial pronouncements of representatives of the hierarchy, but concretely in the initiatives and ministries of women and men of compassion and care.[33] In this context this question arises: Who speaks for or constitutes the church? I take the position that what these women and men "do" contains an important "teaching" value in the particular context of suffering caused by a deadly disease. They are legitimate teachers, motivated in their task of conscience formation primarily by the ethics of care, mercy, and compassion, rather than by the dread of precepts, doctrines, and dogmas. Their praxis, according to Enda McDonagh, exemplifies "the priorities of the reign of God [that place] people before rules, the needs of the sick and the hungry before the concerns of the comfortable and powerful."[34] Thus, the subject of the declaration "This *We* Teach and Do" needs to be understood more inclusively than is normally the case in official pronouncements. In situations where ecclesiological focus continues to favor patriarchy, it is important to emphasize the role of women as constitutive of what *we* teach and what *we* do as the community called church.

Conclusion

The history of HIV/AIDS has witnessed a dramatic transformation in the twenty-first century. Recent reports not only celebrate a downward trend in

[33] Agbonkhianmeghe E. Orobator, *From Crisis to Kairos: The Mission of the Church in the Time of HIV/AIDS, Refugees, and Poverty* (Nairobi, Kenya: Paulines Publications Africa, 2005), 138, 224–27.

[34] Enda McDonagh, "The Reign of God: Signposts for Catholic Moral Theology," in Keenan, *Catholic Ethicists on HIV/AIDS Prevention*, 323.

the rates of HIV infection and AIDS-related deaths, but more significantly they forecast the end of the epidemic. Yet there are significant gaps, including the alarming fact that nineteen million of the thirty-five million people living with HIV/AIDS are ignorant of their sero-status. There also remains a long catalogue of vulnerable populations at risk—in the estimation of UNAIDS—of being left behind: people living with HIV, adolescent girls and young women, prisoners, migrants, people who inject drugs, sex workers, men who have sex with men, transgender people, children and pregnant women living with HIV, displaced persons, people with disabilities, and people aged fifty years and older.[35]

In this situation the ethics of prevention remain pertinent and urgent, as is the task of averting new infections and AIDS-related deaths. The language and understanding of conscience feature as pivotal dimensions of the concomitant ethical discourse. Evidence shows that it is easy to impose rigid boundaries on what constitutes conscience formation. Such boundaries may be skewed by ignorance, stereotypes, and moral hypocrisy, and may overlook the complexities and dilemmas faced by people infected and affected by the disease, the same complexities and dilemmas that frontline ministers of care and practitioners of compassion struggle to deal with while taking into account the multidimensional milieu of people. In addition, the strident or vitriolic rhetoric that oftentimes tarnishes the debate negates the constructive and civil nature and tone of an ethically creative and productive process capable of building the "discursive bridges across our differences" that Linda Hogan advocates in her essay in this volume. Considering the complex contexts of frontline ministers of care and practitioners of compassion, the reality of AIDS discloses factors that such discourse needs to take into account, in particular how institutional precepts articulated from lofty ecclesiastical positions are moderated in their intensity by challenges and complexities of real-life situations and lived experience.

Furthermore, if conscience is a matter of relationality between a human person and God, as *Gaudium et Spes* powerfully affirms, it is the task of the Christian community to stand as a respectful and faithful witness to this sacred act and space of divine-human encounter. More significant, in the final analysis, between exalted moral prescriptions that risk losing pace with reality and a multiplicity of factors conditioning their application to empirical context, I hold that conscience formation primarily designates an exercise in care-*full* accompaniment, compassionate listening, and humble learning.

---

[35] UNAIDS, *The Gap Report* (2014), http://www.unaids.org. Each group mentioned is the topic of a chapter in the report.

13.

Can an Organization Have a Conscience?

Contributions from Social Science to Catholic Social Thought

Daniel K. Finn

Introduction

Can an organization have a conscience? An organization is a particular kind of social structure, one that is planned, coordinated, and purposeful. Thus, we can answer this question only with a clear understanding of the character of social structures. And here we encounter a fundamental problem within Christian theology: the tendency to interpret the impact of social structures as undermining human freedom.

The issues are complex, but a helpful way into them is provided by the view of Cardinal Joseph Ratzinger in his 1984 analysis of liberation theology:

> Nor can one localize evil principally or uniquely in bad social, political, or economic "structures" as though all other evils came from them so that the creation of the "new man" would depend on the establishment of different economic and socio-political structures. To be sure, there are structures which are evil and which cause evil and which we must have the courage to change. Structures, whether they are good or bad, are the result of man's actions and so are consequences more than causes. The root of evil, then, lies in free and responsible persons who have to be converted by the grace of Jesus Christ in order to live

> and act as new creatures in the love of neighbor and in the effective search for justice, self-control, and the exercise of virtue.[1]

This view is quite typical of recent official Catholic teaching on the relation of human freedom and social structures. On the one hand, structures are taken seriously. They can be evil (and hence the talk of sinful social structures elsewhere in magisterial teaching), and they can cause evil. On the other hand, our tradition's theological commitment to human freedom leads Cardinal Ratzinger to emphasize the origins of structures in human action and to stress the importance of free choice in religious conversion. The claim that structures "are consequences more than causes" helps to focus attention on human agency and freedom.

But there are a number of fundamental problems here. First, *how* do structures cause evil? Is it through some inexorable third-party force that violates freedom, or might it not occur *through* the free decisions of persons who live within those social structures? Second, does this view take for granted that social structures are either economic or political? Would things be different if we also understood the parish, the family, and the Holy See as social structures? Third, does conversion typically happen outside social structures? What if we understood preaching, the sacrament of penance, and spiritual direction as occurring within and made possible by (beneficial) social structures? Finally, although the phrase is rhetorically effective, is not the description of structures as "consequences more than causes" impossible to define? Consider some real social structures, such as your parish, a university, Hitler's government, or the Tuesday-night bowling league. Is it helpful to describe these as consequences more than causes?

To understand social structures, Christian theology needs to turn to sociology, a discipline dedicated to understanding structure (the objective relations among persons). Of course, sociology has more than this to contribute to an understanding of organizations in its treatment of culture (ideas, objects, and other things with meaningful content). Unfortunately, the limits of space here require a focus on structure alone.

It is the argument of this essay that once we come to an adequate understanding of social structures, we will also understand two things about organizations. First, they can be characterized by a kind of collective agency, in that it is meaningful to speak of an organization *doing* something. Second, however, organizations do not have anything like a collective consciousness, and they act only in and through the actions of individual persons, most important, those in leadership positions. As a result, although they

[1] Joseph Ratzinger, "Instruction on Certain Aspects of the 'Theology of Liberation,'" IV, no. 15, Congregation for the Doctrine of the Faith, August 6, 1984.

have good and bad effects and can be helpfully described as having moral responsibilities, organizations do not and cannot have a conscience.

Options within Sociology

The first difficulty we face in looking to sociology for a theologically helpful conceptual framework is the diversity of perspectives we find there. The complexity of the options is daunting, and yet the insights of Christian theology help us in choosing an appropriate perspective. Most fundamental in this array of possibilities is the difference between collectivism and individualism, which are polar opposites in social theory that provide two radically different accounts of social ontology, that is, two divergent accounts of what society is understood to be. British sociologist Margaret Archer provides a helpful delineation of these two positions and articulates a critical-realist position superior to both.

The roots of collectivism stretch deep into the history of sociology, with Auguste Comte explaining that "society is no more decomposable into individuals than a geometric surface is into lines, or a line into points."[2] Social forces are seen as so powerful in shaping human behavior that it is naive to attempt to explain that behavior by means of the choices of individuals. Social theories, from this perspective, must be holistic to be adequate, and, as Archer puts it, "individuals are held to be 'indeterminate material' which is unilaterally molded by society, whose holistic properties have complete monopoly over causation."[3] Put in simpler terms, human persons are little more than pawns pushed around on the chessboard of life by social forces. This denial of agency to persons—a rejection of human freedom—renders collectivism an unacceptable position from the point of view of Christian theology.

The polar opposite perspective is individualism. Here too there is a diversity, but the fundamental claim is well summarized by Max Weber, for whom collectivities—whether business firms, families, or government—"must be treated solely as the resultants and modes of organization of the particular acts of individual persons."[4] From this perspective only persons have causal power, and society is reducible to the interaction of those persons. In an extreme form of individualism Friedrich Hayek holds that

---

[2] Auguste Comte, *Systeme de politique positive* (Paris: L. Mathias, 1951), 2:181, cited in Margaret Archer, *Realist Social Theory: The Morphogenetic Approach* (Cambridge: Cambridge University Press, 1995), 3.

[3] Archer, *Realist Social Theory*, 3.

[4] Max Weber, *The Theory of Social and Economic Organization* (New York: Free Press, 1964 [1922]), 102.

"wholes as such . . . are without exception constructions of our mind."[5] Thus, for Hayek, *society, economy, war,* and more are no more than shorthand summaries of the actions and interactions of the individuals involved.

Individualism leaves ample room for an understanding of the freedom of the person, but it greatly overstates that freedom. It eclipses the many ways in which human freedom is conditioned and/or influenced not simply by the actions of other persons but also by the causal impact of social structures within which individuals live out their daily lives.

One simple example of this phenomenon occurs during an election. Once the results are in, we often hear that "the people have spoken." Yet we also know that political parties at the state level exert great effort in trying to redraw the boundaries of election districts favorably, a process called gerrymandering. The party in control attempts to create a few districts where citizens belonging to the opposing party make up a very large majority of the voters and then create more districts where members of their own party make up a small majority of those voting.

In the 2012 Congressional elections, for example, Democratic candidates for the House of Representatives received one million more votes nationwide than did Republican candidates. Yet because of gerrymandering, Republicans ended up with a thirty-five-seat advantage in the House. The point here is not to criticize Republicans, since gerrymandering has a long history among Democrats as well. In fact, because gerrymandering provides politically "safe" districts to some Democrats in the House, many of them are quite happy about it.[6] The point here is to recognize that any attempt to interpret the outcome of elections as simply the results of voters' choices on Election Day exhibits a deep misunderstanding of causality in social life.

Critical realist sociology provides a more accurate account of the relation of agency and structure than does either collectivism or individualism. From this perspective only persons are *agents* (defining this word technically within sociology, as what theologians would call moral agents, since the word in more general parlance can refer even to inert objects, as when one talks about a "chemical agent"). Although they are not formally agents, social structures have independent causal impact on the lives of human

---

[5] Friedrich Hayek, "Scientism and the Study of Society," Part II, *Economica* (February 1943): 43.

[6] For example, Corrine Brown represents Florida's heavily Democratic Fifth Congressional District, one gerrymandered to snake from Jacksonville to Gainesville to Orlando, at points being no wider than a highway. When a Florida judge in 2014 required the legislature to redraw this district because its boundaries were so obviously politically motivated, Brown sided with the Republican legislature in criticizing the ruling. Christopher Ingraham, "A Florida Judge Just Voided the State's Congressional Districts: Here's What You Need to Know," *Washington Post,* July 11, 2014.

agents, even though those structures emerge from and are sustained by the actions of individual agents. To understand this adequately, we need first to examine briefly *emergence* itself as a fundamental process within both the natural and the social world.

What Is Emergence?

Sociologist Christian Smith defines *emergence* as "the process of constituting a new entity with its own particular characteristics through the interactive combination of other, different entities that are necessary to create the new entity but that do not contain the characteristics present in the new entity."[7] The simplest example of emergence is water, which emerges from hydrogen and oxygen but has characteristics different from both. Water will put out a fire, while hydrogen and oxygen will feed it. Similarly, protons and neutrons within the atom emerge from the interaction of up quarks and down quarks. Human consciousness emerges from the electrochemical processes of the brain, and most relevant for this essay, social structures emerge from the interactions of individual persons. In all these cases the new "higher level" thing that emerges has characteristics that would not have been predicted by a simple examination of the "lower level" elements that interact to produce it.

As a result, reductionism must be rejected as a scientific strategy to explain emergent phenomena, since the essence of reductionism is the claim that one can explain a more complex phenomenon by reducing it to the various individual elements from which it emerged. Few people would attempt to explain water or neutrons this way, but sociobiologists regularly attempt to explain human consciousness and morality by means of the characteristics of genes. More relevant to our topic, individualists think they can adequately explain social causality by tracing it to the decisions of individual agents.

The notions of "lower" and "higher" levels should not be misunderstood to mean morally superior or causally more important. Rather, they point to a view of reality as stratified.[8] As with the reductionist view of the world, critical realists understand the fundamental dependence of psychological reality on the biological, and of the biological on the chemical, and of the chemical on the physical, just as there is a stratified hierarchy of the disciplines of psychology, biology, chemistry, and physics within the academy.

[7] Christian Smith, *What Is a Person? Rethinking Humanity, Social Life, and the Moral Good from the Person Up* (Chicago: University of Chicago Press, 2010), 25–26. For a more complete account of emergence than space allows here, see ibid., 25–46.

[8] Roy Bhaskar, *A Realist Theory of Science* (London: Verso, 1975).

But unlike the reductionist view, critical realists understand that there is true novelty at each higher level that cannot be explained simply by reduction to a lower level and that in many cases that higher-level novelty can act back upon the lower-level elements. Most relevant for the focus of this essay is the fact that social structures emerge from the actions of individuals but exist at a higher level than individuals and act back upon them, requiring a careful analysis of the interaction between the two strata.

What Are Social Structures and How Do They Influence Human Action?

What is a social structure? Here too there are options within sociology among which those of us outside of the discipline have to choose.

Douglas Porpora delineates four distinct concepts of social structure to be found within contemporary sociological analysis.[9] First, some sociologists see social structures as patterns of aggregate behavior, a view that tends strongly toward the individualism described above. Second, others understand structures as "lawlike regularities that govern the behavior of social facts," exhibiting a more holistic, even collectivistic view of social life.[10] Third, still others understand structure as a set of rules according to which individuals act, again tending toward a more individualistic perspective. And fourth, the critical-realist view, which Porpora himself defends, understands social structures as "systems of human relationships among social positions."[11] Structures do not have intentionality, only persons do, but those persons enter into preexisting social positions—as an employee, a member of a committee, a patron at a restaurant—each of which is already in relation to other social positions (such as the boss, the committee chair, the waitress). And in each case such a system of relations among positions *is* a social structure. Structures have causal impact in the lives of the agents who have taken on positions within them by presenting those persons with restrictions, enablements, and incentives that condition the agent's choices. Unlike collectivism, there is no determinism here. Individuals are free to ignore those restrictions, enablements, and incentives, though they will typically be worse off for doing so. This insight into how social structures shape human choices resonates with the insights of liberation theology and the arguments of Lisa Fullam and Bryan Massingale elsewhere in this

---

[9] Douglas V. Porpora, "Four Concepts of Social Structure," *Journal for the Theory of Social Behavior* 19/2 (June 1989): 195–212.

[10] Ibid., 195.

[11] Ibid.

volume about how power relationships frequently allow the powerful to exploit the marginalized.

This is the critical-realist view of social structures. This perspective can be employed to understand how hospitals or churches operate, and it is potentially helpful for the essays by Carol Bayley and Archbishop John Quinn in this volume. But let us begin with a more widely accessible example, a retail business.

Consider the situation of a new employee, "Susan," hired as a clerk in housewares at Macy's. The key insight of critical realism here is that she is entering into a preexisting position of a sales associate that is already in relation to other positions, such as customer, co-worker, and boss. Susan experiences an array of restrictions, enablements, and incentives that already characterized those relations long before she was hired.

Among the restrictions she faces are many built into her relation to her boss that are typical of any job, such as the scheduled hours for work and the training necessary at the time of hire. But some restrictions may be tied to the particular culture at Macy's, such as the requirement to dress somewhat elegantly and to embody a thoroughgoing patience, even with an unreasonable customer. These last two restrictions are also present in the relation of clerk to customer, since Macy's customers expect this and some of them might actually walk away if Susan were poorly dressed or impatient in providing service. She will also face a number of enablements, such as a pleasant place to work and an employee discount on quality merchandise.

These restrictions and enablements are then perceived psychologically by Susan as incentives—for example, the incentive to improve the quality of her work wardrobe, to become more effective in leading customers to make a purchase, and to improve her patience to a degree she might never agree to elsewhere in her life. Another set of restrictions, enablements, and incentives characterize the relations between Susan and her co-workers at Macy's, and yet another in her relationship to her supervisor.

Similarly, when "John" walks into Macy's to buy something in housewares, he takes on the social position of customer in relation to Susan. Among the restrictions John faces in that position is that there is no opportunity to negotiate over the price at Macy's, even though that is possible in some other commercial settings. And he faces enablements, such as the variety of options available and Macy's generous returns policy, which create a further incentive for shopping there.

In all these cases the causal impact of social structures consists in how they restrict and enable the choices made by the persons who make decisions within them. There is no determinism here, as Susan could choose to criticize a customer's attitude or refuse to take advantage of her employee discount on clothing or decide to wear jeans to work. Yet such choices are unlikely because Susan will be worse off, perhaps even losing her job, for doing so. This, of course, is why social structures tend to be stable and resist change: there is a price to be paid for not "going along."

The price one might pay from acting out of conscience in spite of structured restrictions is at the center of the moral quandary James Keenan, S.J., cites at the end of his chapter in this volume: an untenured faculty member is invited to appear on a student-organized panel on a controversial topic where that faculty member would be making public statements contrary to official university policy. The analysis of social structures doesn't resolve such problems, but it does render them more tractable by identifying the causal impact of structure through the choices that persons within them make.

Thus, in critical-realist sociology the relation among social positions is the essence of a social structure. This relation is understood to be ontologically real, a *thing* in the world susceptible of scientific analysis.[12]

Critical Realism and Catholic Social Thought

We can now observe more precisely the shortcomings of Cardinal Ratzinger's conception of the relation of social structures and personal freedom. First, while he rightly rejects collectivism in his defense of human freedom and rejects individualism in his ascribing of causal efficacy to social structures, he provides no account of *how* those social structures have causal impact and thus unfortunately resorts to an overly individualistic description of human freedom. Critical realism can improve on this. Social structures have causal impact but never in a deterministic way. Their impact comes only *through* human freedom, only through the choices of agents who experience the restrictions, enablements, and incentives generated by those structures.

---

[12] Here we glimpse an aspect of critical-realist sociology that has its pedigree in critical-realist philosophy of science, as articulated by British philosopher Roy Bhaskar. For Bhaskar, empiricists have been wrong for over two centuries in insisting that the only reliable form of knowledge is that which is sense perceptible. As Bhaskar explains, it was not the law of gravity that caused Newton's apple to fall from the tree to the ground; such a "law" is only a human attempt to summarize how things operate in the world. The cause of the apple's fall was the relation between the apple and the earth. Even though that relation cannot be directly perceived by our senses, it is ontologically real and causally effective. The same holds true for the relation among social positions—the constituents of a social structure. Our five senses don't perceive them, but they are ontologically real, causally effective, and susceptible of scientific study (Bhaskar, *A Realist Theory of Science*).

Second, human freedom is almost always exercised within social structures. If I drive up into the mountains for a hike, I might think of this as time away from the restrictions of everyday life. Yet national parks and forests have rules about how and when I may start a fire, and the very act of hiking arises out of enablements I enjoy as a citizen and as an employee with sufficient resources and free time to take to the mountains.

Thus, the best chance that those "free and responsible persons who have to be converted by the grace of Jesus Christ" will undergo that conversion will occur *within* social structures, as those persons take up the social position of a congregant listening to the word being preached, of a student taking a theology class, of a penitent entering the confessional. Conversion typically occurs in the midst of the restrictions, enablements, and incentives experienced in those preexisting social positions. Economic, social, or political structures are not the only structures Christian theology must account for, although those larger structures are immensely influential, even in matters of personal religious life. As Clement of Alexandria argued eighteen centuries ago, "When a man lacks the necessities of life he cannot possibly fail to be broken in spirit and to neglect the higher things."[13]

Third, and most generally, Cardinal Ratzinger, reflective of most of Catholic theology, did not recognize the stratified nature of reality. More complex "things" emerge out of the interactions of lower-level elements, have characteristics different from those lower-level elements, and in many cases act back upon those lower-level elements. Emergent realities such as social structures are ontologically real things in the world, even if many in our individualistic contemporary culture fail to recognize them as such. Resonating with the insights of liberation theology articulated by Bryan Massingale and Lisa Fullam in this volume, from the perspective of critical realism, a person in a social relation of exploitation is exploited objectively, whether or not that person recognizes the abuse.

How Do Social Structures Change?

The point of those who might think that organizations can have a conscience is that such a conscience can be influential in improving from a moral point of view the behavior of the organization. Yet before making a moral judgment about structural change, we need to look more directly at

---

[13] Clement of Alexandria, "The Rich Man's Salvation," 12–13, *Patrologia Graeca*, 9:616–17, cited in Charles Avila, *Ownership: Early Christian Teaching* (Maryknoll, NY: Orbis Books, 1983), 43.

how social structures do change. This brings us to what Archer has called "the historicity of emergence" of social structures.[14]

As individual persons we encounter social structures—whether the organization we work for, the parish we attend, or the family we were born into—as existing prior to our own participation in them. Yet we also recognize that every social structure has emerged from the interaction of agents, whether the founders of the organization we work for, the charter members of our parish, or our parents. Two things are critically important to recognize in this process of emergence.

The first is that any structure that emerges is not what anyone involved had intended. Agents have differing goals, so the actual outcome will not satisfy anyone completely. And the process of emergence always entails a degree of unpredictability, with no one anticipating everything that eventually occurs. The second characteristic of the emergence of a social structure is that even those "initial" actions to start a new organization occur within the restrictions, enablements, and incentives generated by preexisting social structures. Anyone starting a business firm, a university, a parish, or a family does so as someone already holding a variety of social positions that are in relation to other social positions, and those prior relations among positions generated restrictions, enablements, and incentives that have a causal impact on the choices made.[15] It is literally impossible to go back in history to a time when a social structure emerged from a situation where no social structures had existed before.

Thus, contrary to the impression created by Cardinal Ratzinger's claim that structures are more consequences than causes, individual activity always precedes social structure *and* social structure always precedes individual activity. This is the historicity of emergence of social structures. As a result, when we consider what individual persons do to change a social structure, we must recognize that "agential power is always restricted to remaking, whether this be reproducing or transforming our social inheritance."[16]

As noted above, the fact that agents will pay a price if they resist restrictions or forgo enablements means that most decisions within a social structure tend to sustain it as it is. This tendency toward reproduction of existing structure can be good or bad, depending, of course, on the moral quality of the structure's effects. A highly innovative technology firm faces the very real risk of bureaucratization as it grows. Firms like Google expend great effort to see that the restrictions, opportunities, and

[14] Archer, *Realist Social Theory*, 66.

[15] Ibid., 73.

[16] Ibid., 72.

incentives its employees face will encourage greater creativity and initiative, maintaining the advantages of a small startup to the extent possible. In this way structures can enhance the agency of the participants within them (as universities try to do in requiring faculty members to give grades to students). Of course, structures can also be designed to subvert that agency, as occurs in a police state.

But what might lead to change of a social structure? Most frequently, structural change arises out of a conflict between the interests of persons enjoying many enablements within a structure and the interests of others facing many restrictions. The hazardous factories of the nineteenth century became safer only after workers and their unions pressed national governments for safety standards. Concert orchestras only began hiring women on a par with men after women insisted that auditions should occur with a screen that prevents the search committee from seeing the candidate.[17] In both factories and orchestras an increase in the restrictions faced by those in authority expanded the enablements of an unjustly treated group.

Still, it is quite possible that the interests that agents act on in pressing for structural change may include altruistic ones. Consider the case of Nike, the American manufacturer of athletic footwear and apparel. Because of its importance in producing college-branded sweatshirts, Nike was one of the first targets of the anti-sweatshop student movement in the 1980s and 1990s. Nike suffered public-relations embarrassments and protests at its annual stockholders' meetings until one of the members of its board of directors, Jill Ker Conway, former president of Smith College, volunteered to visit some of the many independently owned factories in Asia that produced Nike's products. As a widely known feminist with a book on the *New York Times* best-seller list, Conway was committed to the well-being of young women.

Interviewing many women workers as well as the men who ran the factories, she reported on various problems with factory procedures as well as on the impact of local culture and structure, where, for example, many fathers would stand outside the factory gates on payday and confiscate the earnings of the young women as they left. As Conway puts it, "I thought there were a number of ways in which the factories could be improved, just through changes in the relationship between workers and management."[18] She proposed, and Nike CEO Phil Knight and the board agreed to create,

[17] Claudia Goldin and Cecilia Rouse, "Orchestrating Impartiality: The Impact of 'Blind' Auditions on Female Musicians," National Bureau of Economic Research (NBER) Working Paper No. 5903, January 1997.

[18] Lynn S. Paine, "A Conversation with Jill Ker Conway," *Harvard Business Review* (July-August 2014).

a board-level committee on corporate responsibility, one that Knight committed himself to join.

With such leadership Nike management insisted on changes in the relationship between managers and workers at the Asian factories, creating a variety of new restrictions and enablements to do so. Plant managers got better training, and ATMs were installed inside the factories so that the women workers could deposit their wages directly into their own bank account before meeting their fathers at the factory gates.[19] At the urging of the committee, Nike has also taken the lead in the development of sustainable and healthy manufacturing processes, such as glues used in shoe manufacture that do not give off toxic fumes. In Conway's twenty-five years on the Nike board the firm turned its public image as a greedy firm, making profits out of sweatshops, into that of a poster child for responsible corporate behavior.

Thus, if we ask what it is that makes it easier for an organization to be good, we should note that social structures change due to a variety of causes. At times they change due to explicit pressure from the dissatisfied, whether external or internal constituencies. Such pressure works best when it artfully alters the set of restrictions, enablements, and incentives faced by those most responsible for the maintenance of the structure.

At other times structures change due to the internal values and priorities of those in positions of leadership. Nike provides one example. The act of the Catholic bishops of Southern Africa to approve of the use of condoms in some situations, reported in this volume by Agbonkhianmeghe Orobator, S.J., is an example of a decision made in the face of church restrictions facing any bishop who might stray from the universal condemnations of condoms by Vatican authorities.

Often, of course, both sorts of forces are at work. Realistic people interested in changing social structures often rely on both pressure and persuasion. Thus, we might assume that if change is to come to the anticonversion laws in India or to the reproductive health laws in the Philippines, described by Eugine Rodrigues, B.S., and Eric Marcelo O. Genilo, S.J., in this volume, a combination of public pressure and rational argument among legislators will likely be the cause.

Organizations with a Conscience?

The *Catechism of the Catholic Church* defines conscience as "a judgment of reason whereby the human person recognizes the moral quality

[19] The author's oral interview with Jill Ker Conway, July 12, 2014.

of a concrete act."[20] Servais Pinckaers, O.P., tells us that when Thomas Aquinas spoke of "the discernment of the moral quality of human acts" he attributed this to "practical reason perfected by the virtue of prudence."[21] In post-Tridentine moral theology, he explains, conscience came to be seen as "the representative of the moral law in the human subject,"[22] reducing the importance of practical reason, but conscience remained a faculty of the human person. And in *Veritatis Splendor*, Pope John Paul II addresses "the precise nature of conscience: it is a moral judgment about man and his actions" (no. 59). In all these accounts conscience requires subjectivity, which an organization lacks, and a capacity for judgment.

Does an organization have the capacity to make judgments? In a hierarchical, "top down" organization those in charge make all decisions, with little or no consultation with others. In such a situation to say the organization made a judgment means nothing more than that the organization's leaders did so. At the other extreme would be a small and perfectly democratic organization, in which all members assemble to debate and decide things, whether by vote or consensus. Here, clearly, the organization is making a judgment. Still, this sort of collective capacity for making a judgment falls short of what seems to be required for a conscience, an integrated consciousness. More work needs to be done on how to parse these distinctions, and as noted earlier, a more complete inquiry would have to take into consideration not simply structure but culture as well.

In critical realism, organizations can be spoken of as wholes, as social structures with a mission. And recognizing that the word *agent* has multiple meanings outside the technical sense employed above (where persons are agents but social structures are not), many critical-realist sociologists talk of the "collective agency" of organizations, whether Macy's or Nike or nation-states. In an important sense, organizations "do" things and thus bear moral responsibilities.[23]

Although organizations have collective agency, they lack any collective consciousness. They are immensely influential through the restrictions, enablements, and incentives that characterize the social relations among positions within them, but they act only through the actions of the individuals within them, whether that is Macy's selling a set of sheets through Susan's actions or Nike's investing in the research of non-toxic glues through the decisions of its board of directors and CEO. Thus,

---

[20] *Catechism of the Catholic Church*, "Moral Conscience" (Collegeville, MN: Liturgical Press, 1994), 1778.

[21] Servais Pinckaers, O.P., *The Pinckaers Reader: Renewing Thomistic Moral Theology* (Washington, DC: Catholic University of America, 2005), 330.

[22] Ibid., 336.

[23] This insight is emphasized by Pope Benedict XVI in *Caritas in Veritate*, no. 34.

while organizations can be quite powerful social structures, they cannot have a conscience.

Another reason to reject the view that organizations have a conscience is to realize that few of us would be tempted to make this claim for an organization in which we hold an important, decision-making position. As a member of the key decision-making body we are not aware of some sort of corporate conscience guiding the group but rather of the interplay of the arguments proposed by the various members, each of whom is consulting his or her own conscience. The group may well have a history of making decisions of a particular sort from a moral perspective, as when Jill Conway argued at the Nike board that "this is not the sort of thing that we do." But this is an appeal to tradition, not a claim that somehow the firm itself possesses a conscience independent of the consciences of its members.

One final argument in favor of the view that organizations do not have a conscience is its practical impact. If we were to say that a university, a business firm, or a parish has a conscience, how would we appeal to that conscience in hopes of making a change? If instead we understand social structures, our focus would be either to put pressure on or to persuade those with decision-making power in the organization to modify the restrictions, enablements, and incentives faced by themselves and others in that organization to alter the choices made.

Conclusion

Can an organization have a conscience? Because an organization is a kind of social structure, and a social structure is a system of human relations among social positions that exist prior to any one person's taking on one of those positions, organizations have causal power through their generation of restrictions, enablements, and incentives. Organizations can have a kind of collective agency, in that we can, for example, attribute to Macy's a policy concerning a dress code for its employees and to Nike the decision to require the factories that produce Nike apparel to install ATMs. And we can helpfully speak of an organization's moral responsibilities (for example, to treat its employees justly or to husband the earth's environmental resources). But an organization has no consciousness and acts only through the actions of individuals within it.[24]

Catholic social thought would be well served to employ a critical-realist understanding of social structures to better understand and critique sinful

[24] See Margaret Archer and Pierpaulo Donati, *The Social Self* (Oxford: Oxford University Press, forthcoming).

social structures in the world. Pope Benedict XVI teaches in *Caritas in Veritate* that "the Church's wisdom has always pointed to the presence of original sin in social conditions and in the structure of society" (no. 34). Even though the word *always* in this sentence is an exaggeration, it is clear that Catholic social teaching now recognizes the powerful effects of social structures. A more perceptive understanding of structure will enable the call of the gospel to have greater impact in the lives of people today.

14.

The Wisdom of Serpents

Conscience, Power, and Politics in the Abortion Controversy

William R. O'Neill, S.J.

"Be wise as serpents and innocent as doves," says Jesus in Matthew 10:16. But there is little wisdom, much less innocence, in today's partisan polemics. Oscar Wilde was right: "Moderation is a fatal thing. Nothing succeeds like excess."[1] We may well wonder, then, Do Jesus's words still speak to us? Yes! But some translation is required if the gospel is to be proclaimed "today, in our hearing" (Lk 4:21).

In the first section I analyze the Roman Catholic Church's turn to modern rights rhetoric in elaborating the "dignity of conscience" for complex, pluralist polities like our own. In the second section I explore the hermeneutical implications of this turn; for rights talk is a two-edged sword, giving the church not only a public voice but maxims for its use: maxims of respect, of recognition, and of responsibility in public reasoning (our "knowing together" or *con-scientia*).[2] Finally, in the third section I apply these maxims to the issue of abortion for Catholic institutions, concluding with a brief excursus on the rubrics of intrinsic evil in public policy.

Re-enchanting the Public Sphere?

From its inception with Leo XIII's epochal encyclical *Rerum Novarum* in 1891, modern Catholic social teaching has defended a rich, religiously

[1] Oscar Wilde, *A Woman of No Importance*, act 3 (1893).

[2] In its original etymological sense, *conscience*, from the Latin *con-scire*, signified "knowing together or with others."

inspired doctrine of the common good (the *bonum commune* of the medieval schoolmen). Only later would the modern rhetoric of human rights be grafted onto the older teleological stock through the travails of theologians like John Courtney Murray, Pietro Pavan, and Jacques Maritain.[3] In a characteristically irenic turn Pope John XXIII resolves the seeming antinomy of personal rights and the common good: *Pacem in Terris* (PT) glosses the pre-modern, perfectionist teleology of *Mater et Magistra* (MM) (depicting the common good as "all those social conditions which favor the full development of human personality" [MM, no. 65]) when it states in deontological terms of the "rights and obligations" implied by the "natural dignity" of conscience. "It is generally accepted today," writes Pope John, "that the common good is best safeguarded when personal rights and duties are guaranteed" (PT, no. 60).

Yet, the council's intention, expressed in *Dignitatis Humanae,* "to develop the doctrine . . . on the inviolable rights of the human person and the constitutional order of society" (no. 1) was long in coming and bitterly contested. Indeed, "the notion of development"[4] is, at best, a euphemism; for the methodological turn from neo-Scholastic theology belies not only Gregory XVI's condemnation of religious liberty as a "crazed absurdity" *(deliramentum)*,[5] but the very ideal of a hierarchically stratified sacral state. As Michael Rosen observes, "It is important to recognize the anti-egalitarian character of so much Catholic thought about dignity in order to appreciate just how great the change was that took place in Catholic social thought around the middle of the twentieth century."[6]

Better, then, to speak of a fundamental reversal of "hermeneutical flow."[7] For where in neo-Scholasticism the dignity of conscience derives from a natural teleological ordering, that is, a "rightful conscience" obedient to Truth, dignity now figures as a regulative ideal, both hermeneutically

---

[3] Cf. *Pacem in Terris,* nos. 53–66, 132–41*;* *Gaudium et Spes,* nos. 25–26, 30; *Dignitatis Humanae*, nos. 6–7; *Populorum Progressio,* nos. 22–24, 43–75; *Sollicitudo Rei Socialis,* nos. 38–40.

[4] See John Courtney Murray, "Meaning of the Document," in *Declaration on Religious Liberty and Declaration on the Relationship of the Church to Non-Christian Religions,* ed. John Courtney Murray and Robert A. Graham (New York: America Press, 1966), 4.

[5] Gregory XVI, *Mirari Vos*, in H. Denzinger and A. Schönmetzer, *Enchiridion Symbolorum*, 32nd ed., no. 2730. Religious liberty figured prominently in Pius IX's "Syllabus of Errors."

[6] Michael Rosen, *Dignity: Its History and Meaning* (Cambridge, MA: Harvard University Press, 2012), 51.

[7] The term is Hans Frei's.

constraining and informing political ends (our public *con-scientia*).[8] Not only are our ends, both personal and collective, constrained by our innate capacity to set them, but they will be reasonable if, and to the degree, that they realize this capacity. In modern Catholic social teaching, human rights (as capabilities of exercising agency) accordingly comprise not only side constraints on policy, but function constitutively in determining it.

Limited internally by the like dignity or intrinsic worth of others, liberty is thus positively oriented to the good of moral community as, in Maritain's words, "a whole composed of wholes,"[9] that is, neither an artifice of interest, as in liberal contractarian thought, nor the "local and ethnocentric" hypostasis of communitarian mores.[10] We realize the limited good of moral community in which all share singly, not en masse, when the "inviolable rights of the human person," including religious liberty, are protected in what Murray defines as "public order."[11] Establishing true religion by imposing distinctively religious duties falls outside the state's proper province for the common good—now chiefly guaranteed in the set of basic, institutional arrangements supporting a rights regime.[12]

In the church's modern doctrine religious reasons do not, then, supplant political and human rights concerns. The divinely mandated "love command" *(agapē)* rather provides the ultimate "grounding reason" for the respect due

---

[8] Dignity rests, then, not in obedience per se, but rather in the capacity to obey or receive God's gracious self-communication. For Karl Rahner's understanding of *potentia obedientalis*, see his "Concerning the Relationship between Nature and Grace," in *Theological Investigations*, vol. 1, trans. Cornelius Ernst, O.P. (Baltimore: Helicon Press, 1961), 297–317; idem, "Nature and Grace," in *Theological Investigations*, vol. 4, trans. Kevin Smith (Baltimore: Helicon Press, 1966), 165–88.

[9] Jacques Maritain, "The Person and the Common Good," in *The Social and the Political Philosophy of Jacques Maritain*, ed. Joseph W. Evans and Leo R. Ward (New York: Charles Scribner's Sons, 1955), 85.

[10] Richard Rorty, "The Priority of Democracy to Philosophy," in *The Virginia Statute for Religious Freedom: Its Evolution and Consequences in American History*, ed. Merrill D. Peterson and Robert C. Vaughan (Cambridge, MA: Cambridge University Press, 1988), 259.

[11] See John Courtney Murray, *We Hold These Truths: Catholic Reflections on the American Proposition* (New York: Sheed and Ward, 1960), 155–74. Cf. idem, "Memo to Cardinal Cushing concerning Contraception Legislation," in *Bridging the Sacred and the Secular: Selected Writings of John Courtney Murray, S.J.*, ed. Leon Hooper (Washington, DC; Georgetown University Press, 1994), 81–86.

[12] See *Dignitatis Humanae,* no. 4. "Positive," correlative duties to preserve and protect agents' basic capabilities (the objects of basic rights) generate such structural imperatives, for example, the state's obligation to guarantee citizens' basic welfare. See also Alan Gewirth, *The Community of Rights* (Chicago: University of Chicago Press, 1996), 106–65.

moral persons. "Love," write the bishops in their post–Vatican II synod, "implies an absolute demand for justice, namely a recognition of the dignity and rights of one's neighbor."[13] Distinctively Christian *duties*, for example, love of enemies, forgiveness, and so forth, presume recognition of basic human *rights* claims, for example, juridical protection of a victim's right to forgive (or withhold forgiveness). The Christian disciple "acts justly" in the prophet's words (Mi 6:8)—even as justice bears the mark of "loving tenderly" (Mi 6:8). But love of the disciple who "walks humbly" with God (Mi 6:8) is never less than just.

One might, of course, still dismiss the church's belated turn to rights as, in Richard Rorty's words, "merely quaint."[14] But there is, I believe, a rich vein to be mined in Pope John's teaching.

Let me elaborate. *Pace,* Jeremy Bentham, the sense of rights rests precisely in their suasive, rhetorical force. Human rights, in turn, show forth our respect for the dignity of conscience, that is, for moral persons capable of forming, revising, and rationally pursuing a conception of the good, while basic human rights preserve the conditions or capabilities of such practically rational (discursive) agency. In ascribing worth rather than mere price to persons as agents, we implicitly valorize the prerequisites of their exercising agency, that is, not only our negative, civil liberties, but basic security and subsistence upheld by the Catholic encyclical tradition.[15] So, too, correlative duties imply more than mere forbearance: a rights' regime likewise requires duties of provision, for example, child nutrition or basic health care and protection against systemic rights' violations.

Fulfilling such rights and duties in "service of the common good," Pope Benedict XVI reminds us in *Caritas in Veritate*, remains "the primary way of charity" (no. 6). Indeed, it is the very service of the common good that demands an option for the poor, that is, those subject to systemic deprivation, whether by class, race, ethnicity, gender, or other.[16] It is precisely our moral/legal entitlement to *equal* respect or consideration that justifies

---

[13] 1971 Synod of Bishops, *Justice in the World,* no. 34.

[14] Richard Rorty, *Contingency, Irony, and Solidarity* (New York: Cambridge University Press, 1989), 45.

[15] See Henry Shue, *Basic Rights: Subsistence, Affluence, and US Foreign Policy* (Princeton, NJ: Princeton University Press, 1980), 5–87.

[16] Redressing such deprivation requires implementing an integral and comprehensive rights regime. For the complex intersection of race, class, and gender, see Bryan N. Massingale's incisive *Racial Justice and the Catholic Church* (Maryknoll, NY: Orbis Books, 2010).

preferential treatment for those whose basic rights are most imperiled.[17] Such a discriminate response finds expression in the graduated legal/moral urgency of differing human rights, that is, the lexical priority of agents' basic rights over other, less exigent claims, for example, property rights, and in the differing correlative duties presumed for realizing the same human rights.[18] Exhibiting the banality of goodness rather than "the ultimate and most sublime values" of our comprehensive (religious) doctrines, such basic human rights constitute the grammar of our practical rational rhetoric.[19] Neither an abstract, thin meta-narrative, nor a culturally determined thick narrative, rights rather configure our narrative *(sittliche)* traditions, permitting us to speak of their limited, moral *(moralisch)* family resemblance.[20] Composing a family of language-games, our well-formed narratives are not rigidly limited but open textured. It is just this family resemblance that undergirds an overlapping consensus regarding what the Preamble to the Universal Declaration of Human Rights calls citizens' "faith in fundamental human rights, in the dignity and worth of the human person." Citizens recognize the justificatory, rhetorical force of such general claim-rights for policy, even if they differ as to the ultimate justification of our common faith, for example, Christian belief in the *imago Dei*. It suffices for deliberative consensus that citizens' best judgments overlap; consensus need not "go all the way down."[21] As we shall see, the redemption of *general* claim-rights, including rights to effective participation, implies citizens' recognition of *differing* comprehensive points of view.

Three Political Maxims

The hermeneutical turn to the dignity of conscience lets the church speak to the modern world in the lingua franca of basic human rights and correlative duties. The institutional provision and protection of such rights, moreover, give rise to the systemic imperatives of the civic common good

---

[17] See Gene Outka, *Agape* (New Haven, CT: Yale University Press, 1972), 20; cf. Ronald Dworkin, *Taking Rights Seriously* (Cambridge, MA: Harvard University Press, 1978), 227.

[18] Cf. John Paul II, *Sollicitudo Rei Socialis*, nos. 42–43.

[19] Ludwig Wittgenstein, *Philosophical Investigations*, 3rd ed. (New York: Macmillan, 1958), pt. 1, pars. 497, 664.

[20] Ibid., pt. 1, pars. 68, 179.

[21] See Donald Davidson, "Actions, Reasons, and Causes," and "Intending," in *Essays on Actions and Events* (Oxford: Clarendon, 1980), 3–19, 83–102, respectively.

and the "option for the poor" it implies—themes expressed in maxims of our public reasoning: respect, recognition, and responsibility. Let me say a brief word about each.

The Maxim of Respect

In the words of *Dignitatis Humanae*: "In the exercise of their rights," citizens of faith "are bound by the moral law to have respect both for the rights of others and for their own duties toward others and for the common welfare of all." The right to religious freedom, we saw, is itself ordered to the common civic good so that citizens "may come to act with greater responsibility in fulfilling their duties in community life" (nos. 7, 8). Freedom, say the council fathers, following Murray, "is to be respected as far as possible and is not to be curtailed except when and insofar as necessary" (no. 7), that is, in accordance with the requisites of public order.[22] In exercising religious liberty, citizens thus "ought at all times to refrain from any manner of action which might seem to carry a hint of coercion or of a kind of persuasion that would be dishonorable or unworthy" (no. 4).

By the same token, in supporting fundamental political positions regarding society's basic structure, citizens of faith must refrain from any "hint of coercion" or dishonorable intimidation. Appealing to worthy persuasion in realizing the mundane common good, the council recalls John Rawls's view that the exercise of coercive political power is proper "only when we sincerely believe that the reasons we offer for our political action may reasonably be accepted by other citizens as a justification of those actions."[23] And foremost among such reasons, we saw, is the protection and provision of basic rights themselves. In a pluralist democracy, liberty—including religious liberty—is legitimately curtailed for the sake of preserving the liberty and basic rights of others.

Persuasion is worthy, then, when we seek public consensus by translating our distinctive religious claims into broadly shared political values such as human rights claims. Let us call this the *maxim of respect*. It is, we may say, the token of admission to the language game of public reason, in which rights figure as warrants or suasive claims, redeemed in public

---

[22] Cf. John Courtney Murray, "This Matter of Religious Freedom," *America* 112 (January 9, 1965): 40.

[23] John Rawls, *Political Liberalism* (New York: Columbia University Press, 1996), xlviff., 217–18; idem, "The Idea of Public Reason Revisited," in *The Law of Peoples* (Cambridge, MA: Harvard University Press, 1999), 135–37.

argument. For in pluralist societies, says Murray, "no minority has the right to impose its own religious or moral views on other groups, through the use of methods of force, coercion, or violence." Yet just so, minority groups enjoy "the right to work toward the elevation of standards of public morality in a pluralist society, through the use of methods of persuasion and pacific argument."[24]

The Maxim of Recognition

But worthy persuasion is not exhausted by speaking. We must also listen, avoiding sectarian polemics and misrepresentation. The charitable interpretation we seek—that our distinctively religious beliefs be translated in terms of human rights—we must offer in turn (Mt 7:12). To the justificatory maxim of respect, we must add a maxim of reasonable interpretation.[25] Citizens generally, and citizens of faith, for example, in Catholic institutions in particular, must exercise a hermeneutics of charity in interpreting public reasons.[26] At times explicit translation of such reasons is not necessary; a *fides implicita* in human rights suffices. But in the give and take of public reasoning, when the interpretation or application of rights is itself contested, the maxim of recognition requires more.

In accordance with their rights to effective participation, citizens, we argued, are equally worthy of representation—each owed "an effort at identification" in public, political reasoning.[27] Christians must, then, seek to interpret their neighbors, for example, Jews, Muslims, Buddhists, or secular humanists, aright; they must, that is, ask what it would mean for their claims to be valid or true from the perspective of our shared political "grammar"—the basic rights we hold in common in accordance with the

---

[24] Murray, *We Hold These Truths*, 168.

[25] "Reasonable" here is a predicate of political reasoning—of political use rather than of religious meaning. A political reason is reasonable if it is formally coherent; normatively cogent (publicly persuasive, for example, invoking rights as warrants); and sincerely held (the reasons justifying the argument explain my holding it—I do not misrepresent my intentions).

[26] Interpreting validity claims entails an extensive application of the principle of charity, whereby the reader assumes the (potential) truth of others' claims against the backdrop of their "patterns of belief" and interprets the sense or meaning of their claims accordingly. See Donald Davidson, "Thought and Talk," in *Inquiries into Truth and Interpretation* (Oxford: Clarendon, 1984), 168. For a critical application of the principle, see Steven Lukes, "Relativism in Its Place," in *Rationality and Relativism*, ed. Martin Hollis and Steven Lukes, 261–305 (Cambridge, MA: MIT Press, 1982).

[27] Bernard Williams, "The Idea of Equality," in *Problems of the Self* (Cambridge, MA: Cambridge University Press, 1973), 236–37.

maxim of respect.[28] And we may, indeed, find the rhetorical tables turned, revealing the lacunae of *our* interpretations.

Worthy persuasion, especially in Catholic institutions, demands such a dialectic of mutual recognition, or what we might term *deliberative tolerance,* a tolerance informed by religious literacy. But even with such a charitable hermeneutics, differences will persist. Agreed-upon public reasons, for example, basic rights, do not exhaust the fund of public reasoning. For, as demonstrated above, rights, though generally compatible, are not self-interpreting. Public reasoning may invoke differing rights of differing weight or scope that conflict in particular cases. And the same right may be fulfilled in differing ways. We may agree about equal educational opportunity for all but differ about the wisdom of affirmative action, or we may agree about affirmative action but prefer race to class or gender. The maxim of recognition does not of itself guarantee agreement. Rather, in Murray's words, our public reasoning presumes the "reasonable disposition to argue our many disagreements in intelligent and temperate fashion."[29]

The Maxim of Responsibility

How, then, do we adjudicate amid our many disagreements in exercising legitimate coercive power? A prudential (consequentially sensitive) note is sounded. For policies, we saw, are governed by basic rights as deontic side-constraints[30] in terms of negative duties of avoiding deprivation, and subject to consequential (teleological) evaluation in terms of positive duties of protection and provision. And since, consistent with the political ideal of the common good, satisfying these latter duties will be relative to prevailing political, economic, social, and cultural circumstances, we may ask this question: Of the set of policies deemed feasible, which will *best* satisfy persons' mutually implicative basic rights—and, in particular, the rights of the most vulnerable?[31] For, as we saw above, respecting agents' equal basic rights entails preferential protection and provision for those whose rights are most imperiled. What policy, program, or practice best

---

[28] Rights thus play a critical role, precisely as the "deep grammar" of our public, political reasoning. Just as grammar configures a well-formed narrative, so rights configure (or re-figure) our political reasoning; worthy persuasion is both regulatively and constitutively governed by the "grammar" of rights.

[29] John Courtney Murray, "The Bad Arguments People Make," *America* (November 3, 1956), 120.

[30] See Robert Nozick, *Anarchy, State, and Utopia* (Oxford: Basil Blackwell, 1974), 28–35.

[31] See Amartya Sen, *On Ethics and Economics* (Oxford: Basil Blackwell, 1987), 73, cf. 47–51, 70–78.

protects the basic rights of the most vulnerable? Let us call this *the maxim of responsibility*.

Deliberative consensus, to be sure, will be halting, incremental at best, and subject to constant revision. As Thomas Aquinas realized, law remains an imperfect instrument. And precisely because public reason mediates across comprehensive doctrines of the good, not all *we* deem morally right can be parsed in terms of rights, much less fittingly legislated; nor are the claims of justice always apparent. Counsels of prudence (Aristotelian *phronēsis*) must prevail as we aim, albeit imperfectly, at the mundane (discursive) common good. For the polity is not the citizen "writ large." While moral (deontic) norms govern personal, conscientious choice (if I believe A to be morally wrong, *I* cannot do it), the common good—or more precisely that aspect of the common good at play in public reasoning—necessarily embraces reasonable difference, that is, differences arising as we apply generally recognized warrants to particular cases. Sometimes we may resolve prima facie conflict, as when we come to see that a basic right to adequate nutrition trumps non-basic rights, such as that to private property. Yet not all reasonable differences, for example, regarding the scope or relative weight of rights, are readily resolved: "Hard cases" are settled only through the public recognition of just why they are hard, that is, that here and now, generally agreed-upon warrants—not simply the venality of one side or the other—are in fact causing the conflict.

If in complex, pluralist polities, the "grammar" of rights grounds legitimate, political consensus, the interpretation (and application) of rights reveals its limits. Wise politics *is* the art of compromise, agreeing where we can, differing where we must: a compromise, not of morality, but rather the compromise morality makes possible. Not all reasons, to be sure, are reasonable; and some, for example, anti-Semitic or racist bias, must be rejected as moral solecisms violating the grammar of public reason. Yet grammar does not of itself constitute speech. Forged in the crucible of public reasoning, wise policy (1) is *constrained* by rights, fulfilling duties of forbearance (where the complex casuistry of cooperation formal/material, remote/proximate, and so on, determines the range of permissible policies), and (2) *constructively* realizes basic rights by fulfilling duties of protection and provision, especially for the most vulnerable. In short, it is not enough to be "innocent as doves," honoring personal conscience (*I* do no harm); we must also be "wise as serpents," aiming, incrementally, at policies that best realize the common good, all things considered.[32]

[32] *Con-scientia*, so conceived, is the exercise of prudence (*phronēsis*, *prudential*) ordered to the mundane common good, in this case, of pluralist, democratic polities.

The Politics of Abortion

There is no simple decision procedure governing public policy. The foregoing maxims rather guide our public reasoning under the regulative ideal of the dignity and worth of the human person, for faithful citizens give a public account of their hope (1 Pt 3:15) precisely as citizens. Let us briefly consider the implications of our analysis for one of the most contentious issues facing Catholic institutions today, the legality of abortion.

The *maxim of respect*, we saw, implies that we translate our distinctive (religious or secular, non-public) beliefs into a persuasive, public idiom of *common* political values, especially basic human rights. And yet, what Glendon calls the strident language of liberal "rights talk" seems to inspire more discord than consensus—an implacable right to life vying with a no less implacable right to choice.[33] Too often, the very appeal to rights is a conversation stopper. As argued above, however, rights are not simply convertible to interests (or benefits due). Indeed, precisely as the grammar of our practical rhetoric, rights function primarily as warrants or suasive claims in public reasoning. Politics may well be, as Thucydides said, "the arena where conscience and power meet . . . until the end of time," but rights trump mere power or coercion, providing a moral template for legal legitimacy.[34]

What, then, of abortion? What would it mean "to argue our many disagreements in intelligent and temperate fashion," as Murray would say, that is, in the common idiom of rights? For those favoring a legal right to abortion, *respect* for the dignity of conscience underscores the force of maternal choice: women cannot be treated as mere vessels, means to nascent life. And yet the logic of rights itself raises the question of the moral status of the embryo and fetus. For precisely in claiming a legal/moral *right* to choice, such choice is removed from the merely private realm. A legal right protecting choice, for example, a right to privacy, cannot be divorced from the other moral rights and duties affected by choice. So too, those opposing such a right must show that the embryo is rightly accorded full moral status (personhood or hominization). Catholics claim moral certainty in virtue of developmental continuity, even if, as the Sacred Congregation for the Doctrine of the Faith's 1974 *Declaration on Procured Abortion* concedes: "It is true that in the Middle Ages, when the opinion was generally held that the spiritual soul was not present until after the first few weeks." . . .

---

[33] Mary Ann Glendon, *A World Made New: Eleanor Roosevelt and the Universal Declaration of Human Rights* (New York: Random House, 2000), 227.

[34] Thucydides, *The Peloponnesian War* (New York: Modern Library, 1951), 331. Cf. Glendon, *A World Made New,* 1.

an important footnote later reads: "This declaration expressly leaves aside the question of the moment when the spiritual soul is infused. . . . It is not within the competence of science to decide between these views, because the existence of an immortal soul is not a question in its field. It is a philosophical problem from which our moral affirmation remains independent" (no. 13n.19).

The strongest arguments for affirming full moral personhood rest rather in traditional casuistic methods of resolving doubt: "It suffices that this presence of the soul be probable (and one can never prove the contrary) in order that the taking of life involve accepting the risk of killing a man, not only waiting for, but already in possession of his soul" (no. 19). As *Donum Vitae* and the recent *Dignitas Personae* contend, the unacceptability of such a risk provides that the "human being is to be respected and treated as a person from the moment of conception; and therefore from the same moment his rights as a person must be recognized, among which in the first place is the inviolable right of every innocent human being to life."[35] Now this is an eminently reasonable argument. But other traditions, including other religious traditions, with their own distinctive casuistries, differ. The questions posed by twinning and recombination prior to implantation, and of spontaneous, natural abortions remain germane for *public* reasoning in a pluralist polity.[36]

Not everyone who accepts abortion, for example, in the case of rape or incest, or to preserve the life of the mother, is party to a "culture of death." The *maxim of recognition* precludes such simple polemics. Nor can we readily assume a meta-casuistry, resolving casuistic doubt. How, then, do faithful citizens address our many disagreements regarding abortion? The *maxim of responsibility* favors that policy which, all things considered, best protects the most vulnerable. In what I have called the hermeneutics of rights, legislation must (1) honor personal conscience, that is, satisfy the conditions of legitimate cooperation consistent with the "negative" duty of forbearance, and (2) promote the public common good by fulfilling "positive" duties of protection and provision, especially for the most vulnerable.

For many citizens the claims of the unborn are for this very reason morally exigent, but no less are the claims of vulnerable women. Now, claim-rights of life *and* of choice (imposing duties of forbearance) militate against any policy of forced abortion or sterilization in curbing population growth.

---

[35] Congregation for the Doctrine of the Faith, *Instruction on Respect for Human Life in Its Origin and on the Dignity of Procreation,* Pt. I, sec. 1.

[36] The possibility of recombination is especially problematic, inasmuch as the ascription of dignity is supervenient upon unique moral personhood; dignity, as in inherent property, is incommensurable and permanent, in the sense that it cannot be forfeited.

Laws systemically violating such basic human rights must be rejected, even in civil disobedience. Yet laws permitting abortion raise a further question. For the casuistry of remote, material cooperation allows me to vote for a permissive law, if I believe my so voting *best* protects the rights of the most vulnerable. John Paul II himself appeals to such prudential logic in his 1995 *Evangelium Vitae*, arguing that one "could licitly support proposals aimed at limiting the harm done by such a law and at lessening its negative consequences. . . . This does not in fact represent an illicit cooperation with an unjust law, but rather a legitimate and proper attempt to limit its evil aspects" (no. 73).

John Paul II is not saying that abortion is permissible for proportionate reasons. The question, rather, is how best to "limit the evil aspects" of prevailing policies, laws, or practices. For in this case the lesser evil *is* the greater good. As John Paul reminds us, such prudential reasoning, legitimately and properly, pertains to abortion policy. Prudence favors every reasonable legal measure "limiting the harm done"—to both fetus *and* vulnerable mother. And among these, surely, is securing the social and economic rights, including healthcare, of women whose poverty and vulnerability remain a leading reason for abortion. Here, too, concern for the unborn cannot be divorced from other basic rights in service of the common good. Just as the constraining role of rights—both of life and of liberty—precludes forced abortion, so the constructive role of rights favors material and psychological support for *any* pregnant woman choosing to bring a child to term.

In either case the maxim of responsibility, integrating liberty and life, dictates a basic, rights-based consensus. But rights, we saw, leave much indeterminate in public reasoning, even for Catholic institutions. Indeed, it is precisely our common grammar that makes sense of difference *not* perspicuously decided by rights, for example, whether elective abortion should be included among protected rights; the legal implications of religious liberty for Catholic institutions; and the fitting mode of deciding either question.[37] Hard cases make bad law, but recognizing them makes good lawyers and even better moralists. For in reasoning back from our differences, we adumbrate the consensus that makes them reasonable. A *rights*-based opposition to abortion, for instance, presumes the general moral salience of rights of life *and* of liberty. The conditions (whether voluntary or coerced) and consequences (material well-being) of pregnancy

[37] John Rawls, *Political Liberalism* (New York: Columbia University Press, 1996), lvi. In footnote 32 on that page, Rawls notes the consonance of his views with those of Cardinal Bernardin in "The Consistent Ethics: What Sort of Framework?" *Origins* 16 (October 30, 1986), 345, 347–50.

matter morally; it is precisely for this reason that many otherwise opposing abortion would permit it in these limit cases.

I may believe that even in the case of rape, embryonic life must be preserved, while conceding the *public* limits of my belief. As we argued above, no meta-casuistry compels citizens of other traditions to adopt a rigorist casuistry forbidding the use of abortificients to prevent implantation. Catholic casuistry is reasonable but not uniquely so. Rape, moreover, is by definition a profound violation of a woman's right to life (security) *and* choice. But such violation generates ancillary rights and duties not generally enjoyed (for example, a refugee's right of non-refoulement predicated on the legal determination of systemic rights' violations). Is it unreasonable, then, to say that redressing the violation of her basic right to life (security), confers a right to choice not otherwise present? The description of rape as "intrinsically evil" precludes any slippery slope where life and liberty are not so threatened. So too, respect for life itself reveals the morally tragic character of cases in which both fetus and mother will die, barring therapeutic abortion. In public reasoning the choice of abortion to preserve life may be irreducibly tragic.[38]

The grammar of rights, I have argued, does not perspicuously decide what we *say* of such issues in public reason: our differing rights-based interpretations. Catholics do not betray their beliefs in conceding this. And so too, for those favoring legal abortion. Reasoning back from our differences reveals the morally fraught nature of abortion in cases not so hard. A public *right* to privacy, after all, is internally limited by kindred rights: liberty, precisely as a right, as Michael Walzer says, is "bonded."[39] Neither are correlative duties merely negative. Contrary to the "hyper-individualism" of American "rights talk," duties of protection and provision constrain my liberty and inform my political ends. As we argued above, advocates of choice, in appealing to maternal vulnerability, cannot summarily dismiss the moral status of the developing fetus. For even here, vulnerability remains gendered, as in feminist criticism of gender-biased abortions under China's "one child" policy. But the attribution of gender bias, no less than

[38] The case is not as simply resolved as some traditional moral theologians believe. For Catholic moral theology implicitly allows for the possibility of "innocent aggression" in developing the *jus in bello* criterion of discrimination: a child soldier, morally innocent, may still be assimilated to the category of combatant. The innocence of such children is already betrayed by sexual violence and trauma. But would we condemn one for killing such a child, when saving one's own family allows no other recourse? The choice, I submit, is irreducibly tragic.

[39] Michael Walzer, *Exodus and Revolution* (New York: Basic Books, 1985), 53, 73–90.

of respect, presumes the existence of a moral subject. Condemning prenatal femicide seems otiose, if *no* moral status is accorded the embryo/fetus.

Just as those opposing legal abortion can acknowledge the force of hard cases, for example, in rape or preserving maternal life, so too those favoring an unqualified legal right to abortion. For partisan of liberty and life alike, public reason is parsimonious. Our common faith in human rights leaves much undecided. It suffices for wise legislation—what we do in "pacific argument"—that our best judgments overlap. We are, after all, playing the same language game. Denying others' good faith, conversely, yields conscience to power: politics as an endless *agon* of interest. And it is this, above all, that Catholic institutions must resist as we continue to, as Murray says, "argue our many disagreements in intelligent and temperate fashion."

A Brief Excursus on "Intrinsic Evil"

But, one might object, is not abortion intrinsically evil, thereby trumping any political or "prudential" compromise? Now actions, behaviors, or practices are deemed "intrinsically evil" *(intrinsece malum)* if they are, writes John Paul II in *Veritatis Splendor*, "*per se* and in themselves, independently of circumstances . . . always seriously wrong by reason of their object. The Second Vatican Council itself, in discussing the respect due to the human persons, gives a number of examples of such acts," for example, "any kind of homicide, genocide, abortion, euthanasia and voluntary suicide . . . mutilation, physical and mental torture and attempts to coerce the spirit . . . subhuman living conditions, arbitrary imprisonment, deportation, slavery, prostitution and trafficking in women and children; degrading conditions of work" (no. 80). A fortiori, no reasonable compromise is possible in such cases, for, as we argued above, such practices systemically distort discourse. John Paul sharply criticized the so-called proportionalist school of moral theologians for failing to recognize the force of such intrinsically evil action. And there is, I believe, wisdom in his critique. For if, and to the degree, actions, practices, or attitudes are fittingly described as entailing a systemic deprivation of basic human rights, as rape, racism, or slavery, to that degree they are intrinsically evil; no further appeal to intentions or circumstances suffices to justify them.[40]

Still, John Paul's critique betrays a certain irony. For the biconditional is not proven: that certain actions, behaviors, or practices, like racism or

---

[40] For those faithful to Aquinas's heritage, it is precisely prudence *(prudentia)* that determines "intrinsic evil," that is, that an action or practice, so described, can never be a fit means for human beatitude. Conscience does not make Kantians of us all.

slavery, are impermissible (intrinsically evil) because they are gravely wrong does not entail that actions, behaviors, or practices are gravely wrong just because they are intrinsically evil or impermissible. Not all actions deemed intrinsically evil in pre-modern, perfectionist teleology, for example, lying, masturbation, contraception, and same-sex relations, are equally grave—not all equally threaten the dignity and rights of conscience. Finally, the most persuasive argument against abortion in public reasoning is *not* that it is intrinsically evil (thereby assimilating it to masturbation or contraception), but that it threatens the basic rights of the most vulnerable. If abortion is gravely wrong, it is so for precisely the same reason that denying healthcare to poor women is wrong. And yet, with respect to abortion, as we have seen, reasonable people may differ; it is precisely these differences that make our public *con-scientia* both possible and necessary.

For if we err in failing to distinguish intrinsic and grave evil, so we err in conflating personal and social choice. If I believe that an action is rightly described as intrinsically evil, in no circumstances can *I* perform it. I cannot do what I regard as morally evil, even in lesser matters, to achieve good (Rom 3:8). Yet as we argued above, personal conscience is not "writ large" on the body politic. Indeed, as Thomas Aquinas recognized, not all wrongful actions are necessarily fit subjects of legislative proscription. A permissive law, we saw above, may be morally flawed, but voting for it does not represent complicity in intrinsic evil, if, writes John Paul, it limits "the harm done." In public choice, after all, the question is not merely *my* forbearance, but how best to resolve our reasonable differences in an intelligent and temperate fashion. And as the US bishops implicitly concede, this is the role of prudence in public reason; it is prudence, after all, that decides whether we should seek to overturn what we regard as an unjust law (the bishops' position on same-sex marriage), seek legal exemption (their position on contraception), or merely tolerate choices we deem immoral (masturbation).

Conclusion

Catholic institutions, such as universities, betray precisely what is "catholic" in their identity when they forsake worthy persuasion. Indeed, undue emphasis upon ecclesial discipline or intramural, ecclesial sanctions, rather than pacific methods of persuasion plays into the very "pro-choice" logic the hierarchical magisterium so opposes. For in pluralist societies, where the maxims fail and public reasoning runs out, what remains is choice (whether of individuals or groups, like the church).

But Catholics do not oppose abortion merely because they are Catholic. Abortion is not a political shibboleth, much less a sectarian marker of identity. Neither are we closet relativists, seeking to impose a sectarian moral truth upon others.[41] Rather, precisely *as* citizens of faith, we must seek to frame our differences (for example, regarding the constituents of basic healthcare, the scope and limits of religious liberty, and fitting modes of participation) within a moral consensus—one, that is, constrained and informed by the political maxims of our *con-scientia*—conscience in the public sphere. A wise (prudential) decision in the case of abortion will recognize that rights we hold in common do, *pro tanto*, conflict, but just so, permit us to make sense of our differences. In the case posed in *Evangelium Vitae*, the very gravity of abortion demands such a prudential assessment of public policy. Not all political compromises are compromises of morality. Some are morally required. For Catholic moral theology, after all, prophecy does not trump prudence (there is no "teleological suspension of the ethical"). Our tradition gives us strong *public* arguments faithful to Jesus's admonition in Matthew 10:16: to protect the innocent, we must be wise.

[41] Where subjectivism denies the validity of general norms, ethical relativism grounds general norms in *particular* validity claims, for example, warrants of sectarian belief systems. Condemning relativism on the basis of such (non-universalizable) claims amounts to a performative contradiction.

Appendix

Conscience, Democracy, and the Service of God in the "Tangle of the Mind"

David E. DeCosse

What if the clashes over conscience between the American Catholic bishops and the Obama Administration are driven in great measure not by anti-Catholicism or by creeping totalitarianism, but by the very model of conscience used by the bishops themselves?

The next year may provide a decisive answer to this question. On January 20, 2012, the Federal Department of Health and Human Services announced that religious institutions would have a year before they would be required to make contraception available at no cost to all female employees. In response, the Catholic Health Association both criticized the HHS statement and called for an "effective national conversation on the appropriate conscience protections in our pluralistic country."[1] Will the church in the next year enter into such a conversation and possibly find solutions that balance the concerns of religious freedom with the respect for democratic equality? How this question is finally answered may well depend on what conceptual model of the Catholic conscience the church brings to the table.

At present, the model of conscience used by most bishops is problematic in two ways. First, it emphasizes obedience, law, and hierarchical authority and thus departs from the Catholic tradition's close linkage of conscience, practical reason, and freedom. Second, on account of this departure, these bishops needlessly lapse into using a sectarian model of

---

A slightly different version of this essay appeared on January 23, 2012, as "Bishops' Conscience Model Makes Light of Practical Reason," http://www.ncronline.org. Reprinted by permission of *National Catholic Reporter*, 115 E. Armour Blvd, Kansas City, MO 64111.

[1] "Catholic Health Association Disappointed with Decision Regarding Women's Preventive Service Regulations," Catholic Health Association of the United States, News Release, January 20, 2012, http://www.chausa.org.

the Catholic conscience ill-suited to the church's mission in a democratic pluralist society like the United States.

When the Catholic bishops today defend conscience, they are defending the idea that within human beings is an uncompromising witness to the universal, objective, exceptionless moral law. Law—moral, natural, and divine law are all different aspects of the same thing—is a crucial category here. The given, ineradicable quality of the moral law derived from reflection on the purposes of human nature is a sign of God's providential ordering of the world. The bishops' close link of moral and divine law informs their conviction—and the conviction of the broader Catholic right in the United States—that these current battles over conscience are part of the larger war that secularism has launched against religion. Law is also crucial as a specific ethical category corresponding to what is obligatory in a universal, objective way.

Here especially the distinctiveness of the bishops' model of conscience comes into view. Where a theologian like Thomas Aquinas writes of conscience combining obedience to moral law and the exercise of practical reason, the bishops heavily favor the former over the latter. On the one hand, this means that conscience is best understood as the way by which we adhere to the moral laws requiring respect always and everywhere—in the bishops' eyes especially meaning turning from what they call the "intrinsic evils" at stake in the use of the artificial means of birth control, in gay marriage, and in taking innocent human life from conception onward. On the other hand, the bishops' emphasis on law as the preeminent category of conscience means that they leave little room for practical reasoning to help the conscience figure out what to do in the face of complexity. Practical reasoning, in this view, is wishy-washy, feckless, diluting the clear demands of the moral law. Or, as Bishop Thomas Paprocki of Springfield, Illinois, said when explaining why Illinois bishops did not seek an exemption from a state law legalizing civil unions for same-sex couples that could have required Catholic Charities to place foster children with such couples: "It would have been seen as, 'We're going to compromise on the principle as long as we get our exception.' We didn't want it to be seen as buying our support."[2]

What has led to the diminished role for practical reason in the way the bishops understand conscience? Two key conceptual matters come to mind, both taken from concerns laid down by Pope John Paul II and Pope Benedict XVI. One is the sharp opposition to the "creative conscience" outlined by John Paul II in the 1993 papal encyclical *Veritatis Splendor*. In that document John Paul criticized any number of developments in Catholic

---

[2] Laurie Goodstein, "Bishops Say Rules on Gay Parents Limit Freedom of Religion," *The New York Times*, December 28, 2011.

moral theology, including one that argued that conscience's use of practical reason in the face of a host of particulars could lay the basis for claiming occasional exceptions to the otherwise universal mandate of the moral law. The pope said that this view of the "creative" possibilities of conscience had things precisely backward. It's not the creative use of practical reason that should determine what is morally required in a particular situation. Rather, it's the moral law—requiring "meticulous observance" (no. 55), as John Paul put it—that determines what reason should conclude that a particular situation demands. In *Veritatis Splendor* John Paul was taking aim at theologians working in the area of interpersonal and, especially, sexual morality. But, I believe, his powerful views have shaped the position of the bishops on the current matters of conscience, which pertain primarily to issues of sexual morality in a political, not interpersonal, context.

Along with the "creative conscience," John Paul also condemned what he called the belief that complex situations could yield a "double status of moral truth." In fact, the issue of double status is another way of articulating what is at stake with the use of the creative conscience. The notion of double status holds that while there may be one truth at a doctrinal or abstract level, there may be another truth—even one proclaiming an exception to a doctrinal truth—that emerges in the face of the complexity of concrete conditions. As with the creative conscience, John Paul dismissed this notion outright. Moral truth is not divisible and, anyhow, the clarifying truth of the moral law holding always and everywhere tells us pretty much everything we need to know about what any concrete situation requires (no. 56).

But the issue of the double status of truth is not only an intra-Catholic matter of moral theology. Instead, it also must be considered in light of the overwhelming emphasis of John Paul and Benedict on the threat to truth spawned by what they regard as the runaway relativism of Western democracies. And this brings us to the second conceptual factor behind the bishops' reduced emphasis on practical reason in the exercise of conscience: the fear that human reason in a democracy like the United States is so damaged by relativism and sin that it is all but incapable of attaining moral truth on its own via an exercise of practical reason. John Paul argued in *Evangelium Vitae* that this dismal capacity of human reason was at the heart of the contemporary "culture of death" at work in a place like the United States (nos. 7–28). Benedict has similarly decried what he has called the way that human reason all too often does not accept truth because it does not really want to know it.[3] Faced with such a negative judgment

[3] Joseph Ratzinger, "The Dignity of the Human Person," in *Commentary on Documents of Vatican II: Volume 5,* ed. Herbert Vorgrimler (New York: Herder and Herder, 1969), 136.

about the capacities of human reason, what is the Catholic conscience to do? Among other things, not assume it has the rightful freedom to exercise too much practical reason in the face of the complex circumstances of democratic life. In the eyes of the Catholic right, this was the downfall of those Catholic Democrats in Congress in 2009 who invoked their own prudential judgment to cast the decisive votes in favor of federal health-care reform—and who, in doing so, defied the official opposition of the American Catholic bishops to the bill on the grounds that it would violate the moral law against abortion.

It is important to note that the close link of conscience and the moral law speaks poignantly to the transcendence of the human spirit. The Arab Spring in 2011; Poland in the 1980s; Selma and Birmingham in the American South in the 1950s and 1960s—the people in the streets in these times and places moved the conscience of the world because they witnessed to a demand for justice that always and everywhere surpasses the claim of oppressive power. By contrast, the problems of conscience now facing American Catholic bishops have nowhere near such stark dimensions. And this is true no matter how often some bishops and their allies on the religious right liken contemporary gay activists to the Ku Klux Klan (as did Cardinal Francis George of Chicago)[4] or see in President Obama the alien spearhead of a war against Catholics (as did columnist Michael Gerson).[5]

In any case the Catholic Church in the United States is not without help in having a model of conscience more suited to the complex challenges of living the gospel in a democratic, pluralist society. The great thirteenth-century Dominican theologian Thomas Aquinas allows for the preeminence of the moral law in the act of conscience but, unlike many bishops, he doesn't collapse the reasoning capacity of conscience into the recognition of the obligation to obey the moral law. Instead, he includes a robust role for practical reason in the process by which conscience judges what is required in a particular situation. Thus, Aquinas speaks of conscience in light of practical reason's use of higher (more speculative) and lower (more factual) knowledge, of wisdom, and of the testimony of the senses.[6] The playwright Robert Bolt beautifully captured this tensive view of conscience caught between the demands of the moral law and the potential of practical reason when, in *A Man for All Seasons*, he has the English Catholic Thomas More say:

---

[4] Brian Slodysko, "Cardinal Defends Comparing Gay Parade Organizers to Ku Klux Klan," *Chicago Tribune*, December 28, 2011.

[5] Michael Gerson, "Obama Turns His Back on Catholics," *The Washington Post*, November 14, 2011.

[6] Thomas Aquinas, *De Veritate,* q.17.a.1, 2.

> God made the angels to show Him splendor, as He made animals for innocence and plants for their simplicity. But Man He made to serve him wittily, in the tangle of his mind. If He suffers us to come to such a case that there is no escaping, then we may stand to our tackle as best we can, and, yes . . . then we can clamor like champions, if we have the spittle for it. But it's God part, not our own, to bring ourselves to such a pass. Our natural business lies in escaping.[7]

For Robert Bolt's Thomas More, the acceptance of the possibilities of practical reason reflects an acceptance of our status as creatures before God. To dismiss practical reason en route to being a martyr before its time is to commit spiritual pride, getting ahead of what divine love may in fact be asking us to do. And there is a lot of good to be done today in such places as Catholic universities and Catholic hospitals. Take the central case in the current conscience struggles: the regulations requiring contraceptive coverage at Catholic institutions. The cries of protest against this regulation often have an assumed air of violation, as if it's self-evident that the regulations will be imposing a direct burden on the Catholic conscience. In fact, though, the moral complicity at issue is at a remove: Catholic institutions would be providing payments for choices that female employees of these institutions may or may not make. Even if we're troubled by the proximity of such payments—aren't they enabling an evil action?—we should recall how the tradition of Catholic practical reasoning provides ways of dealing with such challenges. For instance, what is called the principle of cooperation is used to determine when a Catholic may be involved in a morally acceptable manner in the evil action of another person. The core test of the principle is that one person may not share the intention of the person doing the evil action. Obviously, in the case of the regulations and contraception, this core test is met: the bishops as a matter of conviction do not share the intention of those female employees availing themselves of the healthcare benefit of birth control.

An openness to practical reason here—and to facts like a huge majority of Catholic and American women rejecting the church's doctrine on birth control—might also offer a welcome dose of humility to the church in its reflections on this matter: Is this a prudent place to make a stand? The principle of cooperation also asks whether there is a "proportionate reason" to justify involvement with the moral evil at hand. Here comparison and scaling of values are unavoidable. What may be a sufficient reason to justify cooperation with artificial birth control may not be a sufficient reason to justify involvement with abortion. Here also attention to the full range of

---

7 Robert Bolt, *A Man for All Seasons* (New York: Random House, 1962), 126.

goods at stake in a situation is crucial. So we might ask with an eye toward the fundamental purpose of the institution: Would the failure to provide insurance coverage for birth control impair the morale of female employees and hence inhibit the good to be accomplished by the institution in question? And we might also ask, with an eye toward the values of citizenship: Does the moral ideal of equality before the law mean that if an insurance policy provides prescription coverage to men for Viagra the policy ought also to provide prescription coverage to women for birth control? In any case it is neither relativism nor radical secularism that inspires consideration of such matters. Instead, it is an imperative of the close link of practical reason and conscience long part of the Catholic tradition.

I would like to conclude with one other consequence of the bishops' constrained view of practical reason: the constriction of the freedom of conscience. This is a paradox. After all, the bishops have raised a hue and cry because they are defending the rights of conscience. But, for them, the conscience should be free to adhere to the truth of the universal moral law articulated by the hierarchical teaching office of the church. Moreover, for them, there really aren't many good excuses for not knowing of the need for such adherence. In this they are following John Paul II, who asserted in *Veritatis Splendor* that the hierarchical magisterium of the church "in no way undermines the freedom of conscience" of Christians because "the Magisterium does not bring to the Christian conscience truths which are extraneous to it; rather, it brings to light the truths which it ought already to possess, developing them from the starting point of the primordial act of faith" (no. 64). But what about the freedom of conscience to adhere to a truth not identical with the moral law defined by the hierarchical authority of the church? And what about the freedom to allow one's practical reason to consult empirical data and a wide range of values in determining what conscience should do in a complex matter? Especially if that determination differs from one put forward by the bishops? The model of conscience favored by the bishops in the current disputes has little room for such obvious and significant scenarios. By contrast, it is helpful here to recall another aspect of Thomas Aquinas's theory of conscience that factors squarely into such concerns for freedom: his claim that it is sinful not to follow the subjectively right but objectively wrong conscience.[8] Or, in other words, one is obliged to follow one's conscience if one believes the judgment of one's conscience is true, even if that judgment is, objectively speaking, incorrect.

Thomas's claim has posed a problem for Catholics who insist that an erroneous conscience must be the consequence of a person's culpability. Given that culpability, this line of thinking goes, a person is obliged

[8] Thomas Aquinas, *Summa Theologica* I-II, q.19.a.5.

precisely not to adhere to an erroneous conscience. Beyond this general wariness of the freedom of the erroneous conscience, conservative Catholics can also point to limits that Thomas himself imposes on the freedom of such a conscience. For instance, Thomas says that no one may rightfully pursue such a freedom while claiming not to know that certain egregious actions are always and everywhere against the moral law.[9] Here we encounter a variation on what I noted earlier: that those who claim freedom of conscience to act contrary to intrinsic evils must not know of the moral laws against such evils because they do not want to know of such laws. Theologian Joseph Ratzinger (later Benedict XVI) said as much when he dismissed liberal Catholic post–Vatican II appeals to Thomas's notion of freedom of conscience as being misinformed about Aquinas and regrettably and wholly inspired by modern thought.[10] Here also we can surmise that for many of the bishops the crucial moral laws of which every conscience cannot claim ignorance include those proscriptions against the great intrinsic evils at stake in contemporary American democratic culture—artificial birth control, abortion, and gay marriage. These are the moral laws, as John Paul II noted, that the magisterium has declared and that every Christian conscience "ought already to possess."

So we have a perfect closed circle of conscience. The moral laws against intrinsic evils that every Catholic conscience ought to know are specified by the hierarchical teaching office of the church. Moreover, the correct application or policies related to these moral laws against intrinsic evils—for instance, legislation or regulations related to abortion or gay marriage—are also specified by the hierarchical teaching office. So the Catholic conscience may claim freedom neither from the hierarchically identified intrinsic evils nor from the hierarchically specified policies that best combat such evils. If at some point on this circle you need to break out, you have a free conscience to do so—just not a Catholic free conscience.

There are decisive times and places when the truth of such a closed circle of conscience is necessary. In the face of Hitler's murderous leadership, would that the Catholic hierarchy had spoken out unambiguously in defense of the binding nature of the universal moral law on all Catholic consciences. But today this closed circle of conscience founders on its hierarchical hubris, the greatest measure of which is its identification of the magisterium with the very voice of God. In any case, for purposes of this essay, it is important to note that such a closed circle is only possible by relying on a model of conscience shorn of the capacity of practical reason. And here we can see the enduring relevance of Thomas's model of conscience and of his

[9] Ibid., a.6.

[10] Ratzinger, "The Dignity of the Human Person."

claim that the erroneous conscience is free. For Thomas, what is at stake in any morally complex situation is not only made evident by the clarifying truth of the moral law. Instead, practical reason in all its variety—as wisdom, prudence, science, common sense, knowledge gained from the senses, and so on—must also be brought to bear to determine what is morally obliged. Men and women ought to have the freedom to use such practical reason. Moreover, for Thomas, what provides the basis for the freedom of the erroneous conscience is the great value of practical reason—and not only of obedience to law—in the very constitution of our personhood. As one scholar of Aquinas puts it: "To act morally is not merely to grasp a material good in order to become morally good. To grasp the good in the first place is also to grasp oneself as a being that determines itself freely through reason in order to become such a [morally good] being."[11] Or to paraphrase the plain English of one of the church's great martyrs of conscience: We are to serve God wittily, in the tangle of our minds.

It is time for many Catholic bishops to stop heading for the barricades and start making for the negotiating table to try to figure this thing out. The Catholic conscience demands it.

---

[11] Ludger Honnefelder, "The Evaluation of Goods and the Estimation of Consequences," in *The Ethics of Aquinas*, ed. Stephen Pope (Washington, DC: Georgetown University Press, 2002), 428.

Contributors

Carol Bayley is vice president for ethics and justice education at Dignity Health Care West in San Francisco, California. Her published works include contributions to *Management Mistakes in Healthcare: Identification, Correction, and Prevention* (Cambridge University Press, 2005) and *Accountability: Patient Safety and Policy Reform* (Georgetown University Press, 2004).

Emilce Cuda lectures in the faculty of theology at Pontifical Catholic University in Buenos Aires, Argentina. Her essays have appeared in *Revista Teología* and the recently published *Feminist Catholic Theological Ethics: Conversations in the World Church* (Orbis Books, 2014). She is the author of *Democracia y Catolicisimo en Estados Unidos, 1792–1945* (Agape, 2010).

David E. DeCosse is director of campus ethics programs at the Markkula Center for Applied Ethics at Santa Clara University in Santa Clara, California, where he is also adjunct associate professor in the Department of Religious Studies. His recent work on the intersection of Catholic social thought and contemporary democracy has appeared in *Theological Studies* and *Political Theology*.

Daniel K. Finn is professor of economics and theology and the Clemens Chair in Economics and the Liberal Arts at St. John's University in Collegeville, Minnesota. He has recently published *Distant Markets, Distant Harms: Market Complicity and Christian Ethics* (Oxford University Press, 2014) and *Christian Economic Ethics: History and Implications* (Fortress Press, 2013)

Lisa Fullam is associate professor of moral theology at the Jesuit School of Theology of Santa Clara University in Berkeley, California. She is co-editor of *Ethics and Spirituality: Readings in Moral Theology No. 17* (Paulist Press, 2014) and *Virtue: Readings in Moral Theology, No. 16* (Paulist Press, 2011). She is the author of *The Virtue of Humility: A Thomistic Apologetic* (Mellen, 2009).

Eric Marcelo O. Genilo, S.J., is associate professor of moral theology at Loyola School of Theology in Manila, Philippines. He published *John Cuthbert Ford, S.J.: Moral Theologian at the End of the Manualist Era* (Georgetown University Press, 2007) and contributed to *Transformative Theological Ethics: East Asian Contexts* (Ateneo de Manila University Press, 2010).

Kristin E. Heyer is professor of theology at Boston College. Her books include *Kinship across Borders: A Christian Ethic of Immigration* (Georgetown University Press, 2012) and *Prophetic and Public: The Social Witness of US Catholicism* (Georgetown University Press, 2006). She taught at Santa Clara University from 2009 to 2015.

Linda Hogan is vice provost / chief academic officer and professor of ecumenics at Trinity College in Dublin, Ireland. She has published *Confronting the Truth: Conscience in the Catholic Tradition* (Paulist Press, 2000) and co-edited *Feminist Catholic Theological Ethics: Conversations in the World Church* (Orbis Books, 2014).

James F. Keenan, S.J., is the Founders Professor of Theology at Boston College in Chestnut Hill, Massachusetts. His recent books include *A History of Catholic Moral Theology in the Twentieth Century: From Confessing Sins to Liberating Consciences* (Continuum, 2010) and *Catholic Theological Ethics, Past, Present, and Future: The Trento Conference* (Orbis Books, 2011).

Bryan N. Massingale is professor of theology at Marquette University in Milwaukee, Wisconsin. He published *Racial Justice and the Catholic Church* (Orbis Books, 2010) and recently contributed to *Voting and Holiness: Catholic Perspectives on Political Participation* (Paulist Press, 2012).

William R. O'Neill, S.J., is associate professor of social ethics at the Jesuit School of Theology of Santa Clara University in Berkeley, California. He has authored numerous articles, appearing most recently in the *Journal of the Society of Christian Ethics, Journal of Political Theology, International Journal of Comparative Sociology,* and *Transformative Theological Ethics: East Asian Contexts* (Ateneo de Manila University Press, 2010).

Agbonkhianmeghe E. Orobator, S.J., is the principal of Hekima College in Nairobi, Kenya, and is also lecturer in theology and religious studies there. Previous provincial of the Eastern African Province of the Society of

Jesus, he recently co-edited *Feminist Catholic Theological Ethics: Conversations in the World Church* (Orbis Books, 2014) and edited *Reconciliation, Justice, and Peace: The Second African Synod* (Orbis Books, 2011).

Stephen J. Pope is professor of theology at Boston College in Chestnut Hill, Massachusetts. He has authored *Human Evolution and Christian Ethics* (Cambridge University Press, 2007) and *A Step along the Way: Models of Christian Service* (Orbis Books, 2015) and contributed to the recently published *Restorative Justice, Reconciliation, and Peacebuilding* (Oxford University Press, 2014).

John R. Quinn served as the sixth archbishop of the Archdiocese of San Francisco from 1977 to 1995. He has authored multiple books, including *The Reform of the Papacy* (Crossroad Publishing, 1999) and the recently published *Ever Ancient, Ever New: Structures of Communion in the Church* (Paulist Press, 2013).

Eugine Rodrigues, B.S. (the Congregation of the Sisters of the Little Flower of Bethany in Bangalore, India) received the doctorate in moral theology from the Catholic University of Leuven, Belgium, in 2013. Her dissertation was "Responding to the Threats to Religious Freedom: The Relevance of *Dignitatis Humanae* for India's Multi-Religious Context." She has published articles in the *Vidyajyoti Journal of Theological Reflection* and *Asian Christian Review.*

Osamu Takeuchi, S.J., is dean of the Graduate School of Theology and professor of theology at Sophia University in Tokyo, Japan. His books include *Conscience and Culture: A Dialogue between the West and the East concerning Conscience* (LAP LAMBERT Academic Publishing, 2010) and *Conscience and Personality: A New Understanding of Conscience and Its Inculturation in Japanese Moral Theology* (Kyoyusha, 2003).

Index